THE 'TWENTY-FIVE' CHURCHES OF THE SOUTHWARK DIOCESE

THE 'TWENTY-FIVE' CHURCHES OF THE SOUTHWARK DIOCESE

An inter-war campaign of church-building

Kenneth Richardson
with original illustrations by John Bray

The Ecclesiological Society • 2002

First published 2002

The Ecclesiological Society
c/o The Society of Antiquaries of London
Burlington House
Piccadilly
London W1V 0HS
www.ecclsoc.org

Printed in Great Britain by the Alden Press, Osney Mead, Oxford, UK

ISBN 0 946823 15 4

CONTENTS

The compilation of this volume has, in a sense, been a pioneering project, for there has been no previous attempt to produce a cohesive account of the Southwark Diocese Twenty-five Churches Fund and the ambitious construction programme which it helped to finance. When I first embarked on the necessary research work, it quickly became apparent that sources of information were quite widely dispersed, so that I now have the pleasure of acknowledging with gratitude the help, advice and encouragement which I have unfailingly received from the large number of institutions and individuals I consulted.

Particular thanks are due to the staff of the following repositories whose archives each proved an absolute gold-mine of valuable information: Church of England Record Centre, Council for the Care of Churches (especially their Church Survey Files), London Metropolitan Archives (formerly Greater London Record Office), Royal Institute of British Architects (British Architectural Library and Drawings Collection), and the Surrey Record Office.

Additionally, the staff of Local Studies Libraries in the following London Boroughs each conjured up a considerable amount of useful data: Bexley, Croydon, Greenwich, Kingston-upon-Thames, Lambeth, Lewisham, Merton, Richmond-upon-Thames, Southwark, Sutton and Wandsworth. All this was supplemented by information kindly furnished, sometimes orally, by incumbents, parishioners and others too numerous to single out by name. Their help was equally valuable and is greatly appreciated.

I would also like to express my thanks to John Bray for permission to use his drawings, a small part of his magnificent portfolio of more than five hundred London churches. His drawings are intended to highlight the architectural character of the buildings, and trees and blocking foliage have sometimes been omitted in the interest of recording the structure. Even reduced in size as they are here, his work often gives the measure of a building better than a photograph.

As for the photographs, a good number are my own, because of the lack of material in the public collections. My pictures were often taken under rushed conditions, and certainly with no thought of publication. No-one is more aware of their weaknesses than myself, but I have been persuaded that any photograph is better than none, and, in the hope that this is true, would ask the reader's forbearance.

Because of the diversity of sources, and the sad loss of some parish records over the years, it has not been altogether easy to piece

together the various strands of historical data on individual buildings and sites into a tolerably coherent and balanced whole. More-
over, some of the churches described here have been particularly
well served by published material of one kind or another; but
others scarcely at all. The consequent harvest of relevant facts has
thus been a little more uneven than I would ideally have wished.
Inevitably a few omissions will be noticed by the diligent reader;
some of these are deliberate, in the interests of reasonable concise-
ness, whilst others may have occurred through inadvertence or
ignorance on my part. I tender my apologies for any obvious
shortcomings of this latter kind.

KENNETH V. RICHARDSON

ACKNOWLEDGEMENTS

The author and publishers acknowledge with gratitude the permission of the following to reproduce illustrations and photographs: EMAP Construct, for *The Architect's Journal,* (East Sheen, All Saints, plan); The Builder Group PLC (Putney, St Margaret, drawing; Hackbridge and North Beddington, All Saints, watercolour); Carshalton, The Good Shepherd (drawings); Church of England Record Centre (Castelnau Church Hall, drawing; Eltham St Saviour Church Hall, plan and elevation; Southend, St John the Baptist, architect's sketches of the church); Council for the Care of Churches (Eltham, St Barnabas, photographs of interior; Eltham Park, St Luke, photographs of aisle; New Eltham, All Saints, photograph of east end before restoration; Wallington, St Patrick, early drawing of east end); Downham, St Luke (architect's drawing of interior); East Sheen, All Saints (drawings of the original proposal for the exterior, and of the church with tower); English Heritage, NMR (Southend, St John the Baptist, photographs); Incorporated Church Building Society (Bellingham, St Dunstan, drawing from west; Carshalton, The Good Shepherd, plan; Eltham, St Saviour, plan; Hackbridge and North Beddington, All Saints, watercolour; Mitcham, St Olave, drawing from south; North Sheen, St Philip, plan; St Helier, St Peter, plan and external photograph; Streatham, Holy Redeemer, plan and interior photograph; Tooting, St Augustine, plan); London Borough of Lewisham (Southend, St John the Baptist, photograph of interior showing north chapel); London Borough of Sutton (Carshalton, The Good Shepherd, interior looking east; Cheam, St Alban, interior looking east); London Metropolitan Archives (Bellingham, St Dunstan, plan, east and north elevation, section across nave; St Helier, St Peter, elevations); Mitcham, St Olave (architect's plan and elevations); New Eltham, All Saints (photograph of east end before restoration); Purley Library Local History Collection (Riddlesdown, St James, photograph of interior); RIBA Library Drawings Collection (Eltham Park, St Luke, south elevation; Streatham, Holy Redeemer, watercolour of east end); Riddlesdown, St James (1940s drawing of church, architect's drawing); Southend, St John the Baptist (architect's drawings of interior and exterior); Surrey History Service (Mitcham, St Olave, photograph of sanctuary); Wallington, St Patrick (early drawing of east end); Woodbridge, Mrs Joyce (Eltham, St Saviour Mission Church, interior photograph).

The publishers apologise for any accidental breach of copyright in cases where it has not been possible to establish reproduction rights. If notified, they will correct the matter in any future edition.

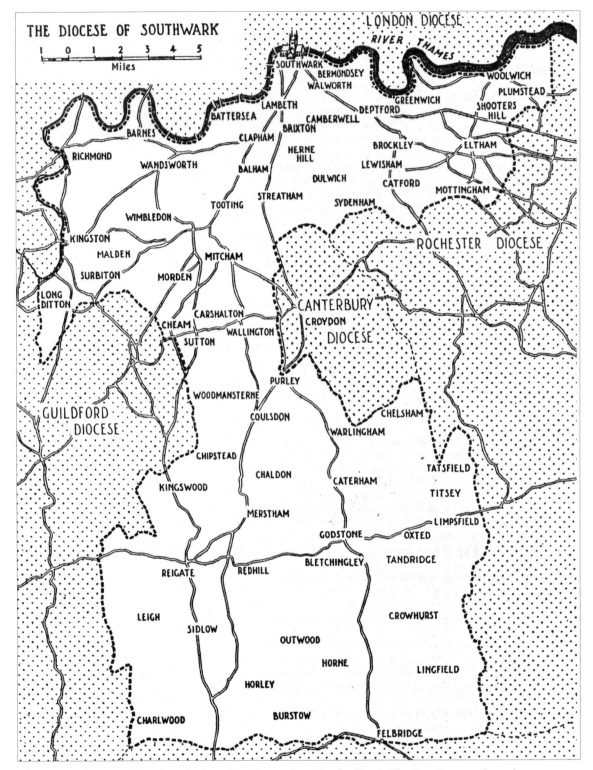

The Diocese of Southwark at about the time of the Twenty-five Churches Fund. The Croydon area, shown here as a detached sector ('peculiar') of the Diocese of Canterbury, was subsequently absorbed into that of Southwark.

THE 'TWENTY-FIVE' CHURCHES

An Introduction and Survey

The Problem

In his successful General Election campaign at the end of 1918, Lloyd George made his famous promise of 'A Land Fit for Heroes to Live In'. One of the principal objectives he had in mind was the provision of suitable housing for the millions of men-at-arms who had survived the first World War and were now to rejoin their families at home.

The problem was that, particularly in the inner cities, four years of strict wartime restrictions on building and maintenance had caused much of the existing housing stock to become badly dilapidated and numerically inadequate. In an attempt to remedy this, a Housing Act was passed in 1919 which conferred responsibility on local authorities for the supply of housing for people of limited means. In London, the County Council responded by purchasing land at several locations on the outskirts of the capital and erecting thereon, during the 1920s and 1930s, a series of huge cottage estates. Additionally the London boroughs pursued similar policies, and the part played by private developers cannot be ignored.

The inevitable result of all these efforts was a mass migration from the run-down inner areas to the new towns. Despite the obvious attractions of better quality housing and more congenial surroundings, the move proved to be a traumatic one for many, involving as it did the break-up of close-knit communities, the need to seek new work in an unfamiliar area or to undertake long journeys to an existing work-place, and, for children, a break in education which might occur at a crucial time. It was indeed a big step into the unknown.

By far the largest part of all the new estates in south London fell within the Anglican Diocese of Southwark, and it was soon realised by the Diocesan authorities that the great population shift, expected to involve some 300,000 people, and its attendant uncertainties,

Cyril Forster Garbett, a photograph taken during his time as Bishop of Southwark.

were matters of major concern to them.[1] It was clearly not possible for the arriving inhabitants of the new estates to build churches for themselves or to support the provision of clergy unaided. Assistance, therefore, had to be provided on a massive scale, and this needed a master plan and a strong guiding hand to organise it and ensure its implementation and success.

'The right man in the right place'[2]

Either by sheer good fortune, or by remarkable foresight within the Anglican Church's corridors of power – possibly a combination of both – a leader with just the right qualities had arrived on the scene in 1919. This was Cyril Forster Garbett.

On his appointment as Bishop of Southwark in that year, Garbett found himself at the head of a Diocese which was not only faced with the twin problems of housing deprivation and impending population migration, each on an enormous scale, but which was utterly ill-equipped to deal with them.[3] There was already a desperate shortage of clergy, and morale amongst those that remained was at a low ebb, because they were overworked and underpaid.[4] But Garbett was not a man to be deterred by such situations: on the contrary, he had long since learned to view problems as opportunities.

Yet, by the time 1925 had arrived, Garbett was to say 'I have been a bishop for six years, and have not yet consecrated a church.'[5] If this might suggest a very lax approach to the problems around him, nothing could have been further from the truth. Right at the outset of his episcopate, Garbett got to grips with the situation. He was aware that to plunge straight away into a campaign to build churches on the projected new estates was clearly not practicable: there were no funds available for the purpose, and insufficient clergy to staff them. His priorities, therefore, were to set about improving the pay and working conditions of the clergy in order to provide a satisfactory basis for recruitment, and to embark on a systematic programme of personal visits to parishes so as to familiarise himself with all corners of his Diocese and to assess the local needs, strengths and weaknesses.

Then began the race against time, to ensure that, as far as practicable, the new estates would have Anglican priests and a place of worship in position to welcome the incoming residents as they arrived. 'If,' as Garbett was to say later, 'the clergy greet and visit the people within a few days of their arrival, if there is a church or hall to which they can invite them, the response is immediate and remarkable. The newcomers are strangers in a strange land: they are far from their old haunts: many old ties have been broken by their removal to a new home: young and old alike need fellowship and friendship, and if the Church is ready at the very outset to offer both, it will become the social and spiritual centre of the new community. But if the Church delays, if it has neither the men nor the buildings until long after the people have settled down, it will never regain the ground which it has lost by its unreadiness.'[6] The degree to which this aim was successfully implemented is illustrated by this comment from an inhabitant of one of the new districts: 'We have three visitors when we first move in – the agent for the beer-house, the book-maker's tout and the parson – and here the parson always manages to call first!'[7]

The Portsea precedent

Ecclesiastical awareness of the impending challenge was already awakening as early as 1899 when the Rural Dean of Lewisham issued a circular pointing out that 'In the now open country district of Southend, in the parish of Lewisham, the London, Chatham and Dover Railway has opened three new stations… In the near future there will be new populations round there to be dealt with.'[8] This area proved to be one of three subjected to major local authority housing activity within the diocese beginning in 1920, the others being Roehampton and Eltham.[9] Of these three, the Lewisham project was by far the largest, involving the construction of over 2,000 dwellings at Bellingham followed by another 6,000 at Downham, with the hamlet of Southend sandwiched between. There, the former proprietary chapel which served the district as its parish church was hopelessly inadequate for the task confronting it, and its reinforcement was recognised as a matter of urgency.

Bishop Garbett had precisely the right experience to point the way forward. Immediately prior to his appointment as Bishop of Southwark, he had completed twenty years of service on Portsea island in Hampshire, ten of them as a curate and another ten as vicar. In 1899 the centrally-placed medieval church at Kingston on the island, which had been demolished in 1843, was succeeded by a large and stately new church, with a seating capacity of 2,000, built to the designs of Sir Arthur Blomfield and considered by some to be his masterpiece. In the years that followed, the church became a byword for its outstandingly successful system of parochial organisation and pastoral care – even though it served a notoriously difficult parish which, in terms of population, was one of the largest, if not the largest, in England. St Mary's at Kingston was the 'mother' church of the parish, and its administrative centre. At strategic points about the parish five 'daughter' or mission churches were successively built, each of them covering its own district and staffed by a team of curates who eventually numbered sixteen. The vicar and his curates lived in and around a Clergy House close by the 'mother' church. It is perhaps a testimony to the quality of the whole operation, particularly as a training ground, that two successive vicars of Portsea went on to become Archbishops – Cosmo Gordon Lang of York and then Canterbury, and Cyril Forster Garbett of York; whilst several of the curates rose to episcopal rank.[10]

Garbett conceived the idea of creating a new 'super-parish', on Portsea lines, to embrace the Bellingham and Downham estates and be centred on Southend. To this end, in 1923 he installed as Vicar there the Revd – later Canon – E. F. Edge Partington, who had been one of his curates at Portsea. A large vicarage and 'mother' church were designed for erection in a focal position at Southend, and 'satellite' churches planned for Bellingham and Downham, thus paving the way for a system of parish administration for the area which, although later modified by the separation of Bellingham and by certain other refinements, today retains at least some of its original features. Edge Partington remained there until 1943. By 1926 he had three assistant priests, covering Bellingham and Downham, and in 1935 there were no fewer than seven to serve what was believed to have become England's most populous parish.

If the Downham and Bellingham estates represented one major challenge, that posed a few years later by the even larger St Helier conurbation was proportionately greater. Here Dr Garbett again tried to establish another Portsea, but his visions of a great united parish were resisted and finally thwarted by opposition.[11]

The quest for funds

The twin constraints which characterised the opening years of Bishop Garbett's episcopate, those of inadequate financial and staffing resources, have already been noted. By 1925, towards the end of a successful five-year Clergy Stipends Appeal and a concurrent Permanent Endowment Scheme,[12] and with his plans for Bellingham and Downham already taking shape, he felt in a strong enough position to launch a determined and comprehensive campaign to provide places of worship for the emerging new centres of population. As the focal point in this campaign, he established the Southwark Diocese Twenty-five Churches Fund, described later as 'perhaps the most spectacular achievement of his episcopate',[13] to be administered with the assistance of his Archdeacons and a specially formed Representative Committee. Canon Edmund Sinker, who, as Secretary of the Diocesan Board of Finance, had been largely responsible for the success of the Appeal for Clergy Stipends, was appointed General Secretary to the Fund; the Revd H. Coxwell White became its Organising Secretary; and Brigadier E. B. Cuthbertson its Treasurer.[14] But it was Garbett himself who was the prime driving force.

The target was to attract, over a period of five years, a total sum of £200,000 – an enormous amount in those days.[15] Of this, half would be expected to be raised directly by local schemes, and the remainder by accumulation into the central Diocesan Fund, from which grants would then be made to the localities concerned. The local schemes would each be run by their own committees, who would also be responsible for the actual building of the church.[16] The campaign, therefore, had to be directed not only at achieving sufficient financial strength in the Diocesan Fund, but also at encouraging the efforts of the local committees. Garbett himself played a significant part in the latter task, for example by personally visiting the areas where new houses were being erected in order to enlist support and instil enthusiasm. And, on a more general scale, he used his influence to the full by addressing meetings, writing articles and taking whatever other opportunities he found for generating publicity for the appeal. He also won sympathetic aid from the Ecclesiastical Commissioners, through whose good offices he was able to secure valuable contributions from various sources, in particular from the City Parochial Charities Fund.

Before the end of 1925, more than £25,000 had already been received by or promised to the Fund.[17] But it was essential to maintain the effort and to give it additional impetus at intervals. There were perhaps three defining moments in this campaign. The first, in February 1926, took the form of a widely reported meeting at London's Mansion House, presided over by the Lord Mayor and attended by numerous influential dignitaries including the Archbishop of Canterbury, Randall Davidson, who threw his weight behind Garbett's own oratory.[18] Then, in November 1927, came a week of prayer and self-denial throughout the Southwark Diocese, during which offerings were solicited at parochial level; these were then presented by local representatives at a packed Thanksgiving Service in Southwark Cathedral and found to total over £19,000, 'an amount which even the most reckless optimist in the Diocese had not even dreamed of'.[19] Garbett had hoped for £10,000. Finally, with the Fund now just £7,000 short of its £100,000 target, a Gift Day was held on 27 June 1928 when Garbett, accompanied by the suffragan Bishops of Kingston and Woolwich, remained in his cathedral from 8 a.m. to 9 p.m. to receive freewill offerings.[20] This event was estimated to have attracted at least 20,000 people and was supported by visits from the Lord Mayor of London in full state panoply and mayors from all boroughs within the Diocese, a 'deputation of Eastern ecclesiastics', and, later, the Lord Lieutenant of Surrey with a trumpet fanfare.[21] At 9 p.m. the target was announced to have been passed. Thus, in less than three years instead of the expected five, the public campaign was brought to an end, though the Twenty-five Churches Fund continued to attract contributions until 1934 when, with receipts totalling over £133,000, it was finally closed and its resources and responsibilities transferred to a successor organisation called the Bishop of Southwark's Council for New Districts.[22] The conclusion of the Appeal was marked on 25 January 1934 by a Thanksgiving Service in Southwark Cathedral, when Dr Garbett – by then Bishop of Winchester – preached the sermon.[23] At this service, 'representatives of the new parishes entered the cathedral in procession, each group being led by a bearer carrying a large wooden cross upon which was inscribed, front and back, the name of the particular parish'.[24] Some of these crosses, which were of distinctive design, still survive: examples are on view in the churches of St Saviour at Eltham and St James's at Merton.

Achievements

What, then, was achieved with the money raised by the Appeal? Its title declares the aim of providing twenty-five churches, but from the outset this was intended as a provisional estimate of requirements rather than as an inflexible definition of limits. There was indeed an early list of exactly twenty-five projects, comprising fourteen new parish churches to be built, six existing ones to be completed or enlarged, and five new mission or district churches with a dual-purpose role as community halls as well as places of worship.[25] For a variety of reasons, not all of these projects materialised: locations were reconsidered, schemes were overtaken by new events, new requirements were added, and in one case, at Morden, local opposition intervened. The final list, published in 1934, was impressive: twenty entirely new churches built, five existing ones completed or enlarged, ten new halls erected, and three sites acquired for future church buildings – a total of thirty-eight projects successfully carried out.[26]

Of course, the work of church extension in the Diocese did not end there. On being set up in 1934, the Bishop's Council for New Districts at once conducted a survey to determine what provision should be made during the next few years for further church building in emerging centres of population. Needs, some of them described as 'immediate', were identified at Cheam, Chessington, Downham, Earlsfield, East Wickham, Eltham, Mitcham, Mottingham, Sanderstead and Warlingham. And so the campaign went on...[27]

Both through his office as Bishop of the Diocese, and through his ultimate control of the grants dispensed from the Twenty-five Churches Fund, Dr Garbett was in a position to exercise a powerful influence over the various strands of ecclesiastical development in the new estates. He was able with very few exceptions to ensure that the dispensation of grants was conditional, as a sort of *quid pro quo*, on patronage of the local living being vested in the Bishop of Southwark. By this means, he could reinforce episcopal control over the style of churchmanship to be practised in the new districts or parishes. Whilst this policy received strong support in some areas, notably those with High Church traditions, it was viewed with suspicion or even outright hostility in some with evangelical leanings.[28] To be fair, Garbett never allowed his own natural inclinations towards Anglo-Catholicism to outweigh strong local tradition: he regarded himself as a 'broad church' man, and he fully respected the value of upholding Anglican evangelical tendencies where these clearly prevailed.[29]

Irrespective of local parochial traditions, he was punctilious in undertaking the function of consecrating new churches, and he was often present when foundation stones were laid, though the important task of wielding the ceremonial trowel was normally entrusted to the care of others such as a suffragan bishop, a benefactor or other lay dignitary, or in some cases to Garbett's own mother.

The dispensation of Diocesan grants for building churches and halls followed to some extent the principle of matching the amounts collected locally for the purpose. But in practice a high degree of flexibility was applied. Where local financial support was strong, boosted perhaps by generous contributions from a landowner or other major benefactor, the amount offered from the Twenty-five Churches Fund might be quite small; conversely, where the task of raising a significant sum within a reasonable period was manifestly quite beyond the resources of the newly arriving inhabitants of, say, a London County Council estate, the Fund's financial help would be on a massive scale. Of prime importance as a motivating force was the need to establish an Anglican presence: to build a church or hall, and to install a priest there.

Ecclesiological perspectives

As has already been stated, the building of individual churches and halls was left to the initiative of local committees; no attempt was made to impose any kind of standard design, though when advice was sought, such as in the selection of a suitable architect, it was given, usually in the form of a short list of suggested options. This absence of bureaucratic control had the beneficial effect of producing a remarkable diversity of approaches to church design, for which the student of ecclesiastical architecture can be grateful. Local building committees appointed their own architects and obtained from them designs they perceived to be appropriate to their requirements; these designs were then submitted to the Diocesan Advisory Committee for acceptance; and finally, if they were for a new parish church, they had to be sanctioned by the Ecclesiastical Commissioners whose consulting architects – Caröe and Passmore at the time – would not only subject the proposed designs and specifications to detailed scrutiny but would inspect the completed building when it was ready for consecration. These measures provided an effective safeguard against shoddy or patently unsatisfactory work, but they could not stifle the production of imaginative or innovative schemes like those of St Saviour's at Eltham and the Barn Church at North Sheen. Because the role of Caröe and Passmore was primarily to ensure the suitability of the building for use as a parish church, they were concerned more with practicalities than with aesthetic values: their expressed reservations about the Barn Church at North Sheen, for example, were on grounds such as the extreme length of the nave and the paucity of light penetrating the windows, rather than on any misgivings about the use of a vernacular concept of architecture. But there were stylistic limits beyond which they were not comfortable, as in the case of J. B. L. Tolhurst's eclectic design for All Saints' Church at East Sheen, which they considered unacceptable.[30]

Garbett himself rarely intervened on matters of design, though he undoubtedly had clear views on the subject, which on occasion he expressed quite forcefully. 'The Church,' he declared in 1930, 'had an unrivalled opportunity for taking the lead in setting a high standard of artistic excellence. Zealous, but ill-instructed restorers had sometimes worked more fatal havoc than the deliberate icono-clast. The interiors of some of the best of their churches were damaged, sometimes half ruined, by tasteless colour and inartistic ornaments and furniture. Clumsy and heavy reredoses, garish tiles and carpets, pretentious pulpits and ridiculous lecterns, hangings and curtains drab in colour, stamped by machine-made ecclesiast-ical designs, windows with insipid and unreal figures, colours on the walls and floors which were in violent discord, cheap and conventional vases and lamps were found in many of our churches and made persistent progress against the worship of God in beauty as well as in holiness. For their sins against beauty they should sometimes have litanies of penitence.'[31]

Notwithstanding Garbett's personal views, the architects em-ployed on the design of the Twenty-five Churches were able, within reason, to induce the adoption of their own individual approaches to what was required; thus they generally managed to stamp their own personalities and idiosyncrasies on the buildings they produced. In consequence, their work ranged stylistically from the determinedly conservative Gothic of H. P. Burke Down-ing at Hackbridge and Tooting to the decidedly avant-garde of Nugent Cachemaille-Day at Eltham. Burke Downing's ideas were bound rigidly by firmly applied principles: he strongly condemned what he saw as a temptation, in the quest to provide church accom-modation as quickly and economically as possible, to lay too much emphasis on cost effectiveness at the expense of quality. 'A church,' he said, 'is not essentially a piece of material equipment as a factory may be for the carrying on of an industry… it has an object much greater than that of serving the convenience of worshippers. It is, or should be, something entering into their worship, something spiritually aiding their worship.' It followed from this, he said, 'that the architect must be given freedom to express himself without the perpetual limiting thought of economy and of how the expenditure will look when divided by the number of sittings provided'. For him, this expression was securely based on his 'love for the English Gothic of the best tradition, which I hold to be the most beautiful, inspiring and devotional for church building…'[32] Those who selected Burke Downing as their architect, therefore, could be assured of receiving a thoroughly traditional Gothic structure of sound design and construction, but it would not come cheaply.

Cachemaille-Day, on the other hand, had no such compulsion to abide by tradition – though it must be pointed out that the ground-plan for his church of St Saviour at Eltham could hardly be more traditional in its design elements: a rectangular nave with aisles, and a squared-off chancel flanked on one side by a chapel and on the other by vestries. In a lecture delivered to the St Paul's Ecclesiological Society on 29 March 1933 he set out what seemed to him to be the salient points underlying a constructive study of modern ecclesiastical architecture. In summary these were, first, the sheer quantity of new churches required in conjunction with the development of new cultural centres in vast and uniform suburban building estates; secondly, finding a true relationship between modern developments in secular art and what must be expected of a specifically Christian art; thirdly, due consideration of the need for economy and speed in church building; and fourthly, the accompanying development of painting, sculpture, and the decorative arts generally, without which he considered a building to be incomplete. He was of a generation which had 'cast away the unconvincing and artificial frills of the less good work of the last century', but he urged that the Church should take a lead in showing 'how new buildings may be clothed with a grace and beauty comparable with those of the past'.[33] Cachemaille-Day's ideas were further expounded at a meeting of the Architecture Club on 6 March 1934, when he pointed out that, because the new housing districts had no civic centre and no public buildings, 'the church could be the centre of a group of buildings for all sorts of activity going on', and it should be able to make 'a real contribution to the question of modernism and traditionalism, because in the Church these characteristics were welded'. The church needed only 'to be a perfectly sincere building which did not in any way try to force itself, and at the same time did not try to introduce archaeological or false eccentricities'.[34]

Sir Charles Nicholson, who designed several of the churches and halls erected with help from the Twenty-five Churches Fund, had been articled to J. D. Sedding and for a time worked with Henry Wilson. He was not inhibited by adherence to traditional style but he had reservations about the modernistic approach. His uncomplicated philosophy found typical expression in his churches at Bellingham and Downham. He described St Dunstan's, Bellingham, as 'of the simplest possible design', without attempting to conform strictly to any 'period' of architecture.[35] But he did not equate simplicity with cheapness, and he later disparaged work which he regarded as 'unduly skimped, especially in the case of roof timbers'. Brick he recognised as the standard material for walls, but called it 'an unfortunate necessity perhaps'. Synthetic materials he viewed with some disfavour: of reinforced concrete he said 'it should not be forgotten that this is a very excellent servant and a very hard master'. He pointed to 'a real danger lest we should forget to build with beauty in our efforts to design with truth', and he added that 'It is always possible that an unbridled desire for novelty may develop into affectation, and that what one generation labels "power" and "originality" may in a few years come to be called "clumsiness" and "oddity".'[36]

Like Nicholson, J. E. Newberry received numerous design commissions for churches in the Twenty-five group, first in partnership with F. H. Greenaway and then with C. W. Fowler. He had earlier been an assistant to J. L. Pearson. His were essentially a 'safe' pair of hands: he produced churches of conventional appearance, based generally on Gothic precepts but constructed with effective use of modern materials. He was a master of spacial effect. Although his churches are sometimes dull and uninspiring outside, their interiors could, at their best, be visually very satisfying. As one commentator put it– albeit in the context of one of Newberry's secular buildings – 'no space is wasted, but a great deal of dignity is obtained by simple sub-division of the space available… one feels that one is in a building which (like Topsy) growed naturally and was inevitable once the plan of the main floor was settled'. Students should not look 'for any unexpected outbreak of originality in design, but for a thoroughly sane and sensible use of the space available, and thought for the purposes for which the building is required'.[37]

For an ecclesiologist's own appraisal of churches in the 1920s and 1930s, and in particular of their furnishings, one need look no further than to the late Stephen Dykes Bower, former President of the Ecclesiological Society. Here are some of his observations, expressed in 1935. 'If the pews are very ugly, as those of varnished pitch pine invariably are, they might be got rid of altogether... chairs are preferable to fixed pews. Their number can be adjusted as required, they do not obscure the architecture to the same extent, and the repetition of their small unit of scale helps to give an impression of size.' He advocates the creation of empty space, as contributing better to a sense of dignity and spaciousness. He says 'There should be nothing shoddy about the furniture of the sanctuary... Much stained glass must, it seems, be endured as a necessary evil and the only thing is to mitigate its unpleasantness as far as possible.' He abhors 'the odious production known as 'cathedral' glass, consisting of opaque tinted panes of different colours.' On colour in a church, 'white is almost always the wisest colour to employ... Lime washing was formerly a regular practice and is fully justified by medieval precedent... there need be little hesitation about applying it over stonework.' On altars, he warns against 'acceptance of the so-called English altar as the inevitably right expression of Anglican propriety. Altars, however, with two candlesticks and a cross, riddels and posts are no more English than continental and we are in no way justified in multiplying them indiscriminately as not merely 'safe' but 'correct'. The only vital questions which should govern the altar are fitness and beauty; and within certain limits of ecclesiology, the decision as to what is appropriate should rest with the architect.' He expresses doubts whether the chancel is always the best place for a choir; a position 'at the side of the chancel, often in what ought to be a chapel, is certainly not the best for the organ.' He advocates the west end as often the best for an organ, with the choir in a gallery at the back or front of the nave.[38]

It may be deduced that Dykes Bower would have approved of much, but by no means all, of what he might have seen had he inspected the interiors of the Southwark Diocese Twenty-five Churches and halls.[39]

As will be clear from a perusal of the following gazetteer pages, no one can reasonably pretend that all of these buildings should be classified as 'great' architecture, nor all of their contents as 'great' art. But, bearing in mind that their completion took place within a period of just ten years, from 1925 to 1934, their diversity is quite remarkable. And it is this diversity, as well as their intrinsic architectural and artistic qualities, that makes these buildings as a whole a subject worthy of study.

Conclusion

It was with some reluctance that, at the age of 57, Garbett accepted his translation from Southwark to Winchester in 1932; and his departure from that see for York ten years later was again the occasion for sadness on his part. In 1955, when still in office as

Archbishop at the age of 80, he recorded in his diary: 'I suppose my best work was at Southwark, restoring discipline, building churches, raising the standard of ordination, establishing synodical government, and in the Lords lifting up my voice against slums and overcrowding.'[40]

In November 1955 he wrote of his decision to retire as Archbishop of York, probably in the following spring. Before doing so, however, he proposed to launch a number of major projects, including a large appeal for new churches to meet the needs of the growing new housing areas.[41] This time, though, it was not to be: he died on 31 December 1955, and his ashes are in the Lady Chapel of York Minster.[42]

GAZETTEER

The gazetteer is arranged alphabetically by place. In choosing the place under which to catalogue each building, account has been taken both of historical and common usage, but in some cases, such as Malden, North Sheen and Kew, there is room for disagreement, not helped by changes in parochial boundaries. Reference to the index will usually help.

Note that, where the place name consists of two elements, it will be found under the first of the two: thus 'North Sheen' is under 'North' rather than 'Sheen'.

The location of each church may be established by reference to the road name given with the entry, or from the website of the Diocese of Southwark, www.dswark.org.

In describing churches, references to points of the compass are to ritual orientation, regardless of the church's geographical alignment.

The majority of the photographs are the author's, and most of the drawings are by John Bray. The sources of other illustrations will be found in the Notes.

BELLINGHAM

St Dunstan, Bellingham Green

New Church, built 1924–5
Architect: Sir C. A. Nicholson
Contractor: Walden & Son, Henley-on-Thames

This was the first church to be built with assistance from the Twenty-five Churches Fund.

The development of a major housing project, under the provisions of the 1919 'Addison' Act, was launched at Bellingham by the London County Council in October 1920 but before a single brick was laid the Anglican Church authorities had inspected the estate plan and reserved a site for a permanent church in a prime position at the heart of the new town. In the absence of immediate funds for its erection, the decision was taken to build first a cheaper structure nearby which could serve as both a temporary mission church and, on a longer term basis, as a hall for social purposes. This building, though simple, was of substantial brick construction and it survives today as the Brookehowse Community Centre; it was designed by Sir Charles Nicholson and erected in 1922, as Bellingham's first place of worship, by William Harbrow of Bermondsey.

Below: Bellingham, St Dunstan from the west.

St Dunstan's, Bellingham Estate – April '88.   John M Bray.

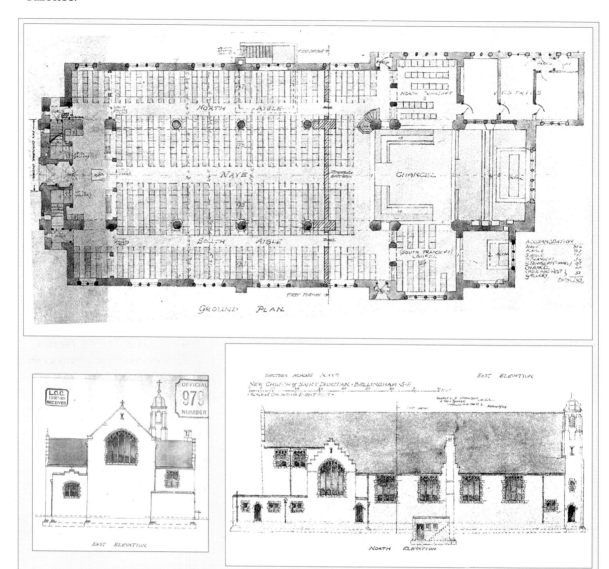

By 1923, over 2,000 dwellings on the estate had been completed, and the site which had been earmarked for the permanent church now overlooked the key focal point from which radiated six roads.

Early in the following year Nicholson produced detailed designs for the church, to be dedicated to St Dunstan, and its foundation stone was laid on 11 October 1924. Nicholson described his designs as being

> on the lines of some of these large late Gothic churches which aim at an effect of internal spaciousness and height rather than one of intricacy and mystery… The architectural detail is also of very simple character and does not attempt to conform strictly to any 'period' of architecture – the detail, except in the

case of the stone columns and windows, being simply a matter of arranging the bricks in such a way as to get a certain amount of variety and relief.

The plan provided for a four-bay aisled nave with a west gallery, and a clerestoried chancel of two bays with a chapel to its south and vestries to the north. The fenestration generally was late Gothic in character, dominated by five-light traceried windows in the east and west walls and in the transept ends. The combined nave and chancel was to have an internal length of about 130 feet, and the building would provide seating for 769 persons.

The church has never been completed to its intended designs and indeed St Dunstan's remains today with no more than the western three bays of its aisled nave, closed off at the east end by a temporary brick wall. This portion provides seating for less than half the planned capacity of the completed church.

Opposite page.

Above: the architect's plan for St Dunstan, east to the right. The plan included transepts, with vestries on the north, and a two-cell chapel on the south.Only the western portion of the church was built. The 'temporary' east wall is also shown on the plan.

Centre: left, the east end as originally conceived; right, the architect's north elevation, with a vertical line showing how the east end was truncated.

Below: the east end as built.

CHOIR, ST. DUNSTAN'S CHURCH, BELLINGHAM GREEN.

Left: an early view of the church from the west, from an old postcard.

Above: interior looking east. Below: the font, remarkable for its small size.

The problem, of course, was that ambitions were not matched by the funds available towards fulfilling them. A sum of £2,000 was provided from the Twenty-five Churches Fund and there were generous donations from other sources but, at the time the church was dedicated on 21 November 1925, receipts were still about £1,000 short of the £10,500 estimated to be the total cost of building even the truncated structure.

The walls of the church are faced externally with red brick, stone being confined to little more than the window surrounds and tracery. The nave roof, which sweeps down across the aisles at a slightly flatter pitch, is covered in grey slates. The best feature is the west front, facing the road: below its five-light Gothic window is a blank arcade of seven round-headed arches; the main portal has a Baroque air, as does the bell turret which is asymmetrically placed to its north and is capped by an ogee-shaped lead-covered cupola.

Within, the stone arcade piers are of square section, set diagonally and with chamfered edges; the pointed arches rest on moulded capitals. The walls are plastered. The roof is of pine, with tie beams and a boarded ceiling, and is decorated in colour. The east end of the north aisle is fitted as a chapel. The large high altar stands behind a full-width communion rail. The vestry originally

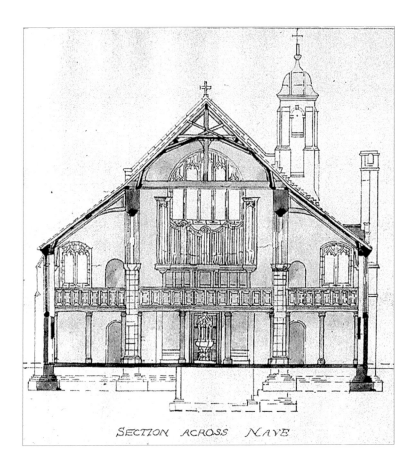

SECTION ACROSS NAVE

The architect's internal elevation of the west end. His intentions for the organ were not realised (see following illustration).

occupied a curtained area on the south side of the building but was later transferred to the west gallery, which extends across both aisles, has a panelled wooden front and is reached by two concrete staircases from the west porch.

The font, centrally placed at the west end, is of some interest. Its octagonal bowl is carved with 'IHS' on one face and floral and foliar designs on the others; its stem and base are also octagonal. The pronounced bevelling of the rim edge is unusual, but its most remarkable feature is its small size. It was found in 1922 in the wooded grounds of Bromley Hall Place, apparently with ferns growing in it, and there seems little doubt that it was one of the many pieces of ornamental stonework which are known to have been introduced there early in the nineteenth century. In effect, it is a scaled-down replica of a typical fifteenth-century church font.

The organ has a complicated history. It was set up in the west gallery at St Dunstan's in 1926, having come from the Chapel Royal at St James's Palace. Sir Charles Nicholson was strongly opposed to its acquisition: he had designed the church's west window to allow for an organ with high towers of pipes rising on each side of it and lower pipes between, so as to avoid blocking the entry of light. The instrument installed had apparently been

The interior, facing west, from an old postcard.

Organ, St. Dunstan's Church, Bellingham Green

designed for chamber use and was tall and narrow-fronted, with four posts enclosing three flats. The case, of which only the front survives, is in a Perpendicular Gothic style, by Hill & Davison, 1837. The organ has been thought to incorporate one of Father Smith's earliest ranks of pipes, but most of the pipework and the three-manual console are by Hill & Son, 1866. The zinc front pipes are decorated with stencil patterns including Royal Arms. Tubular charge-pneumatic action was added in 1900, a few stop alterations were made about 1925, and an overhaul carried out by N. P. Mander in the late 1950s. In 1991 the instrument was restored by F. H. Browne and Sons of Canterbury.

St Dunstan's was not consecrated until 19 November 1939, patronage having been granted to the Bishop of Southwark four weeks earlier. A Consolidated Chapelry was assigned in January 1940, with an area taken from the parishes of St John the Baptist at Southend (Lewisham) and St Michael and All Angels at Bell Green (Lower Sydenham). By this time the Bellingham estate had been further extended to absorb the site of a former golf course to its south.

CARSHALTON BEECHES

The Good Shepherd, Queen Mary's Avenue

New Church, built 1929–30
Architects: Martin Travers & T. F. W. Grant
Contractor: None. Erected by direct labour, with builder Joseph Hastings as Clerk of Works

A mission room, staffed by a lay reader and located in a house in Stanley Road, was succeeded in 1890 by a small iron church, dedicated to the Good Shepherd. This in turn was supplanted ten years later by a larger iron building in Stanley Park Road, the former structure then being re-erected at its rear for use as a hall. Between 1909 and 1912 grants were voted from the City Parochial Charities Fund for the purchase of a site for a new church, but any further ambitions at that time were no doubt stifled by the intervention of the first World War, and the next positive step did not come until the 1920s, when Bishop Garbett visited the parish and promised a grant of £2,000 from the Twenty-five Churches Fund on condition that a start was made within two years on building a permanent church for the district; but he required it to be in a position nearer the centre. In 1928 a one-acre site fronting Queen Anne's Avenue, about one quarter of a mile from the iron church, was conveyed from

The Church of the Good Shepherd, Carshalton Beeches, from the west. Above: a sketch by the architect. Below: a drawing made before the recent addition of an annexe on the south.

The Good Shepherd, Carshalton Beeches – Aug. 94

John M. Bray

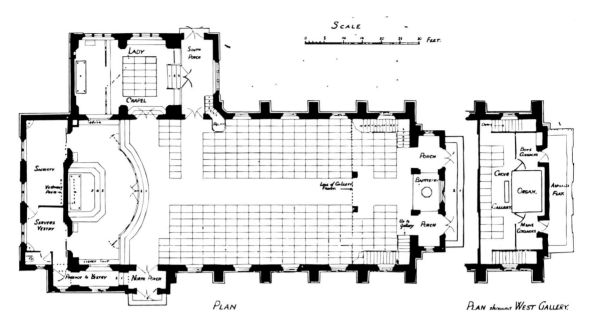

PLAN   PLAN showing WEST GALLERY.

Church of the Good Shepherd, intended plan (the east end is to the left). The south chapel was not built.

Carshalton Urban District Council for the erection of a church, parsonage and parochial hall, and Martin Travers and T. F. W. Grant were engaged as architects for the project; this was, in fact, their first complete joint architectural commission.

At the time the church foundation stone was laid, on 29 June 1929, it was proposed to dedicate the completed building to St Francis of Assisi, but a reversion to the original dedication was later decided. To keep costs down, direct labour was recruited locally and some voluntary aid provided by members of the congregation. As was generally the case with their buildings, the design produced by Travers and Grant was very simple in its constructional elements but showed considerable originality in its embellishments. The architects provided for the construction of a Lady Chapel on the south side and a detached priest's house as well as the main body of the church, but these have never been built.

The church was consecrated on 8 May 1930, whereupon the old iron building was demolished. Unusually, the costs seem to have proved lower than originally expected, totalling no more than £6,060 including architects' fees, with an extra £700 for fittings and furnishings. Of this, £2,000 was contributed from the Twenty-five Churches Fund as promised.

The church was built with a seating capacity of some 380, and has a length of 113 feet and width of 47 feet; the ceiling is 40 feet high. Externally, the walls were constructed of yellow stock bricks, heavily buttressed and pierced by plain rectangular iron-framed windows; the walls were originally whitewashed, apart from a decorative banding of dark red bricks. The roof is continuous over nave and sanctuary and has square clerestory windows in its vertical sides. The west front has a wide single-storey projection, designed to house a baptistry between two entrance porches; this structure is surmounted by a balcony reached from the gallery within. High above, the gable is crowned by a picturesque belfry, which houses a single bell and contributes much to the 'Spanish mission chapel' appearance of the church; its gilded cross was replaced in 1972 after being removed as unsafe two years earlier. The church exterior was intended to be illuminated after dark on feast days.

The interior plan is essentially a simple rectangle without any structural division between nave and sanctuary. There are no aisles. The internal walls, originally distempered, were faced with cement bricks of local manufacture; ominously, the Ecclesiastical Commissioners' examining architects Caröe & Passmore reported in 1930 that they 'seem to be somewhat porous'. In the absence of any interior piers or other internal supports, the roof was stabilised by steel tie-rods resting on the exterior buttresses. It was ceiled in pre-cast plaster, coloured cream, and given a barrel vault which was then carried downwards past the clerestory to the lower side windows in a series of undulating curves which are perhaps the most striking feature of the whole interior design. At the west end, a gallery of steel and concrete was erected for choir and organ, whilst the east wall was given vertical emphasis by a tall shallow recess with a curved top which reflected the line of the barrel vault; within this recess was set a high circular window with green-tinted glass. Placed behind the east wall were the sacristy and vestry, each with a swing door, coloured red and gold, providing direct access to the spacious full-width sanctuary. Enclosing the sanctuary was a curved oak communion rail; this, and the west gallery front and entrance doors, were all given a silver-grey fumed finish.

The church from the south-east, showing the east-end vestries. A long annexe, providing meeting rooms and a chapel, has since been added along the south side.

23

Interior, looking east. Above: the original altar, from a 1941 drawing. Below: an early photograph. The star-shaped light fittings, designed by Martin Travers, have since been removed.

Martin Travers designed many of the furnishings and fittings. Somewhat startling were the extraordinary star-shaped shields encasing the pendant electric lamps which were hung from the ceiling. But the focal point for his artistry was at the east end. At the base of the recess in the end wall he installed an English altar, with four riddel posts, side screens and a low dossal enclosing the communion table, on which were placed six large candlesticks. The rounded riddel posts were surmounted with candle-bearing winged cherubs. The screens and dossal were of pleated woodwork with incised decoration simulating tooled leather, a technique to which Travers added a glowing colour by applying alternate layers of pigment and gilding. The dossal, which Travers said he based on the 'Thornhill' painted leather one formerly in the Law Courts, featured in its centre a circular sun-ray device enclosing the sacred monogram.

Suspended above the altar was a huge rood of Italianate design, against a rectangular background of stained and gilded wood with a pleated or linenfold finish similar to that on the dossal below; mounted on top of the rood was a small roundel depicting the blessing hand of God and the Greek letters alpha and omega. An aumbry, set into the east wall just north of the altar, was given an attractive door bearing the sacred monogram on a lattice design. A hanging lamp, and a small crucifix on the altar, were introduced

into the sanctuary against Travers's wishes; a statue of the Good Shepherd came from the old church.

Martin Travers designed and donated the St Nicholas window in the north wall of the sanctuary, its subdued colours contrasting with the predominant blue and red of his Madonna window on the south side. Two more stained glass windows are at the west end of the church, both quite small: that in the north porch displays a heraldic device representing the See of Southwark, with the initials C. S. for Bishop Cyril (Garbett); while in the south porch Fr Corbould, a Rector of Carshalton, is commemorated by a rebus depicting a rook ('cor') surmounting a cricket ball and two flying stumps ('bowled'). The font was designed with a simple octagonal bowl supported on rectangular panels; it was given an ogee shaped cover with a ball finial. The Cartwright organ, in the gallery above, came from the old church.

The building has had more than its fair share of misfortune since it was erected; and there have been numerous alterations to the interior. The second World War took its toll: the copper roof was lifted and damaged by bomb blast; the vestries at the east end were severely damaged; and the brickwork and doors of the west front were put in need of repair. Reinstatement after the war was accompanied by the conversion of the south porch into a chantry chapel as a memorial to the fallen; its altar, from the former iron church, was later moved to a new position under the gallery. In 1952, a large section of the roof was blown off during a gale, about a third of its copper sheeting being stripped away. An arson attack in 1967 gutted the vestries, destroying most of their contents and damaging much of Travers's work in the sanctuary. Following this, the vestry doors had to be stripped and were then covered in varnish, as also were the altar rails and the gallery woodwork; the roundel which had been mounted on top of the rood was re-sited over the circular east window; and, more significantly, the communion table was brought forward, and its side-screens and front riddel posts removed.

In 1985 the church was found to be suffering from crumbling brickwork and penetrating damp: the outer walls had long since lost their protective paint surface leaving the porous bricks exposed, cracks had appeared in the walls, and the belfry too was crumbling. A major restoration, involving the replacement of much of the brickwork and repairs to the leaking roof, was undertaken by Whitby's Ltd., at cost price on an interest-free extended repayment contract, and the necessary appeal for funds was supported by Sir John Betjeman shortly before he died. Betjeman had a strong affection for the church; one of his poems referred to 'the Travers baroque lime-washed in light', and he whimsically

Aumbry, Good Shepherd, Carshalton Beeches Sept '79. John M Bray.

Original fittings. Above: aumbry door. Below: doorway to gallery.

Door leading to gallery, Good Shepherd, Carshalton Sept '99. John M Bray.

dubbed its characteristics as 'Essoldo moderne in an Hispano-Italian Baroque style'.

A 1984 reordering scheme by Gerald Shenstone & Partners led to more changes. The star-shaped lampshields and last two riddel posts have gone; and the ceiling and its undulating extensions were re-coloured apricot. Externally the south side has acquired a long annexe, designed by architects Carden & Godfrey with James Adam Construction as main contractors. Opened in 2001, it provides meeting rooms and a chapel, in commendable harmony with the original structure, in both its design and the use of materials.

Although there were already 3,000 houses in the area by the 1930s, the Church of the Good Shepherd had to wait until 1965 before achieving parochial status. This delay was largely due to the long-standing opposition of the Rector of Carshalton who, ironically, was that same William Corbould to whom tribute was paid by the rebus window in the church's south porch.

CASTELNAU (Barnes)
Estate Church Hall, Stillingfleet Road

New Hall, built 1929
Architect: Clifton R. Davy
Contractor: W. H. Gaze & Sons Ltd. of Kingston-upon-Thames

In 1824–7 a suspension bridge, the forerunner of the present structure, was thrown across the Thames to link Hammersmith with Barnes. The area to its south, acquired by Major Charles Boileau, was named Castelnau after his ancestral estates near Nimes in France. Early in Queen Victoria's reign he began to build villas on the Barnes road and, in the 1850s, a small chapel of ease was provided there at his expense. In 1868, on a site given by Boileau, Holy Trinity Church was built to the designs of Thomas Allom. A District Chapelry was assigned to it in 1888, and proposals for enlarging the church, first mooted in 1902, were realised in 1913.

By 1928 the population of Holy Trinity parish had soared to some 6,000, by reason of the construction of the London County Council's Castelnau estate of 644 dwellings. The estate, covering over fifty acres, was built in 1926–8; interestingly, some of its streets were named after Deans of St Paul's. At the outset, it was suggested that the population influx might be catered for by a further enlargement of the parish church, but it was quickly realised that separate provision would instead be necessary in the shape of a dual-purpose church hall. A promise of Diocesan help with finance was secured; and negotiations for purchasing a site were under way by January 1927. G. H. Fellowes Prynne was selected as architect for the hall, but he died before taking up the appointment and Clifton Davy was chosen in his stead.

Castelnau, Estate Church Hall, the east end.

Davy's designs provided for a substantial building with a seating capacity of 350. At one end would be a small sanctuary which could be closed off by a folding screen and curtains when not in use; a stage would occupy the other end, with two retiring rooms which could be used for bible classes. Kitchen facilities were also offered. The walls were to be faced externally with multi-coloured bricks, and the tile-covered pitched roof would be supported within on timber posts carrying open timber trusses. Large square-topped windows on either side were to form the main source of natural lighting, supplemented by three stepped lancets in the end wall of the sanctuary.

The designs were quickly approved but determined efforts at fund-raising were needed before building could commence. In January 1929 the building contract was given to W. H. Gaze & Sons Ltd., whose tendered price was £3,887 excluding architect's fees, equipment and furnishing. Towards this the Twenty-five Churches Fund had contributed £1,500. The foundation stone was laid on 27 April 1929, and the sanctuary was dedicated on 25 September.

The second World War had a profound effect on the Hall's fortunes. At the beginning of 1940 the building was 'closed until further notice' to worshippers and was requisitioned for use by Barnes Borough Council as a place of storage. After its 'de-requisitioning' in 1946, it was leased to Surrey County Council and, following extensive renovations, it was reopened for use as a

Above: the interior looking south-east, and the exterior from the north-east. Below: a drawing and plan probably of 1928, showing dual use. The east end is to the left.

PROPOSED · CHURCH · HALL · L·C·C · CASTELNAU · ESTATE · BARNES · S·W·

Youth Centre in July 1947. The lease, initially for five years and then renewable annually, proved to be a long-term arrangement, with the Council taking responsibility for all building repairs other than to the external walls and roof which, along with the chancel and sanctuary, remained the Parish Church Council's liability. Though the latter area had ceased to be used for worship, it was not made available for secular use and was sealed off with a timber screen.

Today, the hall is managed by the London Borough of Richmond-upon-Thames, whose Youth and Community Service operates it as the home of the Castelnau Youth Club. Externally the building appears to have undergone little change, but the interior fittings and decorations are now fully in tune with modern conceptions of popular taste. The chancel is still screened off from the rest of the building.

CHEAM

St Alban the Martyr, Elmbrook Road

New Church, built 1929–30; west end added 1933
Architects: C. J. Marshall & E. A. Swan
Contractors: Stevenson & Glyde of Cheam

A mission church was established in Elmbrook Road, East Cheam, in 1923. A simple building of corrugated iron, with a small bellcote over its western gable, it was re-erected there from its former site in North Cheam as a matter of expediency, but the necessity for its replacement by a permanent church within a few years was already recognised as 'extremely probable', and was being promoted in 1926.

A mile or so to the south-west, nearly four centuries earlier, Nonsuch Palace had been built for King Henry the Eighth. One of its home farms, outliving the palace as Cheam Court Farm, was equipped with some barns and other outbuildings which survived in good condition until threatened with demolition in 1929 to make room for a wider road and modern dwellings. Their fate prompted Charles J. Marshall, a local architect, to suggest that here was the raw material for building a Barn Church similar to the one recently erected at North Sheen. His proposals, backed by a favourable opinion from E. A. Swan, the architect responsible for the North Sheen project, were agreed by the Cheam Parochial Church Council, and the Rector and his Churchwardens promptly acquired demolition rights over the farmhouse, barns, ancillary buildings and garden walling with a view to re-using the most suitable materials; anything unwanted would be sold off, the proceeds being set against expenses.

Opposite: Cheam, St Alban the Martyr, detail.

28

St Alban's Cheam
- Oct '99 — John M Bray.

Meanwhile there were difficulties to be surmounted over the chosen site for the new church. The Twenty-five Churches Fund Committee, to whom application had been made for financial assistance, had delayed a decision while considering the relative merits of the Elmbrook Road site and one further north. They finally settled for the corner of Elmbrook Road and Gander Green Lane, a decision which infuriated the Rector of Sutton, who indignantly complained that this location was too close to his parish boundary, and recalled protests raised in Sutton in 1926 when the proposal was first mooted. His objections were overridden, however, and the architects Marshall and Swan were briefed to prepare designs for a church embodying the best of the acquired materials while retaining the barn characteristics as far as possible.

Once started, progress was well sustained. The contractors, Stevenson & Glyde, who also undertook the demolition work, entered wholeheartedly into the spirit of the enterprise by building the church in the medieval manner, without scaffolding, using a movable platform and derricks. One interesting discovery was that some of the timbers used in the church showed signs of having been employed in other positions before being placed in the early sixteenth century barns. Oak pins which had been used to join woodwork in the old barns were still in excellent condition, and were carefully removed and re-fitted.

The church from the north-east.

St Allan's, Cheam – May '99

John M Bray

The interior looking east (1970s).

The chancel and four bays of the nave were built at this stage, leaving the two westernmost bays, and possibly a baptistry and a choir vestry, to be erected later. The nave was constructed from two of the larger barns, and the aisles from cowsheds. The half-timbered front of one of the smaller barns was incorporated into the upper structure of the gabled organ chamber, whilst chalk blocks and knapped flints from the old farmhouse were used in the lower part. Rich red bricks were re-used to build up the church walls, and old barn tiles to cover the pitched roof, which was pierced by two dormer windows on each side. In a timber shelter on the ridge of the roof was hung a small bell; according to T. P. Stevens it came from St John's College, Battersea, though G. P. Elphick described it as a 'brass ship's bell'. The floor of one of the barns supplied stone flagging for paths outside the church; one of the stones was found to be an old gravestone.

The interior is full of interest. The nave roof, with its massive tie-beams and queen-posts, commands attention. Its timbers were originally made for the barns from fresh wood which sagged in the process of seasoning: hence the rough uneven effect now visible. The lean-to aisle roofs, originally from cowsheds, are carried on beams supported by curved brackets. The upright timber posts which separate nave from aisles have rough curved braces, and rest on brick piers; the tiles capping these, and many of the floor tiles, came from the farmhouse flooring. The organ chamber has Tudor brickwork, from an inglenook and chimney of the old Cheam Court hall, and it displays an upright post with crosses cut into it, an indication that the barn from which it came may at one time have been used for religious purposes, perhaps clandestinely during a period of persecution. The vestry ceiling has great beams taken from the Jacobean floor of the hall of Cheam Court.

Right: the church as first built, from the north. Below: the church from the north-west, after addition of the west end and north porch. Both from old postcards.

The font came from the predecessor of the present St Dunstan's Church at Cheam, where it rested from 1746 to 1864. The aumbry doors were fashioned of wood from a cellar door out of the farmhouse, and carved by Miss Swan of Oxted. A credence table was formed from the top of a staddle – the mushroom-shaped stone structures used on farms to support granaries or stacks and prevent entry by rats.

At the time the church was dedicated on 17 March 1930, the iron mission building which preceded it was left standing for use as a hall, but its demolition was necessary before the new church could be given its final two bays at the west end. A grant of £1,000 had already been allocated from the Twenty-five Churches Fund towards the overall net building costs, but £250 of this award had been withheld pending final completion of the church, so the incentive to press on was there. In January 1931 an appeal was made for additional funds to be collected locally; and by the first half of 1933 the building had been given a north porch with old beams and

a tiled roof, and, with its additional west end, was now complete except for the baptistry and choir vestry which, as structural additions, were abandoned. The church was re-dedicated on 17 June 1933. The building's unusual story was inscribed thus on a stone placed at the new west end: 'This church was built in 1930 of materials from Cheam Court Farm, one of the farms attached to Nonsuch Palace. These old beams were parts of the barns when Queen Elizabeth was at Nonsuch. The glories of Nonsuch have passed away, but the beams of the humble buildings remain and are now around you.'

CHEAM

St Oswald, Brock's Drive

Site for new Hall, acquired 1934
Hall and Church later built outside the aegis of the Twenty-five Churches Fund

In 1923 a Mission Hall was bodily removed from North to East Cheam to serve a district that was 'rapidly growing up of people of very limited means'. Subsequent developments there are described under Cheam, St Alban the Martyr. Ten years later the dismantling of Brock's Fireworks Factory in North Cheam made available a large tract of land for the development of the Park Farm Estate which was to increase the population by about 6,000 in that part of the parish.

The Southwark Diocesan authorities quickly saw the need for restoring the provision there of local facilities for worship, though the Twenty-five Churches Fund was by that time nearing closure. The chosen site, which was bought and vested in the Diocesan Church Trust in 1934, was big enough to permit a hall to be erected on it first, and a larger permanent church to be added alongside when funds permitted.

Designs for both hall and church were prepared by Terence P. Carr. His church hall, constructed of brick with a tiled roof, was planned to function initially as a multi-purpose building, to seat 250 persons, the total cost being estimated at £3,000. The foundation stone was laid on 10 August 1936 and the building was dedicated on 5 March 1937. James Burges & Sons of Wimbledon were the builders.

A permanent church was added on the site in 1952–3 but Carr's designs were not used, the architects being T. F. Ford & Partners. Construction was financed largely by Diocesan funds which became available from a decision not to rebuild the Streatham church of St Anselm which had been destroyed in the second World War. Seating 220 and of 'simple but effective design', the church was provided, above the altar, with a plain wooden cross

Two views of Cheam, St Oswald. Top: hall of 1936–7. Bottom: church built 1952–3.

illuminated by fluorescent strip lighting concealed in alcoves. The exterior, with brick walls and a tiled roof, blends well with that of the adjoining hall.

On the hall's porch, facing Brock's Drive, is a plaque, erected by Sutton Leisure Services, recording the former occupation of the surrounding area by Brock's Firework Factory.

COULSDON

St Francis of Assisi, Rickman Hill

Site for new Church and Hall, purchased 1926; Hall built 1928
Architects: Mathews & Ridley
Contracto: H. Bacon & Sons, Coulsdon

The conventional parish of St Andrew, Coulsdon, was formed in 1906. To serve it, an iron mission building was reconstructed and furnished as a church. The erection of a separate hall followed within two years, but the roles of the two buildings were soon exchanged.

The foundation stone of a permanent church, designed by F. H. Greenaway & J. E. Newberry and dedicated to St Andrew, was laid on 18 April 1914, but the outbreak of war interrupted progress and the building, situated at the corner of Woodmansterne Road and Woodcote Grove Road, was consecrated in an incomplete state on 31 October. Fifty years were to elapse before the west end was finally closed off with a narthex.

In 1925 a mission building for the parish was erected in Rickman Hill, and this was followed a year later by the purchase of a new site there, which was said to be 'adequate for purposes of a church hall and also for the building of a church in the future'. The money for this purchase came from the Twenty-five Churches Fund.

Coulsdon, St Francis (now St Mary and St Shenouda) from the north-west. The building began life as a dual-purpose hall. In this drawing the obscuring foliage has been omitted in order to show the structure of the building.

Work at the site began on 1 June 1928, for the construction of a new hall which, as a 'daughter' to the parish church of St Andrew, was to serve as a dual-purpose building until a permanent church could be afforded. Six weeks later, on 14 July, the foundation stone was laid, and on 15 October the building was dedicated to St Francis: the first dedication, it was said, to this saint in Southwark Diocese. The Twenty-five Churches Fund contributed £1,500 towards the building cost.

In 1943, the building debt having at last been cleared, consideration was given to the possibility of erecting a new purpose-built church on land available behind the hall. Advice was sought as to the choice of a suitable architect but there was of course no hope of real progress during the war years and the idea was abandoned. In the early 1960s a more modest scheme was realised with the construction of a new hall at the rear of the existing building, enabling the original structure to be used solely as a church. This arrangement survived until 12 December 1987, when the final service was held there, the church's closure having been forced by the 'difficulty in finding clergy and a falling congregation'.

In April 1989, after several months of negotiation, the premises were sold to the Coptic Orthodox Church for £550,000, a price said to be a fraction of what could have been commanded on the open market. The Diocese had resisted pressure to sell to property developers, a spokesman saying that 'in the end we are very happy to be able to provide another Christian Church with the premises'. The proceeds from the sale were to be used for refurbishing St Andrew's Church Hall.

The church is now dedicated to St Mary and St Shenouda. It stands on a steeply sloping site, only its ritual north side being fully visible from the road below. This vantage point shows the construction to be of dark multi-coloured brick walls surmounted by a brown tiled main roof which continues unbroken from east to west. There are projecting wings at each end of the building, linked by a long north aisle. Above the aisle is seen a clerestory, set in a wall concealed behind horizontally overlapping timber cladding. A low west porch or narthex contains the centrally-placed main entrance. Above this, in the gable of the main west wall, is a solitary bell on an unprotected bracket; this, if original, was reported by G. P. Elphick (1975) to have been cast at Whitechapel in 1971. At the opposite end, a plain wooden cross crowns the east gable.

Downham, St Barnabas, church (left) and hall (right), from the west.

DOWNHAM

St Barnabas, Downham Way

New Hall, built 1926, and new Church, built 1928–9
Architect: Sir C. A. Nicholson
Contractors: Walden & Son, Henley-on-Thames (the Hall)
  and E. Bowman & Sons, Stamford, Lincolnshire (the Church)

The Hall

The probable need for a church in this area had been foreseen as early as the beginning of 1920, when the news broke that the London County Council was considering embarking on a house-building scheme for the district which would be larger even than that being planned at Bellingham.

The resultant vast and sprawling Downham housing estate which was begun in 1924 presented the Southwark Diocesan authorities with a considerable challenge: the early provision of adequate facilities for worship in the heart of the estate was perceived as essential, and to this end a triangular site was acquired in a good central position on a hill-side facing down the broad spinal route of Downham Way. Finance for its purchase was found with the aid of a grant of £1,000 from the City Parochial Charities Fund, awarded on the recommendation of Bishop Garbett under his Twenty-five Churches scheme. The site was big enough to accommodate church, hall and parsonage and, with the population flooding in, it became a matter of clear and urgent priority to erect first a dual-purpose building which could serve as both church and hall, and to follow this as early as practicable with a larger permanent church, at which stage the original building would be used solely as a hall. This plan followed the precedent set at Bellingham and, once again, Sir Charles Nicholson was selected as architect for both hall and church.

For the hall, Nicholson designed a fairly simple but substantial building; within its overall dimensions of 84 feet by 42 feet it could seat over 400 persons, in a main space of 60 feet by 40 feet, adjoined by a sanctuary at the east end and a stage at the west. The sanctuary, which could be enclosed by three shutters when not in use, was flanked by a vestry and a kitchen, whilst the stage had dressing rooms on either side and a room suitable for committee meetings beneath it. The open timber roof, unusually impressive for a building of this type, was of trussed rafters, with king-posts, struts and purlins. The five-bay 'nave' had narrow passage aisles to north and south, from which it was separated by cylindrical concrete columns with concrete caps. Light was admitted by plain square-headed windows in the aisles and by a series of dormer windows in a large slated roof which swept down in an unbroken line to the outer walls. These walls were faced with 'Old English' Sussex stock bricks.

The foundation stone of this, Downham's first church building, was laid on 19 June 1926 by Stanley L. Powell, who was not only Chairman of the Diocesan Board of Finance, but the principal donor of funds, for he personally contributed £1,500 towards the £4,000 cost of erecting and equipping the building. Six months later, on 22 December, the building was dedicated.

By March 1928 the population of Downham had reached 15,000 and was continuing to grow with undiminished pace. Yet, twelve months later, *The Times* reported that the church hall of St Barnabas was still 'the only public building on the estate' apart from schools. Small wonder, then, that it was #lled every week for the Sunday evening services, and that 2,500 children had 'enrolled in Sunday School classes which have to be held in relays'. The Church of England, said *The Times*, was 'showing the way'.

The consecration of the large permanent church of St Barnabas, on its adjoining site, in the summer of 1929 relieved the pressure on space to some extent, and further help came with the erection of St Luke's Hall to the north-east in 1930. The interior of St Barnabas's Hall was modified in 1936 so as to confine its facilities to secular use

The church hall.

only. The main hall area, with its passage aisles, remained unchanged but, at the east end, the erstwhile sanctuary was walled off and converted into a serving area with a hatch to the main hall and access to a kitchen and storeroom on either side. There was now room in the hall for 376 seats or 300 dancers.

The hall survives in good condition today, though it suffered damage when a flying bomb fell nearby in 1944, and there have been minor alterations since then.

The Church

In November 1927, less than a year after St Barnabas's Church Hall had been opened, Sir Charles Nicholson completed designs for a permanent church to be erected alongside it, and in February 1928 a sum of £8,000 was granted from the Twenty-five Churches Fund for its construction. This was a huge amount, far larger than the normal allocation from this source, and it demonstrated recognition that there was no early prospect of anything like an adequate sum being raised locally.

The builder's contract price of £10,750 thus largely being under-written, early progress was made. Work on the site commenced on 29 May 1928, and the foundation stone was laid on 6 October, consecration following on 13 July 1929. By that time, a further grant of £1,000 had been voted by the Ecclesiastical Commissioners.

As with so many of the 'Twenty-five' churches, particularly Nicholson's, St Barnabas's was still unfinished when it was opened. In this case the vestries, which were planned to be added at the north-east corner, were omitted, and are now unlikely ever to be built according to Nicholson's designs.

The church from the west.

The style of architecture which he employed here has been described variously as 'Byzantine', 'plain Early Christian' and 'on classic lines', but it is probable that Nicholson sought merely, as at Bellingham, to create a spacious building without a conscious attempt to conform strictly to any stylistic precedent. The basic plan is a simple parallelogram, with an aisleless sanctuary projecting from it at one end and a transeptal narthex at the other. Externally, the walls are faced with brick, matching those of the hall; the main roof, which is unbroken from end to end, is covered with red Roman pantiles. The aisle roofs are flat. The windows to aisles, clerestory and chancel are all single lights and very simple. The west front, which faces directly down the lower straight stretch of Downham Way and is thus in a prominent position, has what little ornamentation is externally visible. Its dominant feature is its main portal, which is contained within an outer square frame; above the double timber doors is a plain white tympanum under a rounded arch of moulded brickwork. Over the portal, a large circular window lights the gallery within, and, offset to the south, the main roof gable is broken by a simple brick bellcote, with a lone bell. Each arm of the transeptal narthex has a subsidiary west door, and a series of three small windows just below the roof line.

The spacious interior was praised on its completion for its noble proportions. It, too, is a simple composition, but is given much power and character by the tall cylindrical reinforced concrete columns, of Tuscan derivation, which separate nave from aisles. The building was designed to seat 700; its six-bay nave is about 83 feet long and 54 feet wide across the aisles; whilst the chancel has a length of about 22 feet and a width of 23 feet contracting to 19 feet across the sanctuary. The walls and aisle roofs are plastered; the roof above nave and chancel is open to the apex. In the chancel east wall are set a pair of plain round-headed windows with a string-course over; resting on this is an arcade of three round-headed arches, the outer ones blind and the much larger middle one embracing a plain circular window. There are few other ornamental features in the internal architectural design. At the west end is a full-width gallery, intended to house the choir and organ – though an organ has never been installed there. It has a plain panelled front, and is reached by two concrete staircases from lobbies at the ends of the aisles.

The omission of vestries when the church was built necessitated the erection of temporary facilities at the east end of the north aisle, screened by wooden partitions. After the end of the second World War, the vestries were transferred to the gallery. The east end of the south aisle was initially fitted up as a Lady Chapel; about 1970 this became the Chapel of the Reserved Sacrament, its altar being the one which was originally in the church hall.

Above: interior views taken from the west gallery, looking east. Below: the east end, as re-ordered 1980–81.

St Barnabas, Downham Estate – June '99.   John M Bray ARCA

The interior, looking south-east.

The organ in the north aisle, though modest in size and somewhat rustic in appearance, is quite interesting. It was built originally in 1854 by B. Flight & Sons and installed in the private chapel of Southend Hall at Catford. About 1922 it was apparently moved into the old St John's Chapel there but became redundant when this chapel was succeeded by the new St John's Church a few years later. In 1931 it was purchased from St John's for £50 and transported to St Barnabas's Church to replace its harmonium; the original hand-pumped action was then replaced by an electric pump. As well as keyboards, it once had a hand-operated barrel; this was removed in 1875 but a list of its eight tunes has remained affixed inside the case. Some changes to stops and pipes were made in 1899 and 1909, on the latter occasion by R. Slater, and the instrument was repaired in 1948 by his son S. Slater after bomb damage. A complete overhaul was carried out by Buttolph in 1992–3, when certain alterations made to the pipes in 1899 were reversed and the case was repaired.

In 1962 the fittings were supplemented by pews, choir stalls and a pulpit from the Victorian chapel of Christopher Boone's Almshouses at Lee when that building was sold to the Emmanuel Pentecostal Church.

Like the hall, the church suffered from the effects of the flying bomb which fell nearby in August 1944: all its windows were lost, and its roof was damaged. The parsonage, which had been built in 1938–40 to the designs of Sir C. A. Nicholson and T. J. Rushton, was completely wrecked.

The church interior was reordered in 1980–81, at which stage a platform was set up for the nave altar, a new Lady Chapel was created in the area behind the organ, and a screen was erected at the west end to enclose the narthex.

DOWNHAM
St Luke, Northover

New Hall, built 1930
Architect: Sir C. A. Nicholson
Contractor: Merton Abbey Joinery Works

Even before the completion in 1929 of the sizeable Church of St Barnabas in Downham Way to complement the facilities at its adjacent Hall, it had become apparent that yet more space was needed to cope with the rising demand for Sunday School and church-linked social functions. In 1928, a site for an additional mission hall or church, half a mile to the north-east, was purchased from the London County Council for £600, with grants from the City Parochial Charities Fund. In July 1929 a further C.P.C.F. grant of £1,000 was voted, at Bishop Garbett's request, for erecting a hall on the site, primarily 'to accommodate the overflow of Sunday School children from St Barnabas's Church', but also 'to provide a place for recreative and social activities'. There was no immediate intention to build a church there.

In April 1930, the building contract was placed with the Merton Abbey Joinery Works, and in the following month work was already said to be 'proceeding rapidly'. From the outset the hall was described as a 'temporary' building. With outstanding debts of £900 on St Barnabas's and £1,650 on St John the Baptist at South-end, nothing more ambitious could be afforded, though it was recognised that a permanent church would probably be erected at the site eventually. The building was dedicated as St Luke's Hall on 13 September 1930. The total construction cost was £1,500, with an extra £300 for furnishings and other expenses; the balance in excess of the £1,000 grant from the C.P.C.F. (effectively the Twenty-five Churches Fund's contribution) had to be raised locally. By the time the hall was opened, 360 children had already been enrolled for membership of its Sunday School.

Contemporary reports quote the hall's seating capacity variously as 250 and about 300, but give little information on its appearance at the time of its completion. There is no doubt that it was a strictly utilitarian structure; Sir Charles Nicholson's involvement was probably no more than a general supervisory one. We are told that the interior had an apple green ceiling, whilst the walls were of cream and black, the whole presenting 'a very elegant and pleasing appearance'. The sanctuary, comprising a 'dais on which are the table and lectern', was screened off from the rest of the hall by a curtain when not in use. It was not until St Luke's Day in 1931 that the altar was dedicated; the building was then said to be one of 'three vigorous daughter churches (of St John's at Southend, that is; the other two being St Barnabas's, and St Dunstan's at Bellingham), functioning independently under their priests-in-charge, the entire parochial staff meeting regularly for a weekly "Chapter" in St John's Vicarage'. St Luke's Hall had thus now become fully dual-purpose.

Subsequent developments at the site did not occur until after the closure of the Twenty-five Churches Fund. In 1934 a smaller, additional, hall of timber and asbestos was erected there by William Harbrow of Bermondsey, with financial assistance from the Bishop of Southwark's Council for New Districts and the South London Church Fund. In the following year Sir Charles Nicholson and T. J. Rushton prepared designs for a new permanent church, on part of the same site. Its internal dimensions were about 112 feet by 48 feet; its walls were to be of stock brick, the timber roof being covered with slates; and vestries would be provided in a basement below the sanctuary and north chapel. The estimated cost was £6,000. The necessity for the church was underlined by Bishop Parsons (Dr Garbett's successor at Southwark) who, when the foundation stone was laid on 13 March 1937, said that all church services except weddings had been conducted in the two halls on

Downham, St Luke from the west.

Architect's drawing of the church interior looking east.

the site, while Sunday School classes had been held there in six shifts each Sunday. The church was consecrated on 8 January 1938; it had the distinction of being the only Nicholson church in the area to be fully completed to the architect's designs.

Barely more than three years after the church's consecration, its roof was completely burned out by a wartime incendiary bomb, necessitating the temporary resumption of services in the main hall. In 1942 one aisle of the church was re-roofed with floor timbers and re-opened for worship. The church was fully repaired after the war and is in use today, but both of the halls which preceded it have been supplanted by the brick-built Anthony Toller Memorial Hall and a terrace of small houses.

EAST SHEEN

All Saints, East Sheen Avenue

New Church, built 1928–9
Architects: J. E. Newberry & C. W. Fowler
Contractors: Dove Bros. Ltd., of Islington

Early attempts to establish a permanent church building in this part of the old parish of Mortlake were characterised by much uncertainty in the face of changing circumstances. After several false starts, things seemed to begin moving in earnest in 1924, when Bishop Garbett, aware that the eastern end of the parish was now rapidly expanding its population, urged that efforts should be concentrated there, with the building of All Saints' Church on what appeared to be a satisfactory site. A new Church Building Committee was appointed, and an opinion sought from the Diocesan Advisory Committee as to a suitable architect. From their suggested short-list, J. B. L. Tolhurst was selected and asked to produce

Tolhurst's proposal for All Saints, East Sheen.

designs. These, described at the time as 'both unique and pleasing', passed the Diocesan Advisory Committee's scrutiny.

All should now have been plain sailing but, at this point, complications set in over the conveyance of the land on which the church was to be built. This difficulty had scarcely been resolved when a new stumbling block appeared: Tolhurst's church designs were rejected by the Ecclesiastical Commissioners. Doubts about building costs were already beginning to be expressed; despite the architect's repeated assurances that the church could be erected for £11,000, plus £1,000 for fees and fittings, the lowest building tender received was for nearly £16,000, and Tolhurst was warned that his plans would have to be abandoned unless he could find a way of reducing the expense. Garbett himself regarded the cost as excessive, comparing it unfavourably with that of St Paul's, Furzedown (q.v.), which he had just consecrated. He was also perplexed, he said, by the proposed style of architecture, which featured a 'classical nave with a Gothic clerestory and roof'. It was, indeed, this curious admixture of styles which caused Caröe & Passmore, the architectural advisers to the Ecclesiastical Commissioners, to give an adverse verdict. 'The association,' said they, 'of ribbed vaulting and fan vaulting, carried out in concrete, with the Classical columns and entablature below does not seem to us a happy one'. Surviving drawings clearly point to the influence of Sir Ninian Comper's 'unity by inclusion' principles but, whereas an architect of Comper's stature could gain acceptance for them, Tolhurst could not.

The task of extricating the parish from this unhappy situation fell to the architect W. A. Forsyth, who had just completed the successful enlargement of St Margaret's Church at Putney (q.v.). In securing Tolhurst's disengagement, he later told the Building Committee 'I feel that I saved you from the horrible position of having to worship in a ferro-concrete church, the discomfort and resonance of which would have been intolerable'. Understandably,

Forsyth was disappointed with the subsequent decision to place the design of the church at East Sheen into hands other than his, but the Building Committee, perhaps mindful of Bishop Garbett's reference to St Paul's at Furzedown, went to see another recent church by its architects and decided that this was in line with their aspirations. The church was St Mary's at Sanderstead (q.v.), and the architects were F. H. Greenaway and J. E. Newberry. In 1928 the successors to this practice, J. E. Newberry and C. W. Fowler, were invited to prepare plans for a similar building at East Sheen. This time all went well, Newberry & Fowler soon producing designs which proved generally acceptable. The building contract was awarded to Dove Brothers of Islington who quoted £8,725 excluding heating, lighting, furniture and fittings. The foundation stone was laid on 24 October 1928 by the then Duchess of York, mother to Queen Elizabeth II, and the completed building was consecrated on All Saints' Day, 1 November 1929. By far the greater part of the overall cost of the church, which ultimately reached about £12,700 including fees and 'extras', was met by local efforts, but a grant of £200 was voted from the Twenty-five Churches Fund.

For their money, the parishioners received a typical Newberry church: sound, simple and orthodox, though with one or two original touches to add distinction to the design. In plan, the scheme was for a four-bay nave with north and south aisles, and a chancel flanked on the south side by a chapel, and on the north by choir and clergy vestries and a small sacristy. An organ chamber was fitted above the choir vestry and the return way for communicants.

Interior view of Tolhurst's proposal. Note the Classical columns and entablature supporting a Gothic ribbed vault.

45

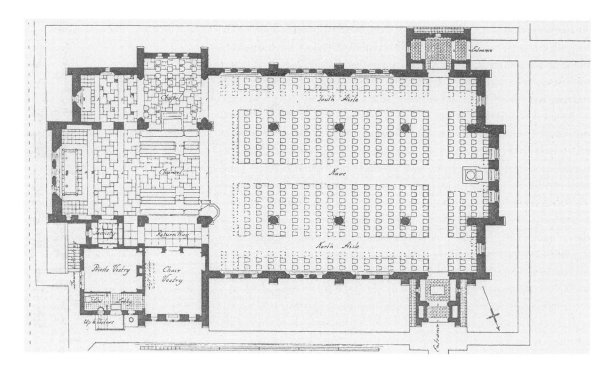

— All Saints', East Sheen — April '99.   — John M Bray A.R.C.A.

At the west end of the church, north and south porches were built, though the original concept provided for a tall tower to be added in place of the north porch; this, however, could not be afforded and has never been erected. The nave, aisles and chancel were all narrow to enhance the impression of height.

As with the Sanderstead church, brick was by far the dominant building material. The outside walls and window surrounds were entirely faced with hand-made multi-coloured bricks, whilst grey-toned facing brick was used internally, except for the arches and responds of the nave, chancel and chapel which were of Bath stone. The thick-tiled roof over nave and chancel was unbroken from end to end, and continued downwards to span both of the aisles, so that there was neither chancel arch nor clerestory. On the ridge over the junction of nave and chancel rose an oak-shingled flèche which served as a bell turret; the bell inside was cast by Mears & Stainbank. Roofing was of Columbian pine, open to the apex and reinforced with tie-beams. The fenestration, entirely of lancets, reflected the chosen architectural style: Early English Gothic. The church could seat up to 526 persons; its overall dimensions were said to be about 113 feet in length and 51 feet across nave and aisles.

Many of the fittings were made from the architects' own designs: these included the altars, riddel posts, communion benches and panelled choir stalls, all simple and of unstained English oak; the altar and processional crosses, candlesticks and alms dish, all executed in pewter; and, at the west end, the Portland stone font, which was square with panel-traceried sides. The font lid was of oak and wrought iron. An aumbry formed a small but attractive feature on the north wall of the sanctuary; it was fitted with a nail-studded door within a moulded arch decorated with minute ball-flower.

Opposite page: East Sheen, All Saints as built. Top: plan, east to the left. Bottom: the church from the north-west.

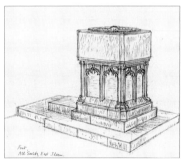

Above: top, aumbry door; bottom, font.

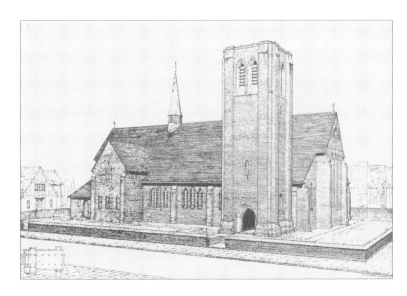

Left: drawing showing the unbuilt tower.

47

Two views of the interior. Top: the south chapel. Bottom: the east end, as re-ordered in 1966–7, but before recent re-arrangement.

An organ was purchased second-hand from Gray & Davison Ltd., who reconstructed and modernised it, adding an electro-magnetic action which enabled it to be played from a detached console on the south side of the chancel. This instrument eventually gave problems and had become unusable by 1947. It was then restored by the John Compton Organ Company who completely renewed the action and positioned a new oak console in the choir stalls; their work was finished in 1950.

In 1960 the church received a new pulpit, in English oak with panelled sides, designed by the architect C. W. Fowler whose joint practice with G. A. Sutton had succeeded that of Newberry & Fowler. By this time, the church had acquired some stained glass. The earliest, in the three lancets forming the chancel east window, bears the artist's mark of Horace Wilkinson and is dated 1932; and the Lady Chapel sanctuary was embellished with memorial glass about 1958.

The church survived the second World War unscathed, but disaster struck on 20 November 1965 when considerable damage was caused by a fire which destroyed the choir vestry and its contents, burnt out the organ and its loft, and spread over about half of the main roof. Repairs were supervised by the architect E. F. Starling, with James Longley & Co. Ltd. of Crawley, Sussex, as the main contractors. The roof had to be repaired and completely re-tiled, and the flèche belfry renewed; the nave floor, which had been damaged by water, had to be replaced; the whole interior had to be cleaned; and the vestries, organ chamber and return way had to be restored. The opportunity was taken to carry out some internal re-ordering. This included replacing and rearranging the seating in the nave; moving the altar forward; and re-positioning the choir stalls to the far east end, so that they faced the altar and congregation. The pulpit also was moved, nearer to the centre of the church. Luckily the stained glass remained intact, but the organ was utterly beyond repair apart from its console which was salvaged. A replacement instrument, originally built in 1911 by Norman & Beard, was secured from the Eden Street Methodist Church in Kingston-upon-Thames, and reconstructed in the organ chamber by Percy Daniel & Co. Ltd. of Clevedon, Somerset, who added some missing pipework and made the console movable. This organ was ready in time for the church's re-dedication on 1 May 1967.

Perhaps the most significant and poignant development of more recent date has been the dedication, on 25 July 1996, of a new stained glass window at the west end of the nave. The work of Alan Younger, it commemorates the young estate agent Suzy Lamplugh, whose disappearance in tragic circumstances ten years earlier had so shocked the nation. Commissioned by her family, the window depicts Christ's Resurrection, signifying the triumph of good over evil and the inspiration to new life. Suzy Lamplugh had been baptised in the church and had sung in its choir.

Under the direction of Patrick Crawford of Caröe and Partners, the east end of the church has now been re-converted to a more traditional appearance, with choir stalls facing each other across the chancel, and the High Altar repositioned closer to the east wall on a new floor of Portland stone.

EAST WICKHAM

St Michael, Upper Wickham Lane

New Church, built 1932–3
Architect: Thomas F. Ford
Contractors: Chapman, Lowry & Puttick Ltd., of Haslemere

With a seating capacity of not much more than 100, East Wickham's medieval church was clearly unable to cope satisfactorily with the demands imposed by the influx of residents into the dwellings erected in the second and third decades of the twentieth century.

The first steps towards erecting a new, larger, church were taken in 1926, when Bishop Garbett consecrated a two-acre plot of land adjoining the old churchyard. But, notwithstanding the existence by this time of the Twenty-five Churches Fund, it soon became

East Wickham, St Michael from the north-west.

Above: top, the east end; bottom, the west end.
Below: the font.

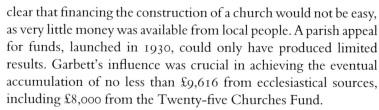

clear that financing the construction of a church would not be easy, as very little money was available from local people. A parish appeal for funds, launched in 1930, could only have produced limited results. Garbett's influence was crucial in achieving the eventual accumulation of no less than £9,616 from ecclesiastical sources, including £8,000 from the Twenty-five Churches Fund.

Early in 1932 Thomas Ford, who had been appointed as architect, submitted design proposals which were accepted subject to a few adjustments including slight increases to the heights of the nave, aisles and bell turret. The building contract was awarded to Chapman, Lowry & Puttick of Haslemere. On 9 July the foundation stone was laid, and construction proceeded at a brisk pace so that the church's consecration was able to take place on 18 February 1933, little more than seven months later. The church was erected some distance back from the road, so as to avoid disturbing the old graveyard surrounding its ancient predecessor.

The architect's brief, to provide a large church at a low cost, inevitably resulted in a simple building on austere lines. In plan, it consisted of a nave of 6½ bays, with corresponding north and south aisles terminating in a pair of west porches. There was no structural chancel but a semi-circular apsidal sanctuary was added at the east end. Vestries protruded from the north-west corner. Within this frame, which extended to a total length of about 131 feet, seats could be provided for over 700 persons.

The building has been described as a Byzantine basilica, modelled on the church of San Apollinare in Ravenna, though without the campanile. Its external appearance is somewhat stark, the dark brick walls being relieved by only minimal decoration, confined to little more than a small round-arched arcade just below the apse roof, and a neatly-chequered pattern of bricks and knapped flints, edged with tiles, used to fill the tympanum over each of the doorways. Set high in the west wall is a cross of white stones which, along with similar stones incorporated into two prominent lamp standards outside the west front, were recovered during excavations for the church's foundations and are possibly the remains of an old manor house. The fenestration, of round-headed lights, is elementary, large single clerestory windows alternating with the smaller triplets in the aisles. The tile-covered main roof, continuous from end to end, has a plain brick bell-cote rising from its north-west corner; the bell, of almost 6 cwt., was reported by R.W.M. Clouston to have been cast by Gillett & Johnston.

The interior is spacious and quite impressive. The architect's expressed aim was 'to obtain a dignified and simple effect, harmonious in colour with nothing to distract the attention from the east end where all the colour and decoration has been concentrated.' The square-sectioned piers of the nave arcades are faced with green

sandstone to a height of about five feet; other structural surfaces are of brick, finished in cream-coated plaster. The semi-circular arches of the arcades spring directly from the piers without capitals. The fine timber roof, open to the apex, has tie-beams. There is a west gallery for organ and choir; accessible from it are two rooms which surmount the porches, one intended as a blowing chamber for the organ, and the other as a music room for the choir.

Original fittings include a stone font, beneath the west gallery; a pair of simple round-headed arches are cut into each side of its octagonal bowl, whilst its pedestal and base have four concave sides alternating with narrower straight ones. The pulpit, also of stone, is semi-octagonal and has small carvings representing the four evangelists. An organ was obtained from Spurden Rutt. A mural painting, to act as a reredos, was intended but not executed.

When the new church opened in 1933, the old one was assigned to serve as a mortuary chapel, and in the 1950s it was adapted as a venue for parish meetings. In 1965 Laurence King prepared designs for converting part of the 'new' parish church for use as a hall and meeting rooms, but this scheme was abandoned in favour of a cheaper alternative financed largely by the Diocese: a separate parish hall, which was put up in 1966 by Kentish Church Builders. The old church was declared redundant in 1971 and was

Above: the pulpit. Below: interior looking east.

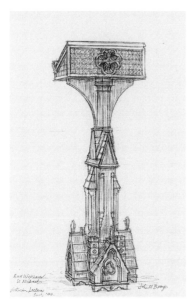

Above: lectern. Below: west door.

subsequently taken over by the Greek Orthodox Church who re-dedicated it to Christ the King. Following the award of a Faculty in 1972, a number of interesting objects were removed from the old church and are now to be seen in the present St Michael's. Mounted on the wall of the north aisle are some notable brasses: of the fourteenth century are John de Bladigdone and his wife Maud, shown as half-effigies, his believed to be the earliest representation on a brass in this country of a man in civilian costume; another, of William Payn and two of his three wives with three children, dates from the sixteenth century and bears on the reverse side an earlier Latin epitaph to John Awncell. On the north aisle floor stand three bells, the oldest of which is inscribed with the date 1660 and the founder's name, John Hodson; another is uninscribed; and the third was cast by S. B. Goslin in 1887, the year of Queen Victoria's Golden Jubilee. Affixed to the panelled front of the west gallery, and re-painted, are the carved Royal Arms of Charles II. These and the 1660 bell were no doubt introduced to celebrate the Restoration. On the nave floor below is an iron coffer, perhaps originally a parish chest but later serving as an alms box; local tradition prefers the story that it was taken from the Spanish Armada in 1588 and given to the church by Admiral Sir John Hawkins. Also at the west end of the church are two Victorian funeral hatchments.

Concurrently with the arrangements made for the transfer of these items from the medieval church, plans were made for re-ordering and redecorating the parish church interior. An initial scheme prepared by R. Covell in 1971 was scaled down to result in the altar being brought forward from the apse, whilst the reredos, the altar rail, the apse panelling and the hanging lights in the chancel were all removed. This wholesale clearance from the sanctuary area gave an added emphasis to the most dominating feature of all the post-war additions to the church interior: a large and strikingly powerful icon set up against the east wall of the apse. This depicts Christ the Divine Word of God in Glory, and was painted in 1973 by Hieromonk Sophrony, a septuagenarian Russian-born monk of the Orthodox Church.

The parish, which had been augmented in 1934 by the absorption of the large Falconwood estate, closely followed by the construction of the Stevens estate to the east, eventually became one of the most heavily populated in the Diocese. On the Stevens estate, St Michael's Mission Church and School were set up in 1938.

ELTHAM

St Barnabas, Rochester Way

Church reconstructed on new site, 1932–3
Architect: Thomas F. Ford
Contractor: W. E. Ismay of Peckham

Few occupants of the constant stream of vehicles negotiating the busy Well Hall roundabout spare even a passing glance at the church nearby. Those delayed at the adjacent traffic lights may, if they are observant, wonder idly at the presence of this High Victorian Gothic building in an environment which is so obviously and exclusively of the twentieth century. But all is not what it seems, and the Church of St Barnabas holds many surprises for the uninitiated.

The outbreak of the first World War led to a vast increase in the production of munitions at Woolwich Arsenal, necessitating the speedy provision of additional housing in the locality to accommodate the many thousands of extra workers who were drafted in. In the course of eleven months during 1915, 1,298 permanent dwellings were built under the supervision of Frank Baines – who was later knighted – to form the Well Hall Garden City which subsequently became known as the Progress Estate. This astonishing achievement was followed by the erection of many hundreds of wooden hutments, one of which was provided by the War Office to serve as a temporary Anglican mission church for the estate. This was superseded in 1916 by a more substantial building which they

Royal Dockyard Chapel, Woolwich, drawing of 1858 from the north-west.

*Right: Scott's interior, drawing of
1867. Below: Ford's rebuilt interior of
1932–3.*

erected on the northern corner of Arbroath Road and Well Hall
Road; the hut continued in use as a hall. The church was still a
temporary one, but it was said to have a 'strong wooden frame work
and roof standing upon concrete foundations'; its walls, 'of coke
breeze two inches thick', were porous and perishable, and the roof
was covered with Ruberoid. It would seat 200 normally but for
special occasions its capacity could be increased to 250.

In 1926 a site for a permanent church, on the southern corner of
Arbroath Road and Well Hall Road, was acquired from the Office
of Works for £500. By the end of 1927, £2,000 had been raised or
promised from various sources for the erection of a church, and the
Bishop of Southwark was nominated as patron. The formation of a
separate District followed in 1928.

The urbanisation of the area, including the construction of
Rochester Way and the Well Hall roundabout, continued into the
1930s, increasing the population of the District to 7,519 at the time
of the 1931 census. It had now become imperative to make a start
on replacing the makeshift church. A new site, facing Rochester
Way close by the roundabout, was purchased for £1,200; the
previous one was sold, and on it was subsequently built the Roman
Catholic Church of St John Fisher & St Thomas More.

In 1932 an offer was made, through the Twenty-five Churches
Fund, of a redundant church at Woolwich Dockyard for re-erec-
tion on the new site. Thomas Ford was the architect chosen for the

project; he had earlier worked in the office of W. A. Forsyth who was himself concurrently engaged in arranging for the transportation of a Victorian church from St Marylebone to Kingsbury in Middlesex. Was this pure coincidence?

Sir George Gilbert Scott had designed the offered building, which was erected as the Royal Dockyard Chapel in 1857–8. Its structural use of cast iron, a feature often found in nonconformist places of worship, was uncommon in Anglican ones though Thomas Rickman had employed it extensively at Everton as early as 1812–14. In plan, the chapel had a chancel with a semicircular apse, and a nave with aisles; a bell turret rose from the east end of the north aisle. The principal entrance was by three doors at the west end. The tall nave had galleries along three sides, to bring the seating capacity up to 1,000 or more. The exterior walls were of red brick, with bands and relieving arches of black brick, and Bath stone dressings. The galleries and arcades were supported on slender iron columns; these were plain up to gallery level, but of twisted 'barley-sugar' pattern above, with gilded vine leaves entwining them. Timber was used abundantly in the roofs over nave, aisles and chancel. The five aisle bays on either side were each gabled transversely.

Eltham, St Barnabas. Above: from the north-east. Below: from the south-east.

St Barnabas, Eltham (originally in Woolwich Dockyard) – March '97. — John M Bray..

The last service in the Dockyard Chapel was held in 1923. For the building's new role at Eltham, Thomas Ford made a number of design changes. The original nave was shortened by one bay, the main west doorway was transferred to the south side, and new vestries were added to the north. The octagonal bell turret, with its brick spire, was repositioned at the east end of the south aisle, and it received a new bell cast by Gillett & Johnston of Croydon in 1933. The nave height was lowered by nine feet, and the galleries were omitted, reducing the overall seating capacity to 561. The interior dimensions were now 106 feet in length, 61 feet width, and 70 feet height to the nave apex. Only the upper portions of the slender internal cast iron pillars were retained; the fine timber main roof and the external red brickwork, stone dressings and roof tiles were all re-used. The old stone font was placed at the west end of the nave. As a modern touch, floodlighting was installed to illuminate the sanctuary.

The rebuilt church was consecrated on 7 October 1933, from which date the District achieved the status of a New Parish. The whole project, executed by W. E. Ismay of Peckham as the contractor, had cost a total of about £13,000, including the site and the purchase of an organ. Of this sum, £8,412 had been contributed through the Twenty-five Churches Fund. The building was the last complete church to be opened with assistance from the Fund.

The temporary church on the north side of Arbroath Road was converted for use as a parish hall; designs and a specification for this purpose were produced by R. A. Watling in 1933. But its days were now numbered, and three years later its site had to be given up for the construction of part of a new private housing estate. Fortunately a replacement site was secured in Rochester Way just west of the 'new' church, and on it was built a brick hall. Its architects were J. Murray Easton and Hamilton Turner, and the contractors T. Rider & Son of Chislehurst. The hall was opened in 1937; it survives today and has achieved local fame as the home of the Howerd Club, named after the late Frankie Howerd who once resided in the parish and had strong connections with the church.

This hall had to be pressed into emergency use for church services in 1944 when St Barnabas's Church was gutted by incendiary bombs during a second World War air raid; only its outer walls and the vestries were left standing. In 1946 a wooden hut, erected within the church walls, was dedicated for worship. It served its purpose for the next ten years. Then, in 1956, the hut was dismantled and services were again transferred to the hall whilst the shattered church was reconstructed. For this latter task, Thomas F. Ford & Partners were called in as architects and W. E. Ismay as contractor – the same team who brought about the rebuilding of the church in 1932–3. Under the direction of Alan Ford, the

St Barnabas after bomb damage, from an old postcard.

Interior after reconstruction.

exterior of the building was reroofed and restored so far as practicable to its pre-war appearance, but the inside was utterly transformed. For an explanation of this, the brief given to the architects needs to be understood: it included the stipulations that the interior should not be as lofty as before since the building had proved difficult and expensive to heat, and that the congregation's seating should be confined to the nave, the aisles being screened off. These requirements, particularly the one restricting the height, ruled out any attempt to reproduce anything like the style and ambience which existed before.

A ceiled barrel vault replaced the former high-pitched open roof; the chancel apse was covered with a semi-dome, and the aisle ceilings were lowered and redesigned. The aisle walls were painted pink. The old twisted iron pillars, which had cracked in the fire, were discarded in favour of square-sectioned columns which divided the nave into four bays; the columns, which were finished with anthemium-decorated caps, supported a full-length entablature on each side. Each aisle bay was screened from the nave by a subsidiary entablature supported on a pair of fluted cylindrical columns, above each of which was placed the kneeling figure of a winged angel, facing the sanctuary. The north aisle contained a small chapel, and the south aisle only the font. The chancel arch was remodelled into semicircular shape.

A large mural, representing Christ in Glory, was painted and presented by Hans Feibusch to fill the semi-dome of the apse. The artist described it as showing 'the Saviour enthroned, with arms outstretched, and surrounded by adoring angels and by clouds which are partly lit up by His glory, but are grey where they face the outer world in which we dwell'. The choir stalls, pews, organ and font came from St Michael's Church, Lant Street, Southwark. The organ, a small two-manual instrument, was built by R. Cope of Camberwell.

Its internal transformation thus complete, the church was reconsecrated on 22 June 1957. The general style of the re-designed interior can perhaps best be summed up as neo-Regency. A contemporary newspaper report described it as 'a light modern interior modelled on lines of classical simplicity'. It is not to everybody's taste, but there is no denying that this church, as it now stands, is remarkable for its double impact: an uncompromisingly Victorian Gothic exterior in a twentieth century setting, and an interior which, to say the least, would have surprised the building's original creator, Sir George Gilbert Scott.

ELTHAM

St Saviour's Mission Hall, Mayerne Road

New Hall, built 1929
Contractor: William Harbrow Ltd., of Bermondsey

The Woolwich Borough Council began building the Page Estate, their first mass housing venture, in 1920, resulting in the erection of over 2,700 dwellings in an area reaching as far south as Eltham Hill. The influx of residents eventually led to the decision, in 1928, to provide a temporary church near Eltham Green, as a mission attached to Eltham's parish church of St John the Baptist. Consent for such a building, licensed initially for five years, was granted by the London County Council for erection in Westhorne Avenue at its junction with Lionel Road, but this proposal had to be abandoned because of 'certain unforeseen legal and other difficulties'. An alternative site in Mayerne Road, close by Eltham Green, was soon purchased for £500 with help from the Twenty-five Churches Fund, and construction began at the beginning of 1929.

By 8 March the builders, William Harbrow Ltd., had reportedly already roofed the structure and, as St Saviour's Mission Church, it was dedicated on 12 May 1929. A further grant of £500 from the Twenty-five Churches Fund contributed towards meeting the cost of £1,246.

By this time the Page Estate carried a population estimated at 6,000. A mere two years later, when a new District was constituted, Bishop Garbett observed that the 'whole aspect was changed by the prospect of a large addition of houses on the Middle Park Estate', where over 2,000 dwellings were to be built by the Woolwich Council on the south side of Eltham Hill. Clearly, whilst the Mission Church was adequate for the Page Estate residents, it could not be expected to encompass the new population as well and was not geographically central to it. This led to the decision to

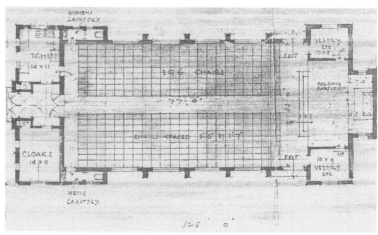

Eltham, St Saviour, original plan for mission hall, with east to the right.

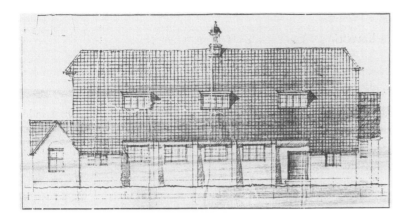

Original design, south elevation.

create a new parish of St Saviour and to erect a new permanent church within the Middle Park Estate. (See Eltham, St Saviour.)

After the Middle Park church was opened in 1933, the Mission building in Mayerne Road became its parish hall but, at least for the Middle Park residents, this arrangement had its drawbacks, the then Bishop of Southwark commenting in 1936 on its distance from the church on the far side of a busy main road.

On 6 March 1957 the hall was re-dedicated as St George's Mission Church, with the intention that it should once again perform a dual-purpose function as a place of worship and social activity for Page Estate residents, and in particular should relieve the children there from the hazard of crossing the busy Eltham Hill to attend Sunday School. This proved a false dawn for, within a few months, the hall's use as a church was finally terminated, though Sunday School continued for a while to function there. In 1961 a new hall was opened next to St Saviour's Church in Middle Park Avenue; the building in Mayerne Road was demolished, and flats were erected on the site.

Unsigned and undated drawings, comprising a plan and side elevation of the 'Proposed Mission Building for Eltham Green Estate', were lodged with the Ecclesiastical Commissioners but probably relate to the hall intended originally to be sited in Westhorne Avenue. They illustrate a building about 100 feet long overall with a seating capacity of nearly 400. What was provided in Mayerne Road was a simple, smaller structure with seats for 300 worshippers and a sanctuary which could be closed off by folding doors. An organ chamber and a vestry were also fitted and, on the date of its dedication in 1929, the hall was equipped with altar rails, lectern and font, as well as a small organ. In the sanctuary were said to be two striking paintings by Sybil Parker entitled 'Soldiers of the Cross', and a sanctuary chair inscribed with the date 1625; their fate is not recorded.

The hall's structure seems to have been largely of timber. A wooden cross surmounted the red roof at each end.

East end, photographed in 1957. Note the folding partition to close off the sanctuary.

ELTHAM
St Saviour, Middle Park Avenue

New Church, built 1932–3
Architect: N. F. Cachemaille-Day
Contractors: Pitcher Construction Co. Ltd., of Holloway, London

The conception of this, the most widely known of all the churches built with help from the Twenty-five Churches Fund, arose from the Woolwich Borough Council's decision to construct an estate of 2,000 houses on the ancient royal hunting ground of Middle Park adjoining Eltham Palace. The erection of these houses began in 1931. In that same year Dr Garbett secured the formation of a new ecclesiastical district from the parishes of St John and St Peter, Eltham, with patronage assigned to the Bishop of Southwark; but he first had to overcome opposition from the Reformation Church Trust who at the time were patrons of St John's. Arrangements were then put in train for funding the purchase of a site on the new estate and for erecting a permanent new church thereon; but by the time the church's foundation stone was laid, on 19 November 1932, Garbett had been translated to the see of Winchester and it was Bishop Parsons, his successor at Southwark, who was influential in the choice of Nugent Cachemaille-Day as architect.

Eltham, St Saviour from the north-east.

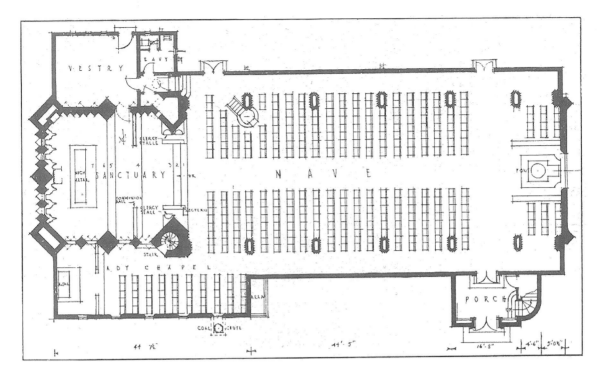

Cachemaille-Day's design, produced while a member of the practice of Welch, Cachemaille-Day & Lander, won the RIBA's London Architecture Medal and Diploma for 1933; St Saviour's was said to be the first church building to receive that distinction. The full scheme included a hall and committee rooms as well as the church, but only the church was built.

Construction proceeded rapidly, the completed church being consecrated on 1 July 1933, less than eight months after the foundation stone was laid. The total cost, including furnishings, fittings and fees, reached about £11,000, towards which £7,000 was contributed from the Twenty-five Churches Fund and substantial sums from other ecclesiastical charities. At the time of consecration, only 400 of the planned 2,000 houses on the estate had been occupied.

The church, intended to seat some 500 worshippers, was built upon what was for its date an utterly conventional ground plan, providing for a simple rectangular nave which, measuring about 86 feet by 44 feet rising to a height of about 40 feet, closely approached double cube proportions. Also provided were narrow passage aisles, and an aisleless chancel, about 28 feet square, flanked on its ritual north side by a Lady Chapel of 42 feet by 15 feet, and on its south by a clergy vestry. There was provision for a choir and organ in a west gallery, and for a projecting porch in the north-west corner with a choir vestry over. What emerged from this basic plan, however, was far from conventional.

Plan (east to the left), showing how the tower is raised over the sanctuary. Not shown are a gallery at the west end, with a central space for the choir, with the organ divided between north and south; and a choir vestry above the porch.

Early postcards, with views from the north-east (top) and south-west (bottom).

The design principles were described as being 'to no small extent affected by the desire to make a permanent fireproof structure of which the upkeep costs should be as little as possible'. The architect added that 'no attempt has been made to reproduce any historical style on the one hand nor to be unusual on the other hand, but rather to treat modern materials in a simple way and let them give a quality to the building of their own'. The result, in the words of the architect's associate Felix Lander, was a building 'largely of reinforced concrete cased in brickwork, with a reinforced concrete roof'. The foundations and pier cores were of reinforced concrete, and the windows were framed in pre-cast concrete except for those in the sanctuary which were leaded.

Externally, the impression is of a grimly gaunt fortress with a severely angular outline relieved only by minor brick ornamentation above the tower windows. The square tower's resemblance to a medieval castle keep is heightened by the long cylindrical stair

turret, lit only by small window slits, at its north-west corner. The outer walls, all of dark purple-grey sand-faced brick, are pierced by pairs of tall narrow clerestory windows which, together with the plain triangular-sectioned buttresses, give a powerful vertical emphasis to the design.

Inside, the nave walls are plastered between the piers, but the prevalent surface textures are brick, concrete and glass. Attention is at once drawn to the chancel where, notwithstanding the bare brick walls, most of the colour and spectacular effects are concentrated. Here the space is carried up to a height of about 45 feet where, under the tower, it is ceiled with patterned wallboard, coloured blue. Height is gained because of the omission of an intended room above. Set into the east wall are two pairs of tall slender windows filled with intensely glowing patterned glass, predominantly in vivid blue shades, the work of Mellowes & Co. Ltd. Behind the high altar, which retains its original frontal, rises a grey concrete reredos, with squared-off pinnacles echoing the zigzag rhythm of the east wall's brickwork; its centrepiece is a majestic nine-feet high figure, sculptured by Donald Hastings in white concrete, of the Saviour holding the world in His left hand whilst blessing it with His right. Suspended from the ceiling is a huge cross, strongly coloured in black, red, green, gold and silver, and displaying symbols of the crucifixion; like the altar ornaments, frontals and hangings, it was supplied by J. Wippell & Co. Ltd. The altar rails, reading desk and clergy stalls are all of brick, as is the impressive pulpit, designed by Cachemaille-Day, which clasps the first pier on the south side of the nave; here again, in desk and pulpit, the zigzag motif is used to decorative effect in the brickwork. A plain horizontal disc above the pulpit serves as a sounding-board; perhaps it was added in response to a comment from Caröe & Passmore, the Ecclesiastical Commissioners' consultants, that the 'form of construction adopted renders the building somewhat resonant and

The interior looking east.

experiments are being made with a view to the improvement of the acoustics'.

The nave is only slightly less lofty than the chancel. Its flat ceiling is supported on transverse beams which are surfaced with granite aggregate, whilst the ceiling panels are of concrete poured onto a layer of fragmented glass to produce a mosaic-like effect. The wall piers are of grey brickwork laid, as elsewhere, to form a zigzag surface. The low passage aisles are functional and in themselves of little visual impact, but affixed to a pier at the west end of the south aisle is one of the distinctive painted wooden crosses which were presented to churches built with aid from the Twenty-five Churches Fund.

The west gallery is divided into three sections: a central space for the choir, and enclosed chambers on either side for the organ, which was built by R. Spurden Rutt & Co. Ltd.; the instrument is now played from a detached console on the north side of the nave. Below the gallery is the massive lead-lined font, a cast concrete cube sculptured by Donald Hastings.

In the Lady Chapel, the reredos, also of grey concrete, depicts the Resurrection in relief. Built into the wall to its south is a fragment of minutely carved stone said to have come from Southwark Cathedral. The small square windows on the north side are filled with strongly coloured glass, mainly blue.

The building has acquired the reputation of being something of a landmark in English church design. Inevitably, parallels have been drawn with Albi Cathedral, and there has been much comment from architectural historians. The advice of one clergyman of the 1930s was 'to make a pilgrimage to St Saviour's, but to say a little prayer en route for strength to bear the sight!' And some of the early tenants of the Middle Park Estate dubbed it 'The Prison', or 'The Church with the Zip Fasteners' – an allusion to its long thin side windows.

A new parish hall was built next to the church in 1961. In the 1990s a thorough restoration, aimed at returning the church as closely as possible to its original appearance, has been skilfully carried out under Ian Picken of Gerald Shenstone & Partners.

– St. Saviour's, Eltham – Lady Chapel reredos – Oct '99 John M. Bray.

Above: wooden cross, a surviving example of those presented to churches built by the Twenty-five Churches Fund. Left: reredos in the Lady Chapel.

ELTHAM PARK
St Luke, Westmount Road

Completion in 1933–4 of Church partly built 1906–7 to designs
of Temple Moore
Architect: J. B. L. Tolhurst
Contractors: R. Mansell Ltd. of Croydon

Between 1900 and 1914 the Scottish developer Cameron Corbett
built an estate of solidly constructed houses on some 340 acres of
land he had acquired to the south of Shooter's Hill. In 1902 a site for
an Anglican church and hall was purchased from Corbett, and the
formation of a separate ecclesiastical District for the area was
recommended in the following year. In May 1904 the first service
was held within the new estate, in an upstairs room of a private
house. Four months later a dual-purpose hall, designated St Luke's
Mission Church, Well Hall, was opened. Built facing Westmount
Road by William Harbrow of Bermondsey, it was about fifty feet
long and cost £752.

Measures to establish a permanent church building proceeded
rapidly: in 1905 a fund-raising scheme was launched and Temple
Moore was appointed architect. His designs, for a complete church
to seat 733, were exhibited at the Royal Academy in 1906. He
proposed erecting, on a curiously asymmetrical plan, a building of
fourteenth century Gothic style, with exterior walls of red brick
and stone dressings, and a tile-covered main roof. As usual with this
architect, it is in its spacial mastery that the church was lifted out of
the ordinary; Goodhart-Rendel noted St Luke's as an example 'of
the grandeur that Moore knew so well how to extract from bare
shapes and homely materials'. The building was of no great size, yet
the nobility of the internal design, which belied the modest exterior, was achieved with conspicuous assurance through the use of

Eltham Park, St Luke from the west,
as conceived by Temple Moore.

massive arcades. Just two broad bays separated the nave from the north aisle, with three bays covering the same length on the south side. This latter system was continued eastwards by one further bay to flank the southern side of the chancel, which was given a corresponding arch on the north. The plain north arcade was made to spring from great oblong stone-faced piers with moulded capitals, whilst the south arcade was designed with square stone piers and plain arches. A continuous barrel vault covered both nave and chancel; above this, the external roof was supported on splendidly prodigious timbering. There was no provision for a chancel arch. A small bell tower was to stand at the east end of the south aisle and to the south of the clergy vestry – one of two which were to adjoin the sanctuary. The tower's ground-floor stage was to form a recess for the altar of a side chapel.

In the event, Temple Moore's south aisle and tower were omitted, the south arcade being bricked up with temporary walling into which was inserted a two-light traceried window for each bay. The foundation stone was laid on 14 July 1906, and the partly completed church was dedicated on 6 July 1907; Goddard of Dorking was the builder. Consecration had to wait for a further year because of complications over the patronage deed; the assignment of a District Chapelry followed early in 1909. In 1918 an appeal was launched with the aim of completing the church to Temple Moore's designs, but progress was slow and the architect himself died in 1920. In 1923 J. B. L. Tolhurst, who was appointed in his place, submitted new plans, including a tower in the south-west corner, but building tenders were nearly double what had been expected and the proposals were set aside whilst energies were concentrated on enlarging the original mission building which,

Right: the interior looking east.
Below: the interior looking north–west across Temple Moore's nave.

since the construction of the church alongside, had served as a parish hall. These extensions, designed by J. J. Taylor and built by W. Pollock of Mottingham, were opened in 1926.

A final appeal for funds to complete the church was begun in 1930, and this time, with the aid of grants secured from various ecclesiastical sources including the Twenty-five Churches Fund, it was found possible to proceed. Revised proposals, prepared by Tolhurst, were approved in 1932: these provided for the addition of a south aisle, baptistry, Lady Chapel and vestries, but the 60-foot tower suggested earlier was to be replaced by a porch, saving over £2,000. Some internal changes were also approved but these had to be abandoned because of an unexpected further call on financial resources in 1933, when the east wall of the old hall was found to be

St. Luke's Eltham Park

Left: the interior looking south-east across the nave towards Tolhurst's Lady Chapel.

Below: The pulpit, designed by Temple Moore.

in danger of collapse, necessitating its removal and the shortening and reconstruction of the building's east end.

R. Mansell Ltd. of Croydon, who were awarded the church building contract, began work in August 1933, and Tolhurst's additions were consecrated on 17 February 1934. The total cost was £6,785 including furnishing as well as the architect's and surveyor's fees. Care was taken to match the construction materials with those of the original work of 1906–7: the buttressed external walls were of Kentish red brick with mouldings and window tracery of Portland and Bath stone. The aisle windows comprised four which had formerly pierced the temporary walling blocking the south arcade, and additional ones designed to a similar pattern. The Lady Chapel, at the east end of the new aisle, was given a much bolder

Right: Tolhurst's elevation for the new south aisle; the tower was not built. Below: the aisle from the south-east, shortly after completion.

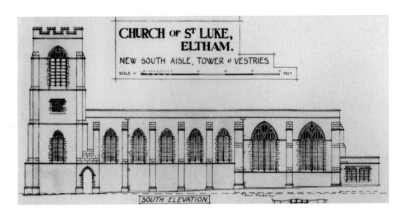

CHURCH OF ST LUKE, ELTHAM.

NEW SOUTH AISLE, TOWER & VESTRIES.

SOUTH ELEVATION

pair of four-light south windows with tracery of fifteenth century Perpendicular derivation, and one of three lights in its east wall. The aisle's flat roof, panelled within and carried on moulded beams and carved brackets, was unbroken from end to end except for a carved arch brace marking the junction with the chapel. Aisle and chapel were each 19 feet wide internally, the aisle being 60 feet in length and the chapel 34 feet. The vestries were placed transversely across the east end, extending behind the chancel for almost the full width of the church. The baptistry, adjoining the new south-west porch, received an octagonal font of Beer stone to replace the old second-hand one.

In the second World War considerable damage was suffered by both church and hall: over 2,000 tiles had to be replaced or renewed on the church roof, and all windows, including some stained glass work, were broken on the north side and west end.

The church retains some fittings designed by Temple Moore. These include the oak choir stalls, pulpit, sanctuary rails, and altar

with its curtains, frontal and furnishings, all given at the outset, and the aumbry in the north wall of the sanctuary. Temple Moore also designed a rood beam and cross in 1913 but neither this nor a revised scheme, prepared by him a year later for a rood screen omitting the cross, was executed. Instead, a carved oak chancel screen was partly erected in 1915 by Dart & Francis Ltd. of Crediton to the designs of Hedley and Douglas Pollock; this, 25 feet wide and 14½ feet high, was initially completed only at the north end, the remaining work being confined mainly to the frame and some of the mouldings. Construction was finished in 1921 with pierced Perpendicular tracery and a panelled dado designed by W. S. Weatherley. A carved oak war memorial, also designed by Weatherley, was placed on the north wall of the sanctuary in 1919. Another memorial, a tablet in brass which was dedicated in the previous year, commemorates Sir George and Lady Vyvyan who were early benefactors of the church.

An organ was first set up in the church in 1907. This, a small instrument by Brindley & Foster bought from St Barnabas's, Rotherhithe, was replaced in 1917 by a two-manual organ rebuilt by A. Noterman. The present electronic instrument was installed following the grant of a faculty in 1978, and was redesigned and rebuilt in 1997.

In the north aisle is a stained glass window depicting Christ Amidst the Doctors, erected in 1923; the craftsman and donor was C. J. Woodward. A three-light window, made and presented by Margaret Cowell, was placed in the Children's Corner in 1931; its main subject is The Good Shepherd. Tempora paintings were added to the walls below. More stained glass was inserted in the chancel east windows in 1958.

Other fittings in the original Temple Moore part of the church include an oak panelled reredos, installed in 1954, and a carved litany desk incorporating emblems representing Southwark Diocese and St Luke. This latter piece was made at the Faithcraft works and dedicated in 1943. The altar table in Tolhurst's Lady Chapel was given a frontal and curtains designed by the architect. A timber screen, separating the chapel from the south aisle, was set up in 1948 as a memorial to civilians killed in air raids in the second World War. It was made by Allen of Oxford.

Since 1979 various modifications and improvements have been made to the church interior, generally designed and executed with great sensitivity; Ursula Bowyer was the architect. These have included the addition of a panelled nave altar and platform, new west doors with an internal screen, and toilet and kitchen facilities in the former north-west porch.

Below: two internal views of the aisle, dating from the time of its construction.

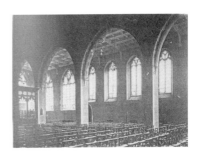

FURZEDOWN (Streatham)
St Paul, Welham Road

New Church, built 1925–6
Architects: F. H . Greenaway & J. E. Newberry
Contractors: James Burges & Sons, of Wimbledon

A new Mission District, intended primarily to serve the developing Links Estate on the site of a former golf course, was established in 1910; its first services were held in the library of Furzedown House, to the north. In January 1911 Sir Charles Seely, the owner of the Furzedown estate, conveyed part of his land to the Ecclesiastical Commissioners as a site for the construction of a permanent church, a parsonage and a mission hall or parish room. The plot was a large one, covering nearly 7,000 square yards with frontages of over 300 feet to Welham Road and 250 feet to Chillerton Road. The architects F. H. Greenaway and J. E. Newberry were commissioned to produce designs for a dual-purpose mission hall and this building, a permanent structure of brick and stone which survives today, was erected alongside Chillerton Road in 1911, and became known as the Seely Hall.

In 1914 Greenaway and Newberry prepared designs for an ambitious new church for the area, but the first World War caused them to be shelved and, after hostilities ceased, priority was given to the erection, in 1920, of St Andrew's Mission Hall in Links Road; this, a building of timber and asbestos, was replaced by a new hall complex in the 1970s.

An Ecclesiastical District of St Paul, Furzedown, to supplant the erstwhile Mission District, was formed in 1923 from parishes in Streatham Park, Mitcham and Tooting Graveney, whereupon the Seely Hall functioned in effect as a parish church. Then, on 6 June 1925, the foundation stone was laid of a new permanent church which was to be built according to revised proposals which had been submitted by Greenaway and Newberry. Described as 'simple

Furzedown, St Paul, from the east (taken from an old postcard).

View from the south-west.

and plain almost to severity', the new designs were estimated to cost £13,619 to implement, including the architects' fees and expenses but not furniture: cheaper indeed than the £34,273 required for completing the pre-war scheme. Towards the building costs, which eventually totalled just over £14,000 in all, more than £3,000 had been contributed by a Trust Fund which had been inaugurated by Sir Charles Seely before he died in 1915; there were grants also from the Twenty-five Churches Appeal and other ecclesiastical sources, as well as a substantial sum raised by local effort.

On St Matthew's Day, 21 September 1926, the finished church was consecrated and given formal parochial status. The successful building tender, from James Burges & Sons of Wimbledon, had actually revealed a margin below the architects' cost estimate, and this was used for constructing the nave and chancel arcades in Portland and Bath stone instead of brick and plaster. In style, the new church was based on thirteenth century Gothic precepts. The walls were of Fletton bricks, faced externally with brown Crowborough bricks unrelieved by any stone dressings. Lancets were used for fenestration throughout, tall stepped lights dominating the east wall of the chancel, and unstepped ones at the west end of the nave; elsewhere, smaller lights were grouped either in pairs or in triplets. The roof, continuous from east to west and embracing the aisles, was covered in flat hand-made red tiles. Above the nave, and offset to the south, was erected a small timber gabled bellcote.

The church plan was orthodox: a five-bay rectangular nave with north and south aisles; a chancel adjoined on its north side by a chapel, and on its south by a return way for communicants and by vestries and a sacristy surmounted by an organ loft. The main entrance porch was placed at the western end of the south aisle, and

The interior looking east, before 1970.

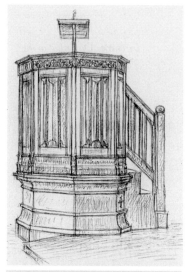

Top: oak pulpit of 1931. Bottom: marble font, designed by Sir Aston Webb.

a smaller porch was added in a corresponding position on the north side. Small transeptal arms were provided over the chapel and organ loft, with a semi-octagonal stair turret for access to the latter.

Inside, the total seating capacity was 621. The nave was about 78 feet long and 23 feet wide; each aisle was about 74 feet by 14 feet, and the chancel about 37½ feet by 21½ feet. The interior walls were plastered; the roofs, of Oregon or Columbian pine, were open to the apex. The architects designed many fittings for the church, including oak panelling in the chancel, altar rails with decorative detailing, and choir stall fronts. At the west end of the nave, the marble font, given by the Seely family, came from their chapel at Sherwood Lodge, Nottingham, and was designed by Sir Aston Webb. Later additions included a carved oak pulpit, made in 1931 by James Burges & Sons to the designs of J. E. Newberry. The three stepped lancets forming the east window of the chancel contain glass by Martin Travers, on the theme of Te Deum Laudamus; his original work here, of 1937, was mostly destroyed by bomb blast in the second World War which led to the temporary closure of the church, but in 1952 the windows were carefully restored to their original design and colour during war damage repairs. For this work, Travers is said to have used the same drawings as for a similar window at St Andrew's Church, Langley Mill, in Derbyshire. There is stained glass also in the Lady Chapel; this, designed by a Miss Chance, depicts the Blessed Virgin Mary and Child and is a memorial to members of the Chance family. The present organ, installed in 1973, was placed at the east end of the south aisle during the course of internal reordering which saw the conversion of the former organ chamber into additional vestry space; the choir was moved into the south aisle about the same time.

The vicarage was built in 1926–7 by James Burges & Sons, on land facing Chillerton Road which had been given by Wandsworth Borough Council in exchange for the originally allotted site to the west of the church in Welham Road. J. E. Newberry was again the architect.

HACKBRIDGE AND NORTH BEDDINGTON
All Saints, London Road

New Church, built 1928–30
Architect: H. P. Burke Downing
Contractor: Stanley Ellis Ltd., Guildford

In 1887 Nathaniel Bridges, lord of the manor of Wallington, conveyed to the Vicar of Beddington and other trustees a parcel of land at Beddington Corner for use as the site of a church and parsonage. Here a temporary church of timber and corrugated iron was established in 1893 and dedicated to All Saints. A Conventional District

Left: watercolours of the proposed church submitted by Burke Downing to the Royal Academy exhibition of 1927. Notice the difference in fenestration from what was finally built, shown below.

The church as built. Left: the west end. Below: the east end.

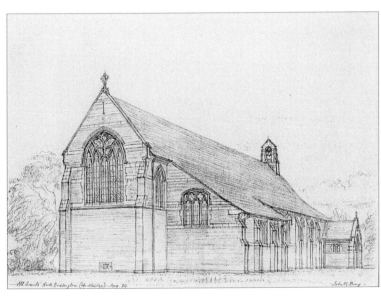

The church exterior, from old postcards. Right: from the south-west. Below: from the south-east.

was assigned in 1916, in which year a priest-in-charge was appointed with instructions to organise a new parish and erect a permanent church. A new site for this purpose, a little to the south and on the main Mitcham to Carshalton road, was acquired for £750 in 1921, grants towards the cost of its purchase having been secured from the City Parochial Charities Fund. Of 1¼ acres, this site was large enough to enable space to be reserved additionally for a new church hall and a parsonage. H. P. Burke Downing was selected as architect, and he produced initial designs in 1922 for a large church to seat about 750 persons. Fund raising efforts began in earnest in 1924, but within two years ambitions were cut back and Burke Downing was instructed to prepare new designs for a simpler church seating no more than about 400. A target date for the building's completion and opening was set for the winter of 1926/27; this proved over-optimistic but progress no doubt

received some impetus from a comment in the Incorporated Church Building Society's report for 1928 that 'the existing iron building was in a deplorable condition, and could not last more than another year'. The architect's revised designs were approved by the Ecclesiastical Commissioners in February 1928, and the foundation stone was laid on 9 July in that year.

The completed church was opened without ceremony, its first service being held on 23 March 1930; consecration, which had been deferred until the building debt had been much reduced, did not take place until 19 May 1931.

The provision of funds for building the permanent church had begun quite promisingly, with the prospect in 1922 of grants of £1,000 each from the Diocese and the South London Church Fund. By March 1926 £5,020 was said to be 'in hand', of which £2,000 had been allocated from the Twenty-five Churches Fund. In 1928, building costs were estimated at £9,270. Between then and 1930 further grants had been secured from ecclesiastical sources, but these sums, together with local contributions, still left a deficiency exceeding £2,000. A strip of the land acquired in 1921, which had been earmarked as the parsonage site, was sold in 1930 for £650 and, by the time the church was consecrated, only £428 remained owing.

Burke Downing's approved designs were, inevitably for this architect, in the Gothic style and said to 'have a character of simplicity combined with dignity'. They consisted of a five-bay nave with north and south aisles, and a chancel with a chapel on its north side and vestries to its south. Nave and aisles were about 73½ feet long and 38¼ feet wide, and the chancel 35¼ feet long and 18¼ feet wide. An organ chamber was placed above the choir vestry. Entrance porches were provided at the western end of each aisle,

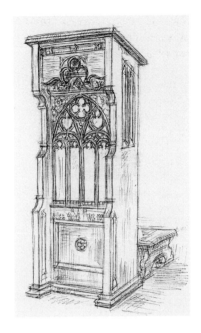

Above: lectern. Left: the interior looking east.

Right: altar rails. Below: top, the font, of English alabaster; bottom, the pulpit.

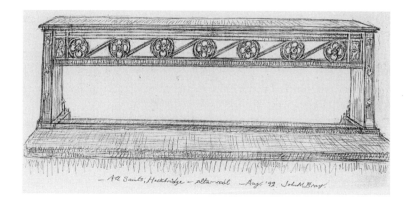

and an additional door was inserted at the eastern and of the north aisle. There was seating capacity for 394 adults.

Externally the walls were faced with purple brown Crowborough bricks, with stone dressings to the doors and windows. The roof, covered in dark red hand-made tiles, was continuous over nave and chancel and was carried down across the aisles, though at a shallower pitch. The 1922 designs had included a rose window high in the east wall and a bell turret on the north side, but the later version omitted these and placed a modest bellcote over the west gable. The traceried oak doors were fitted with hand-wrought ironwork.

Within, the walls were plastered. The arcade piers and arches were constructed of white stone. Stone was used also for paving the chancel, sanctuary and chapel in colour, and the nave and aisle gangways in white. The roof was of open construction, in Oregon pine; all beams were wood-pinned, no nails being used.

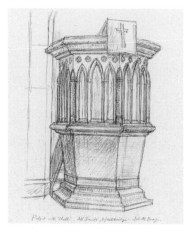

The altar in the chapel was brought from the old church where it had been placed in 1910; it had been given by the Vicar and Churchwardens of St Michael's, Bandon Hill, South Beddington. The temporary altar which served the 'iron' church from the beginning in 1893 had been re-fashioned into a wooden chest which was now placed in the organ loft. The organ and bell from the old church were not retained; a small temporary organ, bought for £45 in 1941, was later replaced by an eighteenth-century chamber organ. Other fittings set up in the church included a font of English alabaster, and a small statue of the Blessed Virgin Mary brought from France by a soldier in the first World War and placed above the 1914–18 War Memorial in the chapel. The chapel screen was 'new' in 1952. Two stone brackets, above the entrance to the chancel, were intended to support a Rood. The window over the chapel altar came from the 'iron' church; prior to this it had been in Beddington Parish Church (St Mary's). Another window, of three lights depicting the Shepherds in the Manger, the Virgin Mary and the Wise Men offering gifts, commemorated George Henry Hitchings (d.1926), his son and daughter.

Unusually for one of the Twenty-five churches, patronage of the living was not surrendered to the Bishop of Southwark until 1933, two years after consecration. In the following year a Consolidated Chapelry, taken from the parishes of Beddington, Mitcham and Carshalton, was assigned, under the name of North Beddington, and this was re-styled Hackbridge and North Beddington in 1969. By 1937 the population of the New Parish was said to have topped 6,000.

MALDEN

St James, Bodley Road

New Church, built 1932–3
Architects: J. E. Newberry & C. W. Fowler
Contractors: Joseph Dorey & Co. Ltd., of Brentford

Malden's first church dedicated to St James was a temporary one erected in Poplar Walk – now Poplar Grove – early in the 1860s. It was quickly superseded by Christ Church in Coombe Road. In 1904 a Mission Church was established in Burlington Road as a 'daughter' of Christ Church, with a revived dedication to St James; a simple brick structure with pointed windows and a west porch. Built by E. Buckingham & Sons of New Malden to the designs of Vincent Davison, it had a seating capacity of about 250.

This provision served the Anglicans of New Malden for a quarter of a century, but at the beginning of 1929 the vicar of St John's, Malden, reported discussions with representatives of Christ Church on the siting of a new church on the boundaries of Old and New Malden. With the support of Bishop Garbett, Oxford's Merton College, the landowners, were persuaded to offer a plot close to the new Kingston Arterial Road with frontages of about 198 feet to Bodley Road and 95 feet to Malden Road, with the proviso that church building should start within seven years. This condition was agreed and the land was conveyed to the Ecclesiastical Commissioners on 31 October 1929. By the end of the year, a new ecclesiastical district was formed from parts of the parish of Malden and that of New Malden and Coombe, and a strip from St Saviour's, Raynes Park; a generous grant towards the cost of a new church was promised from the Twenty-five Churches Fund; and the Bishop of Southwark was nominated as patron. This last hurdle was not cleared without opposition, for concerns were expressed by supporters of the local evangelical tradition; but these seem to have been laid to rest by Archdeacon R. C. Joynt of Kingston.

In 1930 a Church Building Fund appeal was launched, and events gathered pace with the appointment of Newberry & Fowler

Malden, the Mission Church of St James, from an old postcard.

as architects in 1931. With commendable foresight, a plot adjoining the church site was purchased for the erection, at some future date, of an additional hall; and grants for this and towards the cost of building a church were secured from the City Parochial Charities Fund. In May 1932 the architects' designs and specification were cleared by Caröe & Passmore for the Ecclesiastical Commissioners' approval, and the building contract was then awarded to Joseph Dorey & Co. Ltd. whose tendered price was £9,870. Preliminary work began, appropriately, on St James's Day, 25 July, and the foundation stone was laid on 8 October. By this time, £8,900 had been committed to the Building Fund, of which £6,150 represented grants, including £3,000 from the Twenty-five Churches Fund. But all this was not enough to cover the builders' contract, let alone the ancillary expenses such as architects' fees and the provision of heating, lighting, furniture and fittings. To ease this problem, a suggestion was made that the church should be built in portions, but this was abandoned when it was calculated that £500 overall could be saved by pressing on with completing the whole building.

The finished church was consecrated on 20 September 1933. For its date, its design was conventional and conservative, being based on fifteenth-century Perpendicular Gothic traditions, but it was unusual amongst the 'Twenty-five' churches in being given a tower worthy of the name; this, a four-stage structure on the south side, was described by its designer, J. E. Newberry, as 'of moderate height' and 'utilitarian as well as aesthetic'. Its external effect of loftiness is somewhat diminished by the tall chancel, to which vertical emphasis was added by placing the clerestory windows just below roof level. The church's construction was almost entirely of brick: multi-coloured outside and a light sand-lime formulation within; the use of stone was confined to the tracery windows. In plan, the building was given a five-bay nave, 74 feet long, with narrow north and south aisles; a chancel of 43 feet with an apsidal east end; a morning chapel on the north side with a sanctuary opening out from a transeptal arm; and a sacristy on the south side, with choir and clergy vestries. The tower, rising above the choir vestry, housed a ladies' vestry, organ and ringing chambers, and the belfry in which was placed a single 5½ cwt bell cast by Mears & Stainbank. The bell-founders had apparently quoted £736 for casting and hanging a ring of eight bells, but the congregation made do with just one until 1958 when an electric peal was installed. North and south porches were added at the west end of the church. The nave and chancel roofs, continuous from end to end, were of British Columbian pine, covered in Welsh green slates; lean-to roofs sheltered the aisles. The west front was dominated by a large seven-light window with Perpendicular Gothic tracery and a similarly styled window of five lights was placed in the north transept. Also traceried were the five-light aisle windows and the smaller ones at clerestory level which were inserted in the nave walls as well as in the chancel. The interior height was enhanced by the relatively narrow width and by the treatment of the nave arcades: above the main system of arches, separating the nave from

Opposite: the church of St James, from the south-east, from an old postcard. Below: the west end of the church.

— St. James', New Malden – Nov. '99   — John M. Bray.

Right: the exterior from the south-east.
Below: the interior, looking east,
showing the apse as modified by J.
Sebastian Comper in 1958.

the aisles, rose a secondary system of flattened pointed arches springing from small brick shafts. These upper arches were pierced with the clerestory windows. The main piers were simple and devoid of capitals. Seating capacity was assessed at 554.

Interior fittings included an octagonal stone font decorated with deeply-cut quatrefoils, behind which, set in the nave's west wall,

was a piece of moulded stone from Southwark Cathedral. The chancel altar, communion benches and choir stalls, all in oak, were designed by the architects. The unusual oak tip-up seats in the nave are still in place and especially noteworthy. A three-manual organ, which was 'all of fifty years old' when bought for £100 in 1932, was restored and modernised for the church by Henry Speechly & Sons for £700. A building debt of £1,900 still had to be faced at the time of the church's consecration – the final overall cost including the organ reached £12,522 – but by the end of 1935 this had been cleared and attention was being given to completing the furniture and fittings. An oak pulpit, designed by J. E. Newberry and set up in 1935, was supplemented in 1938 by a pair of clergy stalls, also Newberry's work, and wooden sanctuary gates to match the communion rail. Outside the church, a 'granolithic' kerb was laid down to enclose the grounds.

The church did not escape serious injury in the war years that followed. On 20 June 1944 the west end was wrecked by blast from a flying bomb which landed nearby. Roof timbers were particularly affected, much glass was shattered, and some of the furniture smitten, the lectern beyond repair. Regrettably, hooliganism was responsible for further damage to the font and organ. Altogether the destruction was assessed as 'so severe that permanent restoration is obviously far off'. Consideration was given to shutting the nave off from the aisles and continuing worship there temporarily but it was decided to hold services at the hall in Burlington Road – the former Mission Church – until restoration could be carried out. This arrangement continued until 1947 when the church was re-dedicated and brought back into use after the completion of temporary repairs; these included re-facing the font's stonework as well as recommissioning the organ and the general rehabilitation of the east end.

Refurbishing continued through the 1950s and beyond. Restoration of the church fabric was finally completed in 1954, to the specification of the architect C. W. Fowler. In the same year a new aumbry, sanctuary lamp and altar frontal were dedicated, together with a striking new font cover. This last piece of equipment, surprisingly Classical in its inspiration, was designed with niches to house coloured wooden figures representing the Blessed Virgin with the Holy Infant Jesus, St James attired as a pilgrim and St Nicholas as the patron saint of children.

Next came a scheme, completed in 1958, to decorate the chancel sanctuary, for which J. Sebastian Comper was the chosen architect. This, to quote from the church's Jubilee booklet, transformed the apse 'from its original Cistercian simplicity into the elaboration of design and heraldic work which the visitor now sees'. The three blind arches in the apse walls were plastered over and their heads

The interior. Above: the original oak tip-up seats. Below: top, looking east; bottom, the north chapel.

The font, with its later cover, the niches still unfilled.

filled with reticulated tracery; below were placed a series of nine coloured shields symbolising, from the north side to the south, Merton College, Oxford; Canterbury; St James; the Chi Ro monogram; the Holy Trinity; alpha and omega; St George; the Diocese of Southwark; and the Borough of Malden. Further tracery adorned the panels beneath.

A statue of the Madonna and Child was placed in the Lady Chapel in 1965. This, an early work by the sculptor Raphael Maklouf, was executed by him in plaster, and cast in bronze at the Camberwell School of Art.

There are two stained glass windows by John Hayward: the Weaver memorial window, of 1967, in the south porch, and the three-light Curry family memorial window installed in 1973 in the east wall of the Lady Chapel. The Stations of the Cross, and the icon of St James at the east end of the south aisle, were added in 1983. The original organ was replaced in 1970 by a three-manual Copeman Hart electronic instrument which was dismantled in 1993.

The Burlington Road Mission Church, which was put to use as a parish hall when the present St James's was built, was badly damaged by fire in 1936 but reinstated soon after. In 1937 a second hall, designed by A. Cox, was built by F. Hartfree Ltd. in Green Lane and this was extended two years later. The Burlington Road hall was sold to the Police Federation in 1964, and then demolished. The proceeds were used for financing the construction in 1965–6 of a new hall on a site, which had been purchased in 1931 for £375, adjoining the north side of the church. This building was designed by A. J. Tolhurst and erected in brick by Courtney & Fairbairn. An earlier scheme for a prefabricated building failed to attract the requisite funds.

MERTON
St James the Apostle, Beaford Grove

Site for new church, hall and parsonage house, acquired 1933
Hall & church later built outside the aegis of the Twenty-five Churches Fund

Beaford Grove in Merton appears to have been under consideration as a site for a church as long ago as 1907, for in that year the architect J. Alick Thomas produced proposals for a new stone-built Gothic church, with alternative designs for a tower and aisles, to be built there and dedicated to St James. These plans do not seem, however, to have progressed beyond the drawing board, and twenty years elapsed before the appearance in the Southwark Diocesan Directory of a reference to the Merton district in the context of new churches being required.

In 1931 the local tennis and sports club supplied immediate needs by making available their corrugated iron hut for temporary use as a mission room, to be served by curates and lay ministers of St Mary's parish. This was situated off Cannon Hill Lane, in what is now Buckleigh Avenue. Then, by the end of 1931, grants of £750 from the Twenty-five Churches Fund and £250 from the City Parochial Charities Fund were secured for the purchase from Merton and Morden Urban District Council of an adjoining site for erecting a church, parish hall and vicarage. These grants left £290 still to be raised from other sources, and the site was not finally conveyed until January 1933.

In 1934 a dual-purpose Church Hall was constructed on the site by Limpus & Son Ltd. of Kingston and Surbiton, the architect being Thomas F. Ford. The Diocese was said to have contributed £2,500 towards the cost. It is a substantial building of brick with an attractive octagonal bell tower.

A new Conventional District, to include parts of Merton parish and that of St Saviour, Raynes Park, was assigned to St James's in November 1938. In the same year, Thomas Ford produced preliminary designs for a permanent church and vicarage. These were revised in 1939 but the outbreak of the second World War prevented any further progress.

In 1951 a Legal District was formed to replace the former Conventional District, and preparations for building a permanent church were again put in hand. Financial considerations caused more delays but eventually the Diocese were able to contribute £27,000, including 'ported payments' by the War Damage Commission arising from claims relating to Christ Church at Lee and St Paul's at Forest Hill in south-east London. New designs were

The wooden cross given to Merton, St James the Apostle as one of the churches founded under the auspices of the Twenty-five Churches Fund. The cross is now on display in the porch.

Merton, St James the Apostle, hall of 1934 and church of 1957.

provided by Thomas Ford, and construction finally began in 1956, the contractors being C. H. Runnalls Sons Ltd. Built of brick, with a tower and spirelet placed in the ritual north-west corner, the church was consecrated in June 1957. It contains a large three-part mural by Hans Feibusch (1958), an organ by N. P. Mander (1958) and glass by John Hayward (1963 and 1965). It also has the distinction of displaying, in its entrance porch, a large blue-painted wooden cross with a central cream circle bearing the church's name. One of these was given to each of the 'Twenty-five', but it is rare to find any still on open view.

MITCHAM

St Olave, Church Walk.

New Hall, built 1927–8
Architects: Chart, Son & Reading
Contractors: Merton Abbey Joinery Works

New Church, built 1930–31.
Architect: Arthur C. Martin.
Contractors: Hall, Beddall & Co., of Pitfield Wharf, London S.E.1.

The Hall

'Lonesome' was the name applied to this part of St Mark's parish in Mitcham, because (if the usually reliable T. P. Stevens is to be believed) 'no one lived there and few passed that way'. The name still lingers but by 1927 the area was lonesome no longer, for a Diocesan Mission District was being established there by Bishop Garbett to serve the people already in residence whose numbers would shortly be swollen from 6,000 to 10,000. The construction of a Mission Hall, to be used as a temporary church, was already under way, with financial support from the Twenty-five Churches Fund. In November of the same year the first missionary priest was instituted to the District, with responsibility for the residents of Lonesome and the new estate of Long Thornton Park.

On 26 January (not on 26 June as has frequently been mis-reported) the new Mission Hall was dedicated and licensed for Divine Worship by the Bishop. The occasion will have been one of the more memorable among Garbett's many such engagements, for it was marked by pouring rain. The local roads had not yet been made up, which prevented the Bishop's car from getting anywhere near the site of the hall, so the remainder of the journey had to be made on foot over railway sleepers which, with every step, were almost submerged in the quagmire of mud.

The site, in the centre of the thickly-populated part of the new estate, was spacious enough to provide for the future erection of a permanent church and a parsonage.

The hall, while described at the time as 'substantially built, and not of the tin tabernacle style', was in fact a very simple building, being timber-framed with wall coverings of asbestos sheeting. The open timber roof, continuous from east to west and pierced by a series of small louvres, had a boarded ceiling and was covered externally with red asbestos tiles. The main body of the hall, which measured 50 feet by 30 feet, functioned as the nave during church services, and was supplemented by a narrower chancel which could be shuttered off when not in use, a vestry and a kitchen. The designed seating capacity, wholly in chairs, was up to 400, a remarkable total for so small a building.

Most of the furniture arrived as gifts. From East Horsley Church came the pulpit, and from St Paul's at Furzedown a font, lectern, desk and bell. St Peter's Church at Streatham contributed a brass lectern, and a two-manual reed organ was presented by the Deaconess Institution at Clapham.

In 1930 the pulpit was passed on to the newly-built hall at Streatham Vale, forerunner of the Church of the Holy Redeemer (q.v.). In its place was set up temporarily the old pulpit from the demolished Church of St Olave at Tooley Street in Southwark, except for the stairway and the wood carving round the base. These were to be attached on the pulpit's eventual transfer to the new permanent church which was by now in course of construction.

On completion of the new church in 1931, the dual-purpose hall became the parish hall. In the second World War it was requisitioned and put to use as a British Restaurant. In 1943 the accommodation there was said to be 'both inadequate and unsuitable', and the decision was made to set up a fund for building a new hall and rooms after the war. By 1949 the structure was described as 'in a bad way', but it somehow survived for two more decades and was still there, 'in poor condition', in 1970.

In 1968 plans were unveiled for redeveloping the church grounds so as to incorporate a new parish hall reached from the church by a covered way. David Bush, who was appointed architect, refined the scheme to include provision for ancillary rooms as well as houses and a car park. The proposals, with others concerning the reordering of the church interior, were the subject of much discussion and amendment until, in 1976, the church land was finally sold for building, the proceeds being used for financing the construction of the new hall on a site between the church and the neighbouring Rowan Road Recreation Ground. The hall was in use by November 1976 although not formally opened and dedicated until 17 January 1977.

St Olave's, Mitcham. —John M Bray.

Mitcham, St Olave from the north.

The Church

On historical and architectural grounds, this church is undoubtedly one of the most rewarding of the Southwark 'Twenty-five'. Its dedication to a seafaring saint may seem surprising but is explained by a link with the former church of St Olave in Tooley Street, Southwark.

In October 1927 Bishop Garbett reported to the Ecclesiastical Commissioners that the Trustees of St Olave's proposed to use a sum of £5,000 to £6,000, expected to arise from the disposal of the old church, for the purpose of building a new one in St Mark's parish, Mitcham, to serve a rapidly increasing population. The proposals were subject to two conditions: that the resultant New District, when formed, should be known as St Olave's, and that patronage of the living should be vested in the Crown, St Olave's in Southwark having been a Crown living since 1543. Garbett, already aware of the need to provide additional facilities for worship in the area, which was centred on Long Thornton Park, must have been delighted, even though the proposal's realisation would preclude the Bishop of Southwark from claiming patronage. He had no hesitation in offering a grant from the Twenty-five Churches Fund towards the balance of building costs. As has been related, he had taken the preliminary steps of approving the formation of a Diocesan Missionary District and the construction of a temporary building for use as church and hall pending a more permanent arrangement.

The church in Tooley Street had reached the end of its useful life. The medieval structure had partly collapsed in 1736/37, but was rebuilt to Henry Flitcroft's designs and reopened in 1740. In 1843 it was severely damaged by fire but was again rehabilitated, then in 1918 it was declared redundant and demolition was sanctioned. The whole site was sold for the construction of a warehouse, and the tower, the church's last surviving fragment, was destroyed in 1928.

In Mitcham, 1928 saw the opening of a local Building Fund to help with the erection of the proposed new church. Land for the site, extending 200 feet by roughly 175 feet, was 'given freely', and in November 1929 a New District was constituted. In the preceding April the priest-in-charge had expressed doubts whether the time was yet ripe to establish a permanent church building with its ongoing financial implications, but the Bishop of Woolwich, who chaired the newly formed building committee, would not brook any delay and urged the construction of a Basilican type of church to seat 400 to 500. Arthur C. Martin was appointed as architect, apparently on the strength of good work done at Sandhurst and on King's College Hostel in Vincent Square, Westminster, and by July in 1929 he had submitted designs for a church seating 500 and allowing for possible enlargement when required. £7,000 was now said to be available from the sale of St Olave's in Tooley Street, a further £650 had been raised locally, and a grant had been promised from the Twenty-five Churches Fund.

The church from the south.

Architect's drawing of the church from the south.

Arthur Martin's designs were, for their date, unconventional. They provided for a nave of two bays, shallow transepts, a chancel with a Lady Chapel on its north side, and a west porch and vestibule under a tall west tower. But it was the treatment and style of the structure based on this essentially simple plan which evoked the comment, when the church came to be built, that it was 'like no other in Christendom'. The inspiration was clearly Byzantine, as evidenced by the central dome – though this was to be encased in a broad tower – and by its eight supporting columns. The main construction materials would be brick and reinforced concrete.

To its credit, the Building Committee was not overawed by the originality of the designs, though there were divergences of opinion, and the proposals were approved subject to the roof being pointed, not flat as designed. The complete church was estimated to cost a daunting £17,000, but it was decided in the first instance to omit the Lady Chapel, the west bay of the nave and the west tower which could be added on later; it was thought that these economies would reduce the estimated cost to about £10,000 and still provide seating for 400.

A revised design incorporating a ridged roof was submitted but was smartly rejected by both the Central Advisory Committee and the Twenty-five Churches Fund Committee, who found that the alteration 'had seriously impaired the particular style and architectural beauty of the original design'. By the end of 1929 a reversion to the original flat roof was agreed and sanctioned, and tenders were invited for building the truncated church. Unfortunately the lowest tender was for about £14,000 but the architect suggested modifications, including a smaller sanctuary, to reduce building costs to £11,000. This was referred to Bishop Garbett who agreed that up to £12,500 could be spent so as to retain as much as possible

The intended west elevation (not built).

WEST ELEVATION

90

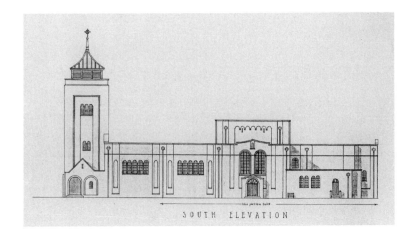

The intended south elevation. The westernmost bay and tower were not built.

SOUTH ELEVATION

of the original design. Towards this sum a further grant of £500 would be made from the Twenty-five Churches Fund to enhance its total contribution to £2,628, and there would be assistance from the Incorporated Church Building Society, but at least £1,000 would have to be raised locally over the next three to four years. Garbett himself was keen to bring Arthur Martin's designs to realisation, calling them 'excellent'. The building contract was thereupon awarded to Hall, Beddall & Co. whose revised tender was £11,287, to which would have to be added the architect's fees and other expenses.

Plan (east to the right), including the unbuilt westernmost elements.

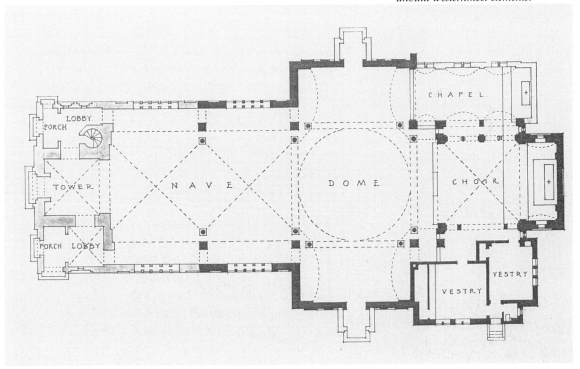

On 3 May 1930 the foundation stone was laid by Garbett's mother in the presence of the Bishop himself and of the Bishops of Woolwich and Dover. The assembled company were a little more fortunate than those who had attended the dedication of the church hall two years earlier for, although a thunderstorm broke, it waited until immediately after the proceedings had ended.

Contemporary reports assert that 380,000 bricks were used in the construction of the church. The walls, rising from a heavy bed of concrete sunk into the clay site, were capped by parapets edged with moulded artificial stone and, except for the vestries, the whole church was domed and vaulted in concrete, the flat roofs being finished with asphalt. Temporary brick walls were erected at the west end of the truncated nave and on the north side of the chancel, to allow for a future west extension and a Lady Chapel when required.

On 17 January 1931 the church was consecrated, Garbett as usual conducting the ceremony. He expressed himself as 'delight-ed' with the church, and had no regrets that its birth had come about through the demise of St Olave's in Southwark. 'That old church,' said he, 'had nothing of interest except its name. It was not

The interior looking east.

Interior of St Olave's, Mitcham—May '99

interesting historically nor architecturally, nor was it then of any practical value… [it] was standing empty and useless and, in the circumstances, it was only right that it should be sold and the money put to use.'

Garbett's enthusiasm does not seem to have been entirely mirrored in other quarters, however: one local comment, made at the time of the church's consecration, asserted that 'misunderstandings and grave allegations were disquieting at St Olave's, but it now looks as though the church will advance calmly as an Anglo-Catholic centre'; evidence, this, of earlier conflict over the prospective style of churchmanship.

Despite the lack of half of the intended nave, the church's profile, as viewed from the neighbouring park, is long and squat, but at close quarters the severity of its uniform brown-red brick and its sharply defined external angles and wide tower is seen to be mitigated by detailing such as the round-headed windows and blind arcading, the ornamental rainwater heads embossed 'Saint Olave 1930' and a slightly concave outline to the moulded end parapets, this last motif being used also to crown the moulded heads of doorways. All windows are simple and brick-framed.

Caröe & Passmore found the nave, as erected, to be about 61 feet long and the chancel about 34 feet, both having a width of 45 feet. The shallow transepts measured about 11 feet deep and 32 feet wide. Choir and clergy vestries were provided on the south side of the chancel, with a small organ chamber over the choir vestry. There was seating for 512, all in chairs. But these prosaic details hardly do justice to an interior offering such a striking contrast to the asceticism seen outside. The overall impression is of broad sweeping curves. The dominant architectural feature is the

Pulpit and north wall of chancel.

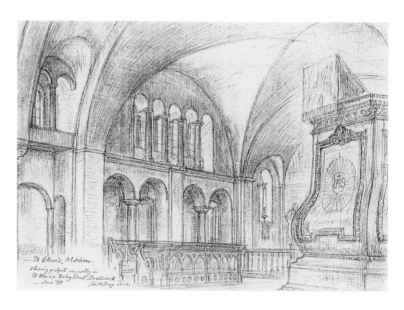

One of the bells from the original St Olave's, now hanging between the nave and north transept.

crossing, crowned by a large saucer dome rising, to a height of 40 feet, above wide curving arches which spring from four pairs of smooth cylindrical concrete columns. These columns from the outset provided almost the only note of colour, a pale blue which, with their moulded Byzantine capitals of blue and gold, stood out against the background of plastered walls, vaults and arches which were of plain white except for a pale primrose edging.

Some of the furnishings and other equipment came from St Olave's Church at Southwark, having been donated by the Trustees. These included the fine early eighteenth century oak pulpit, of tulip shape, which since 1928 had found a temporary home in the Hall; a white marble font, also of the eighteenth century; an oak table fashioned from the one-time sounding board of the old pulpit; and some silver-gilt communion plate comprising a chalice of 1630 and a flagon and alms dish each of 1688. To these gifts were added four eighteenth-century pewter collection plates, some oak choir stalls, and a panelled wood altar made by two local craftsmen. A second-hand organ was purchased from Rest, Cartwright & Sons and then modernised. The Trustees of the old St Olave's also presented three bells from the demolished church. Two of these, a great tenor of 19¾ cwt. and one of 5 cwt., had been cast by C. &. G. Mears of London in 1844; the third, inscribed 'Mr. Nicholas Flower Churchwarden 1719', was a sanctus or clock bell of 2¼ cwt. cast by Richard Phelps of Whitechapel, a predecessor of the Mears firm. The biggest bell was considered too heavy for use until the projected west tower was added to Mitcham's new church, but it was accepted together with the lightest of the three, the middle one being given to Mears & Stainbank's Whitechapel Foundry to defray the cost of fitting and erecting the others. It was decided to fix the tenor bell across the external angle of the nave and north transept, where it still remains, and to suspend the smaller beneath the interior dome; but the latter now hangs externally from a bracket fixed to the east wall of the crossing tower.

As is often the case with buildings of unusual design, there were a few teething problems. As early as March 1931 it was observed that the eight interior columns had lost some of their pristine beauty, for blue paint was peeling off each of them, whilst the outer walls of the church were becoming 'spattered and streaked with chalk', a sign that damp was attacking the bricks. Four years later, cracks were appearing in the church ceiling. But these setbacks were overcome, and the 1930s as a whole were a period of much positive development. The population of the District, which was recorded in the 1931 Census as 8,473, looked set to double, with the erection of Council housing in Meopham Road, the sale of Norbury golf course for building, and the expected sale of Tooting Bec golf course. In 1936 the Sherwood Park area was severed from St Olave's to become a new parish, and the Ascension Church Hall was dedicated there, Terence Carr producing designs for a new church to accompany it. In the following year a vicarage for St Olave's, also designed by Carr, was built by Hudson Bros. of Clapham Junction.

Meanwhile the south transept of St Olave's Church, which had been provided with an altar, was refurnished in 1934 and styled the Chapel of Our Patron Saint Olaf; it now contained a painting of St Olaf and Viking Ships, by a local artist named Skilbeck.

Next year a statue of the Virgin Mary and Child was acquired and this was placed in the north transept when, in 1939, it was

The east end in the 1960s, before the subsequent re-ordering. [Copyright of Surrey History Service.]

converted for use as a Lady Chapel. The font, which had stood there, was removed to the west end of the nave. Minor internal adjustments and rearrangements were made in the 1940s, and in 1951 wall plaques representing the Stations of the Cross were set up. In 1955 major repairs and renovations were carried out under the architect Graham Crump, the main contractors being W. J. Brooker Ltd. Subsequent developments included the replacement in 1956 of the high altar dossal by a Christus Rex crucifix featuring a small kneeling figure of St Olave at its foot; the reconstruction of the organ in 1961 by Rest, Cartwright & Sons, using most of the existing pipework; and the provision in 1967 of new oak kneeling rails, made by Tom Jones, in the two chapels.

In 1969 the entire church was reroofed by R. H. Hope & Co., a task which revealed defects in the brickwork of the parapets. Expensive maintenance operations such as these needed money. About the same time a scheme was formulated to sell part of the church grounds for redevelopment to provide housing, a car park and a new vicarage. David Bush was called in as architect and, after much refinement, his proposals were submitted to the Town Planning authorities in 1971. Then followed the deconsecration of parts of the churchyard to enable building work to proceed.

David Bush was also engaged to produce a scheme for liturgically reordering the church interior. In 1972 his initial ideas for seating 'in the round', with a nave altar near the eastern rim of the circle, were tried experimentally in conjunction with the conversion of the chancel into a Lady Chapel and the re-siting of much other furniture. This aroused considerable opposition but a compromise scheme was worked out which accepted the principle of a nave altar but discarded many of the other alterations. In 1978 the west wall of the church was given a new brick porch and vestibule, designed by John Harris: a virtual acceptance, this, that the planned west end of the nave and its terminal tower would now never be built. Three years later, in connection with the church's jubilee celebrations, a portable font was introduced into the north transept and the nave sanctuary was given emphasis by raising the altar on a platform and installing new communion rails; this latter work was likewise devised by the architect John Harris.

Today, the church interior is more richly tinted than was originally the case: the old white surfaces are now cream, the eight cylindrical columns are a much darker shade of blue, and the newer furnishings are generally infused with colour.

MORDEN

St George, Central Road

Proposed New Church

This project must be accounted one of Bishop Garbett's failures. Certainly its outcome, after a lengthy period of wrangling and uncertainty, was a major disappointment to him, and there is no record that he ever set foot inside the building once it was erected.

Faced with the daunting problem of providing adequate facilities for worship for the huge population expected to arrive in the London County Council's new 'cottage estate' of St Helier, Garbett laid plans for erecting three churches and two church halls within the bounds of a single parish to be created from parts of Carshalton, Morden and the Benhilton district of Sutton. There was no objection from Carshalton or Sutton, but the proposals were viewed unfavourably at St Lawrence's, Morden, whose Parish Church Council, led by their new Rector, the Revd A. J. Culwick, in October 1927 voiced their opposition to the idea of segregating part of their parish. Little progress was made in 1928 towards resolving the impasse, but steps were initiated by the Rector to seek a site for a new church building and to open a local fund to finance its erection; a dual-purpose hall was envisaged to begin with. A subsequent application for a cash grant from the Twenty-five Churches Fund brought a response requesting submission of definite proposals including those for a church as well as a church hall. The architects Douglass Mathews & Ridley were thereupon asked to draw up rough plans but the stumbling block remained that, whereas the Twenty-five Churches Committee recommended absorption of part of Morden into the proposed new St Helier parish in accordance with Garbett's wishes, the Morden parish authorities and their patrons were still adamant that no such division should take place.

With obvious reluctance on both sides, an apparent compromise was reached by the end of 1929 under which Bishop Garbett conditionally accepted that control of the 'central portion' of Morden parish, which was to contain part of the St Helier estate, could remain with St Lawrence's, but the Ravensbury area to the east must be given up. On this basis, and subject to satisfactory arrangements being made for building a church, a grant of £2,000 from the Twenty-five Churches Fund was agreed in principle. But the Bishop clearly retained doubts about the credibility of such an arrangement, as he questioned the ability of St Lawrence's parish to raise sufficient funds for completing the enterprise.

Early in 1930 St Lawrence's secured from the L.C.C. a suitable site, adjoining the then existing rectory in Central Road, and William Pite was selected as architect for the new church. It soon

Right: the hall, now church, of St George, from the west. Below: the modern hall, attached to the church.

emerged that an anonymous benefactor had come forward who was prepared to finance the building of both a church and a hall and to help with the provision of a vicarage and an endowment for the new benefice. This offer was conditional on the maintenance in the new district of the existing evangelical traditions of Morden parish, and on patronage being vested in nominated trustees including the Rector of Morden. These conditions cannot have pleased Bishop Garbett who was known to have anglo-catholic leanings and had expected patronage to be given to the Diocese, but he was realistic enough to see the advantages of the proposals and, after further negotiations, he broadly accepted the scheme with some modification as to patronage.

That year saw further delays while boundaries were argued over, and by the end of the year signs were beginning to emerge that the plans might become unstuck. The donor was now suggesting that only a hall should be built to begin with, and that he would notify the Bishop after two years whether he would be able to proceed with the completion of the scheme. In March 1931 the Rector had to tell his P.C.C. that the donor was 'unable to fulfil his promises'. To make the best of a frustrating situation, it was decided to proceed with building a hall as quickly as possible and to launch a public appeal for the necessary funds: £4,000 was needed to supplement both the £2,000 already raised and an interest-free loan of £1,000 which had been offered by one of the patrons. For this more modest scheme, T. N. Ashford was appointed architect and the builders were C. H. Gibson Ltd. of Thornton Heath. No help was forthcoming from the Twenty-five Churches Fund, though a prospect remained of its assistance with the cost of erecting a permanent church, provided one could be built within two years.

Work on the hall was under way by June 1931, and on 27 February in the following year it was dedicated by the Bishop of Woolwich. Garbett was conspicuously absent. A simple brick structure designed to seat about 250, it was barely adequate for its task.

Subsequent developments can be briefly summarised. The two-year period of grace allowed by the Twenty-five Churches Committee lapsed without any start being made on building a church. In 1935 proposals were drawn up for a church to seat 250 initially and 550 on completion, but these were abandoned. A temporary solution was eventually achieved when, on 5 January 1938, the Bishop of Woolwich dedicated for use as a church a wooden building which had been erected close to the hall. This survived severe damage by fire in 1947, and it still exists today. In 1976 a new structure, containing an entrance lobby, lounge and kitchen, was put up to link the two earlier buildings; the original brick hall was refurbished and renovated, and converted for use as a church; and the former wooden church was made into a Family Centre. The architect was Malcolm Thomas and the builders J. Kidd & Son (Builders) Ltd. of Clapham Park. The whole complex was re-dedicated by Bishop Stockwood on 22 June 1976 as St George's Church and Family Centre.

MOTSPUR PARK
Holy Cross, Douglas Avenue
Proposed New Church

There is no evidence that any money was paid from the Twenty-five Churches Fund in support of this project. However, it was certainly on the Fund's preliminary list for financial assistance, as is clear from its inclusion, as Holy Cross, Raynes Park, in details published in the Southwark Diocesan Directories for the years 1927 through to 1930. For that reason, it is appropriate to give a brief historical summary here.

A mission district had been established at Raynes Park in 1900 from part of the ancient parish of Merton. In 1906, on a site in Grand Drive near Raynes Park railway station, the partly completed church of St Saviour was consecrated to serve the area: it was the first church to be built in the newly constituted Diocese of Southwark. A District Chapelry was assigned to it in the following year, when a separate site in Douglas Avenue was secured for mission buildings to cover the West Barnes part of the new District. In 1908 a second-hand iron building was erected there and opened as the Holy Cross Mission Hall, to be ministered by a curate from St Saviour's. The next development came in 1914, when a new

Holy Cross, Motspur Park, built in 1949.

stone-built hall in Douglas Avenue was dedicated for use as a place of worship until a permanent church could be constructed on the site of the iron building, which was to be retained meanwhile for social purposes. The new hall was lengthened in 1921. A scheme to build a parsonage house on adjoining land was promulgated in 1926, the intention being to follow this with the erection of the proposed permanent church. This will have been the stage when a financial contribution from the Twenty-five Churches Fund came under consideration. The proposals, however, did not reach fruition, and there was no reference to them in the Fund's list of churches and halls built, or assistance promised, in the Southwark Diocesan Directory for 1931–2. Similarly, the final definitive list, published in 1934, of churches, halls and sites supported from the Fund excluded any mention of the Holy Cross. Possibly the change of heart arose from the acquisition in 1929 of a site, on the far side of the new Kingston bypass, for the proposed church of St James, New Malden.

Disaster struck twice in the second World War. In September 1940 the original iron mission hall was 'bombed out of existence'. Worse, the stone church building was itself destroyed by a flying bomb in 1944. Rebuilding plans were put into effect after the war, and a new church, simple and unpretentious, was designed by R. G. C. Covell and dedicated on 29 January 1949. In it were placed two communion rails which, according to T. P. Stevens in the *Southwark Diocesan Gazette*, came from a Queen Anne mansion at Diss in Norfolk; and a prominent rood made by students of Kingston School of Art.

A Conventional District was created for the area in 1966, under the name of the Holy Cross, Motspur Park.

NEW ELTHAM
All Saints, Bercta Road

Enlargement in 1930–31 of church partly built 1898
   to designs of P. Dollar
Architect: Thomas F. Ford
Contractors: John Garrett & Son Ltd. of Balham

The first public services for Anglicans in this part of Eltham, known then as Pope Street, were held in 1880 at premises in Novar Road by the vicar of Holy Trinity in whose parish it was. In 1884 All Saints' Pope Street Mission Hall was built and opened in Avery Hill Road; a dual-purpose structure for worship and social functions, it could accommodate 150 persons. A site for a permanent church, adjoining Bercta Road, was acquired in 1892 but another six years elapsed before building proceeded, and even then construction was left incomplete when consecration took place on 17 November 1898.

The architect was Peter Dollar; the portion of his design to be erected comprised an aisled nave with buttressed red-brick walls relieved by stone dressings. Set into each side of the high-pitched roof were two dormer windows, each of five arched lights. Triple lancet windows gave light to the low aisles. At the east end a small apsidal structure served as a temporary chancel, timber-framed and encased in corrugated iron sheeting. The church bell was crudely housed in a simple rectangular box with louvred sides, perched on thin timber supports outside the stopped-up east wall of the north aisle. Inside the church, the arcades separating the wide three-bay nave from the aisles rested on piers of alternate circular and octagonal sections. Seating was provided for 300.

There were no further significant developments until after the first World War; in 1922 New Eltham was designated a Conventional District with its own priest-in-charge, and an appeal was soon launched for £10,000 to complete the church, build a new hall and purchase a parsonage house. The hall came first: a brick building placed transversely opposite the west end of the church, it was designed by Walter P. Silvester and opened on 10 January 1925, replacing the former mission hall in Avery Hill Road.

The fund-raising campaign to meet the expense of enlarging the church now gathered pace and, in 1929, despite the objections of the Vicar of Holy Trinity, a separate New District was carved out of his parish. Peter Dollar submitted new proposals for completing the church but these were rejected in favour of a scheme put forward by Thomas F. Ford. The building contract was awarded to John Garrett & Son Ltd. of Balham whose tendered price was £6,010, and by August 1930 the new work was put in hand. The added portions were consecrated on 16 May 1931, and the New

New Eltham, All Saints, in its incomplete state before enlargement in 1930–31. Top: the east end. Bottom: from the north-west, a view which can be compared with the drawing below. (Detail from an old postcard.)

The view from the north-west, after completion to Ford's designs.

The exterior. Top: from the south, showing the chancel and morning chapel behind obscuring hoardings. Bottom: from the north showing the porch and other additions of 1930–31.

Parish of All Saints came into being. Patronage was conferred on the Bishop of Southwark in consideration of a £2,000 contribution from the Twenty-five Churches Fund towards the building costs.

Ford's designs, generally Perpendicular Gothic in style, provided for a new chancel with a morning chapel to its south, and an organ chamber and vestries for the clergy and choir to its north. A porch and clergy entrance were also placed on the north side, and a new door was inserted at the east end of the existing south aisle. An intended west porch was not built at this stage, recourse being made to a temporary corrugated iron accretion. The new parts were faced, like the old, with walls of red brick, Bath stone being used for dressings. The chancel roof, lower than that of the nave, was covered by red tiles as was the main chapel roof which was transversely gabled. The nave and aisles were re-roofed and small ventilators introduced in place of the original dormers. Two more windows were added for the north aisle. Tall three-light windows with Perpendicular tracery were provided in the east wall of the chancel and the south wall of the chapel.

Inside, the church now had an estimated seating capacity of 522. The distinctive chancel arcades, each of one pointed arch between two smaller ones, rested on hexagonal-sectioned piers. The two capitals to the chancel arch, originally plain, were now carved. The chancel roof was supported on massive crenellated tie-beams with king-posts.

Some of the old internal fittings were moved to different positions. The organ was re-erected in the new organ chamber; a two-manual instrument by Henry Jones & Sons of South Kensington, it had been acquired for £300 in 1901. The high altar was removed to the south chapel along with its altar rails which were now picked

A view into the south chapel from the north.

All Saints, New Eltham – July '99 — John M.Bray

out in gilt. Outside, the church bell was given a slightly more dignified position, though unprotected from the weather, and is now visible near the parapet on the south side of the chapel. According to G. P. Elphick, it weighs 2¾ cwt; cast originally by John Warner & Sons, it was shotblasted and rehung by the White-chapel Bell Foundry. Other fittings, installed in 1931 or soon after, included an 'English' high altar, a reredos for the Lady Chapel, and a wooden pulpit carved with Perpendicular Gothic detailing. In the chapel, which is now dedicated to Our Lady and St Aidan, is a striking wall memorial to the Revd Canon Arthur C. Norledge (1886–1964), the first vicar, and his wife. In the south window of this chapel are richly coloured pictorial glass panels from the short-lived St Aidan's Church at nearby Edgebury, which closed at the end of 1974.

In 1937 a proposal to replace the corrugated iron porch with a permanent new west end, increasing the seating capacity by 48, was put into effect. Thomas F. Ford was again the architect, and John Garrett & Son Ltd. the contractors. The alterations, designed to be in harmony with the rest of the architecture, involved blocking up the west doorway and inserting a three-light traceried window in its stead; above this was placed a much larger Perpendicular window of six lights. A new brick porch was built at the west end of the north aisle. The total cost was £1,200 including cleaning down the church and paving the churchyard between the west end and the parish hall. Within the church, the west end of the nave was now converted into a baptistry.

The church survived the second World War, but not entirely unscathed: in 1944 the south aisle, Lady Chapel, organ and hall were all damaged by blast from a flying bomb which landed nearby, and a stained glass window was reduced to fragments. Post-war developments included the enlargement of the parish in 1954 by annexation of parts from the Annunciation, Chislehurst, and Christ Church, Sidcup. An interesting innovation was the introduction, in 1974, of facilities enabling local Roman Catholics to use the church as a Mass Centre; this provision continues.

To mark the church's centenary, Caroline Benyon was commissioned to design new glass for the centre light of the chancel's east window. This, with a splendidly effective standing figure of Christ as its centrepiece, was installed in 1999.

NORTH SHEEN (Kew)

St Philip the Apostle and All Saints, Marksbury Avenue

New Church, built 1928–9
Architect: Edward A. Swan
Contractor: J. J. Fuller of Chiswick

'No church has had more loving care given to its building and furnishing… The church is not only unique in itself, but it is a fitting memorial to the two devoted Churchpeople who first thought of it, and who, by their enthusiasm, loving care, and self-sacrifice, made it possible to build it.'

So said Bishop Garbett, though he might fairly have bestowed the credit among several members of the two families, interlinked by marriage, whose combined efforts brought the church into life: the Hoares and the Lamberts.

A local historian, Uvedale Lambert, and his wife Cecily née Hoare, who resided at South Park Farm, Blechingley in Surrey, owned a redundant timber barn at Stonehall Farm, Hurst Green, near Oxted. In 1926, aware of the Southwark Diocese's plan to erect twenty-five new churches, they offered the barn for conversion. Garbett, who became personally involved in the ensuing discussions, asked for definite plans, and the architect Edward Swan, who had done much other work for Uvedale Lambert, was engaged to produce them. Early in 1927, the plans were approved by Garbett, and the decision was taken to rebuild the barn, at a site in North Sheen, as a memorial to members of the Hoare family of Stansted House, Godstone.

At that time, the North Sheen district was served by a dual-purpose Mission Hall, dedicated to St Peter, which had been erected in 1910. To resolve a period of uncertainty about the district's status, the Diocese agreed in 1926 to the establishment of a Diocesan Mission District, subject to local support for a fund to build a church on a site provided by an estate developer named Hugh Leyborne Popham. This site was quite a generous one, measuring some 215 feet by 160 feet at the junction of Marksbury and Atwood Avenues.

Tenders were now invited for the delicate operations of dismantling the barn, carefully identifying the timbers and other materials to be reused, carting them to the new site, and reconstructing them there according to the architect's directions. The contract was awarded to J. J. Fuller of Chiswick, whose estimated cost was about £5,000, excluding fittings. Towards this sum, £2,500 was granted from the Twenty-five Churches Fund, conditional on patronage being vested in the Bishop of Southwark, and on the church being dedicated to St Philip the Apostle and All Saints instead of perpetuating the Mission Hall's dedication to St Peter. But before the foundation stone was laid, on St Philip's Day, 1 May 1928, by Mrs. Philip Hoare – Cecily Lambert's sister-in-law – there were lengthy negotiations with the Ecclesiastical Commissioners, whose consultants Caröe & Passmore were patently unhappy with some aspects of the design proposals, particularly the unusual

North Sheen, St Philip the Apostle and All Saints from the south-west.

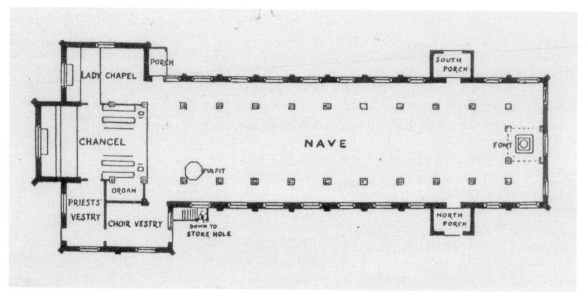

Above: plan of the church, east to the left. Below: two views of the chancel.

proportions of the nave and the design and disposal of the windows. It cannot have been often that they were required to assess a former barn's suitability for use as a parish church!

The barn, as it stood at Stonehall Farm, was an L-shaped structure, some 120 feet long, which had latterly been used for housing farm implements and hay. It was considered to date from at least as early as the seventeenth century, possibly the sixteenth, and there was evidence, exemplified by the large number of mortise holes, that some of its beams and rafters may originally have been ship's timbers. When its demolition began, on 31 January 1928, the decision was taken also to pull down the adjacent stables and to use their timber for widening the church's aisles. Whilst the barn's timbers were, so far as possible, restored to their original positions as the church was being built, some modifications had to be made and some additional components were incorporated, though care was taken to ensure that their design and materials were in keeping with the reused elements. The original L-shape of the barn was straightened out. The rubble stone plinth on which the church was constructed was taken from the barn, but the old weatherboard walling was replaced by bricks which, together with the roof tiles, were baked at Daneshill, Basingstoke, by Walter Hoare, a cousin of Uvedale Lambert. The specially toned red bricks were two inches thick and laid in English bond, consistent with the practice at the time the barn was built. Bath stone dressings were used for the mullioned windows, which the stonemason, George Baker of Oxted, based on the design of those at the great house of Compton Wynyates. Additional dormer windows, four on each side, were inserted into the roof, which was extended at shallower pitch to embrace the widened aisles. Over the west gable was placed a small timber-framed belfry, its diminutive spire being modelled on that of Martyr Worthy Church near Winchester. The single bell, of 2½ cwt and said by G. P. Elphick to have a 'good tone', came from Holy Trinity Church at Wandsworth.

Three porches were constructed, using oak from the barn. The main pair, giving access to the nave, were paved with smooth blue slates, more than two inches thick, taken from the barn's threshing floor.

In contrast to the church's exterior, which tends to be modest and self-effacing, the inside presents a visual impact which is almost breathtaking with its forest of ancient timbering. The long narrow nave is punctuated by 24 square-cut oak piers, resting on square brick bases to gain greater height; many of the piers were said to be already 'gnarled with age, and worn thin in places where cattle have rubbed against them'. They support an impressive roof, of unseasoned oak, with tie-beams and queen-posts; this is continuous from east to west and open to the apex.

The chancel was screened from the vestries and intended organ chamber on its north side by an arrangement of timber framing and brick nogging; whilst the corresponding timber-framing on the

Above: the barn-like roof. Below: interior looking east.

Illustration (of the 1930s) of the Lady Chapel sanctuary as designed by Hugh Easton.

south side was left partly open between the chancel and a small morning chapel.

The baptistry was centrally placed at the west end, below the belfry. The tower-frame which supported the latter was copied from that at Tandridge Church near Oxted; its four massive supports were cut from oak on Uvedale Lambert's estate at Blechingley.

Some of the original fittings merit notice; not all of them survive in their primary positions. The square grey font, inspired by a thirteenth century one at Aldenham, Hertfordshire, is of Surrey marble dug from Lambert's South Park Farm and cut by George Baker; it rests on a cylindrical stem with four detached shafts. The oak pulpit is a replica of the one in Hereford Cathedral, said to date from 1480, from which Bishop Croft denounced the behaviour of Puritan soldiers in Cromwell's time. It was carved and presented by Geoffrey Hoare in memory of Sir Archer Croft, his father-in-law. At the east end, the sanctuary walls were lined with old oak panelling reported to have come from a manor house at Banstead. The High Altar incorporates more oak panelling, of linenfold design and said to be Tudor in origin. The Jacobean oak altar rails came from Writtle Church in Essex. A priest's chair, designed and given by the architect E. A. Swan, was fashioned in oak from the Stansted estate. The choir stalls were likewise of oak from Stansted, given by Mrs. Philip Hoare. Their poppyheads came from the City church of St Dunstan-in-the-West; discarded during renovations about 1860, they were bought by Henry Gerard Hoare, formerly of Stansted House, and presented by Hoare's Bank whose premises in Fleet Street were almost opposite the church. Two oak lecterns were also given by the Bank.

Thus furnished, the new church was consecrated on 4 February 1929. A District Chapelry was assigned in 1930. Sadly, Uvedale Lambert never lived to see his barn's reincarnation: he had died on 6 June 1928 and was buried at Blechingley. At Garbett's suggestion, his name was included on the Hoare family memorial tablet, erected at the west end. The Hoares had been generous financial contributors towards the cost of the structure, which reached about £6,770 including cartage, heating and architect's fees. This outlay had provided a church, nearly 140 feet long, which could seat 435 people.

In memory of Uvedale and Cecily Lambert, the morning chapel on the south side of the chancel was furnished as a Lady Chapel in 1933. Designed by Hugh Easton and executed – except for the reredos – by C. Hammond, it was panelled with cedar from a tree in Godstone churchyard which fell in a snowstorm at Christmas 1927; the same tree yielded wood for sanctuary chairs. The reredos, made by Easton and central to his scheme, comprised a framed bas-relief panel depicting the Madonna and Child surrounded by children. The silvered wooden candlesticks which were placed on the oak altar table were, again, designed by Easton.

The provision of an organ caused some difficulty. Uvedale Lambert had made it clear that he did not wish the church to be 'over-organed' and, with this in mind, a small organ chamber considered ample for the purpose was initially set up on the north side with advice from the organ builders Walker & Sons. It proved inadequate for a second-hand instrument was eventually purchased, which had to be sited further west, in the north aisle. This organ was reconditioned and installed by Henry Willis & Sons in 1936. Consequential adjustments included repositioning the pulpit and converting the originally intended organ chamber into a storage recess which in 1950 was partly concealed behind a screen of timber framing and brick nogging similar to that on the south side.

The font at North Sheen, based on a thirteenth-century precedent.

Other changes have included the replacement in 1955 of the original foundation stone, which was rapidly wearing out, and the introduction in 1956 of a font cover, or rather lid, of carved oak, assembled by Harold C. Broad; its bronze fittings, featuring an elaborate cross, were made by Thomas Harrington & Sons of Enfield. The transomed five-light east window has stained glass commemorating the young daughter of a former incumbent.

The old Mission Hall, which since the Barn Church's construction had continued in service as the parish hall, was sold in 1966 to the Roman Catholic Church of Our Lady Queen of Peace for use as a Chapel of Ease. The proceeds contributed to the cost of erecting a new hall, opened in 1967, on part of the vicarage garden and land adjoining the east end of the church; its architect was George E. Cassidy and the main contractors Martin & Thorpe.

Recent improvements to the church interior include the provision of new heating, lighting and draught-proofing; the installation of new seating; and the erection of a screen and gallery towards the west end, dividing the long nave into a 'worship area', and a parish room. Oak has been employed in the constructional work, to ensure consistency with the original interior.

The Southwark Diocesan Directory now lists the church under the place-name of Kew instead of North Sheen.

OLD MALDEN
Proposed New Church

Plans for financing the building of an additional church for Old Malden never progressed beyond the tentative stage. This location, along with New Malden and Raynes Park (Holy Cross), was included in the Southwark Diocesan Directory's first list, published in 1927, of churches to be built with assistance from the

Twenty-five Churches Fund. The list was said to be 'open to revision, and should not be regarded as final', but these three locations again all appeared in the following year's list, and once more in the 1929–30 edition which reported additionally that a site had been secured at New Malden. Yet Old Malden and Raynes Park were both absent from the list for 1931–2, and neither had been reinstated when the final list was produced in 1934.

Though the original proposals, concerning this area administered by the Malden and Coombe District Council, were rather vague, they were clearly prompted by the remarkable expansion of its population: by 1905 there were nearly 8,000 residents; in 1928, the year following the opening of the Kingston by-pass, there were said to be over 20,000, and the number reached 25,000 in 1931.

Already, in 1925, the vicar of Old Malden had warned of the need for a new church in the parish to serve the neighbourhood of Motspur Park, and by the next year the purchase of a site was under consideration. Plans were far from firm, however, and in 1927 it was admitted that these proposals might quite possibly be dropped and a new plan substituted. A year later came the announcement that preliminary arrangements were being made to purchase a site on the arterial road, i.e. the new Kingston by-pass, 'opposite the jam factory'; and these arrangements evolved through negotiation with the landowners, Oxford's Merton College, into the acquisition of the plot upon which the church of St James, Malden (originally styled 'New Malden'), was built. It was this sizeable church, suitably positioned to serve the needs of new residents over a wide area, which no doubt rendered unnecessary the erection of another place of worship closer to Old Malden, thereby causing the tentative plans to be dropped.

Subsequent developments in this district are described under Malden, St James, and Motspur Park, Holy Cross.

PURLEY

St Swithun, Grovelands Road

New Hall, built 1928–9
Architect: S. Jupp
Contractor: Shopland & Co. Ltd., of Sutton

The parish of Woodcote was created in 1911, from part of the former lands of the Carews of Beddington. The first church to serve the district, an iron building, had been erected in 1905, and was followed in 1910 by a permanent stone-faced structure designed by G. H. Fellowes Prynne. Services in the Brighton Road area of the district had been begun in a private house in 1908 by Church Army chaplains, whose congregation moved a few months later to a new mission hall in Lansdowne Road.

In 1926 it was decided to make provision for a permanent new church building to cover the Brighton Road area. A steeply sloping site was acquired in 1927 at the corner of Downlands Road and Grovelands Road, and a fund was opened for the erection initially of a hall which would serve also as a temporary church until a permanent one could be built. S. Jupp, of the practice of Elms & Jupp, was appointed as architect. Grants totalling £750 were subsequently secured from the Twenty-five Churches Fund towards the estimated building cost of £2,255 including furnishing and architect's fees, and the foundation stone was laid on 8 December 1928.

The completed building, which was dedicated on 25 April 1929, was designed as a simple parallelogram in plan, with a small narrower projection at one end. Though of modest size, with a seating capacity of 200, it was said to be the largest hall which could be accommodated on the site if space were to be left for building a permanent church. Its walls were of brick, punctuated by plain square-headed windows; on the ridge of the thick-tiled roof was placed a tile-hung timber turret with a flèche. The hall today is almost completely screened from the adjoining Grovelands Road by trees and a tall hedge. It was licensed for banns and marriages in 1934.

Progress towards erecting a permanent church on the site was encouraged by the award in 1937 of a £1,000 grant from the Bishop of Southwark's Council for New Districts. Early in 1939 N. F. Cachemaille-Day, who had been appointed architect, produced designs for a church to seat around 350 people at an estimated cost in the region of £6,000. It was to have a mansard roof resting on low brick walls; the choir vestry would be housed in a basement, taking

advantage of the falling ground level. The church was to be built in three stages, the first of which would consist of chancel, chapel, vestries and two bays of the nave. The foundation stone was laid at a full masonic ceremony on 15 July 1939, and the walls had been built to a height of some six feet when the second World War erupted and all building work had to be stopped.

In 1949 the project was revived under a new architect, David Nye, but four more years elapsed before a building licence was granted. The partly-completed walls of Cachemaille-Day's church were then demolished and a new structure was erected with funds mostly provided by the transfer of war damage payments totalling £15,000 from two bombed London churches which were not rebuilt: St Peter's at Greenwich and Holy Trinity at Blackheath. This indebtedness is acknowledged on tablets set up in the porch and in a window at the west end which was designed to symbolise St Peter and the Holy Trinity with St Swithun and St Mark.

The new church, credited to D. Evelyn Nye & Partners, was dedicated on 3 April 1954. Of restrained design, the building has brick walls and buttresses, the latter with a pronounced batter; windows are narrow and square-topped. The chancel terminates with a five-sided apse, in one wall of which is set the foundation stone from Cachemaille-Day's church. The copper-clad roof has a small octagonal turret over the chancel, surmounted by a cross. The simple aisleless interior, designed to seat 281, is characterised by big elliptical transverse arches. In 1981 an organ was acquired from the chapel of the demolished former Reedham School. The building's setting, at a much lower level than the hall, is attractive in a well-maintained garden.

St Swithun's achieved parochial status in August 1961, and the church was formally consecrated on 14 October in that year.

PUTNEY

St Margaret, Putney Park Lane

Enlargement in 1925–6 of church built originally in early 1870s
Architect: W. A. Forsyth
Contractors: F. G. Minter Ltd. of Putney

This church has an unusual history: it began life as a Baptist chapel, was later occupied by Presbyterians, then fell into disuse, and was finally acquired by the Anglicans who adapted it as a chapel of ease for Putney parish and then developed it to the dignity of a parochial church.

The identity of the building's original architect is uncertain. It is likely that its design was influenced by Colonel Alexander Croll, a Civil Engineer who in 1869 had purchased Granard Lodge in Putney Park Lane. He had the chapel built in its grounds by 1873 as a memorial to his mother, and he maintained a Baptist minister there who acted as his chaplain. In 1877 the then minister, Samuel H. Booth, left to become effectively the first full-time secretary of the Baptist Union and, in the same year, a much larger Baptist church was opened about a mile away in Werter Road. In 1879 Croll sold part of his Granard Lodge estate, including the chapel, to the Presbyterians with the stipulation that the building was to be used 'as a Protestant Church only or for Church Schools'. Two years later the rest of the estate was acquired from Croll by Seth Taylor.

The Presbyterians seem to have had lively connections during their occupation of the chapel, for their worshippers are reported to have included the radical John Bright, and Ramsay Macdonald is said to have been a member of a debating society formed by one of its ministers. But in 1898 they also moved to a larger church, built for them in Upper Richmond Road, whereupon the Granard chapel and the land on which it stood were bought by Seth Taylor. The chapel now ceased to be used for worship although, with the transfer of its ownership to him, Taylor had been assigned rights over the two pews which had formerly been reserved for Colonel Croll.

By 1910 there was mounting concern among Anglicans about the inadequacy of facilities for worship for the rapidly increasing population of Putney parish. In October of that year Seth Taylor responded by presenting the Granard chapel to the parish for use as a chapel of ease, and he undertook to make annual contributions to the stipend of a curate in charge; additional land adjoining the chapel site was conveyed in 1911. Conditions were attached to the gift; the building was to be used for the liturgy and rites of the Church of England only; a seat in it was to be reserved for the residents of Granard; any external structural alterations should be subject to Taylor's approval; and he should nominate the architect employed for such alterations.

The building at that time had an aisleless nave with shallow apsed transeptal arms. It was orientated from north to south, with the chancel at the north end. From the ritual south-west corner rose a small bell tower with an octagonal top storey surmounted by a spire. G. P. Elphick records the bell as being of 2 cwt. and inscribed 'W. Blews & Sons 1871'. The entrance porch or narthex adjoining the tower was approached by climbing a steep flight of steps, a feature made necessary because the nave floor sloped sharply downward towards the chancel to allow headroom for a meeting chamber in the basement area at the porch end. Externally the chapel had an undeniably picturesque appearance; the style was of course Gothic.

Putney, St Margaret from the south-west, from an old postcard. Note the original steps to the elevated west entrance, removed in 1912.

Some repairs and alterations were made, at a total cost of £1,950, before the building was opened for Anglican worship. The contractors were T. H. Adamson & Sons of Putney, and the architect was Alfred Gilson Humphry, Seth Taylor's nominee. Internally, the sloping nave floor was removed and replaced by a level one laid on steel joists in concrete; a lobby wall was taken out; a new heating chamber and apparatus were installed; electric lighting was substituted for gas; dilapidated seats were replaced by new oak seating; and a font was brought in from the parish church. Outside, the porch and its approach steps were removed, and a new flat-topped narthex built, this being faced with stone; and the ivy on the walls was 'neatly trimmed'. The chapel would now seat about 250 persons, but already it was recognised that a need for enlargement would soon arise.

Thus renewed and refurbished, the chapel was consecrated on 5 October 1912; its dedication to St Margaret was 'in deference to the wishes of' Seth Taylor. Proposals to extend the building were rapidly set in train and, only a year later, were agreed in principle with Taylor. The choice of architect for the enlargement was not entirely clear-cut: the parochial authorities apparently favoured Atkinson & Alexander but Taylor expressed himself as virtually under an obligation to secure the appointment once again of A. G. Humphry. Taylor suggested persuading the two practices to co-operate as Joint Architects. Discussions ensued on the question of financing the project, expected to cost over £4,500, but the first World War intervened, giving rise to building restrictions, and the proposals had to be set aside.

Seth Taylor died in 1917, and was commemorated by a brass wall tablet set up in the chapel; but his family remained supportive and they contributed generously towards the provision of an endowment fund in 1918. In 1920 the building was licensed for marriages, and by 1923 a clergy house had been established and a temporary hall built next to the chapel for parochial use. But the most significant development in this period was the purchase by the London County Council of the Dover House estate, on the west side of Putney Park Lane, for the erection of housing; this, which became known as the Roehampton Estate, was to increase the local population to a number approaching 10,000, and it provided an irresistible impetus for proceeding with the enlargement of the chapel and constituting a separate parish for the district.

Bishop Garbett was in no doubt that the chapel as it stood was now far too small for the needs of the area, and he at first declined to countenance the creation of a new parish until the building had been 'considerably enlarged and made more worthy of serving as the future Parish Church'. To this end he later offered a grant of up to £500 from the Twenty-five Churches Fund, though such was the response to the appeal for funds that only £200 was ultimately taken up from this source. However, notwithstanding Garbett's views, application for the creation of a separate District was pursued and, following a survey by Caröe & Passmore, consulting architects to the Ecclesiastical Commissioners, a Consolidated Chapelry was assigned on 12 October 1923, long before any start had been made to the necessary building work. Patronage was surrendered by the Vicar of Putney to the Bishop of Southwark.

The report of Caröe & Passmore's survey to determine the suitability of the building for use as a parish church is interesting for its description of the structure as it then was. They found that the nave was about 65 feet long and 30 feet wide, with shallow semi-octagonal transepts, and a shallow recess or sanctuary at the ritual east end containing an altar. There was no structural chancel, the choir seats being placed in the nave to the east of the transepts. There were small clergy vestries on either side of the sanctuary. At the west end was the main porch, with a small subsidiary porch in the south-west corner surmounted by a turret containing a clock and bell and roofed with a slated spire. A basement below the west end of the chapel contained a large choir vestry and a heating chamber. The walls, internally plastered, were faced outside with Kentish ragstone and Bath stone dressings; they were well buttressed but 'much overgrown with ivy'. The open main roof, 'somewhat lightly constructed of stained and varnished deal', was plastered on the backs of rafters and collars, and had a covering of Welsh slates with ornamental crested ridge tiles. The porch's flat roof was covered with lead, and the sanctuary roof ceiled with stained and varnished boarding. The nave seating and choir seats were of oak and there was an oak pulpit. At the west end was a stone font with an oak cover. Other fittings included an altar rail and lectern of brass, and a small organ in the south transept. The chapel could seat 256 persons in all. Subject to certain specified repairs, the building was adjudged suitable for use as a parish church.

The enlargement of the building proved to be a protracted and contentious exercise. It appears that Garbett's advice was sought as to the choice of architect and, without specifically making a recommendation, he commented that H. P. Burke Downing had done very good work and was a brother of an Ecclesiastical Commissioner. In fact the architect's brother was Sir Stanford Downing, the influential Secretary to the Commissioners. Burke Downing was promptly invited to produce proposals for increasing the church's seating capacity to about 750, whilst preserving its existing character. His suggested addition at the ritual east end, to cost between £11,000 and £12,000, immediately set the alarm bells ringing and caused Burke Downing to be told that the churchwardens were 'staggered at the cost'. The architect's offer that the

Burke Downing's proposal for the east end, shown at the Royal Academy Exhibition of 1924.

The exterior. Top: from the south, with the enlargements at the east end just peeping above the foliage. Bottom: from the north, showing transept and dormers added in 1925–6.

work be completed in stages was rejected but a reduction in seating capacity to 500–550 and the omission of a proposed side chapel and other features were put into consideration. Above all, it was insisted that the general character of the present church 'must be strictly maintained' and 'the existing building must not be interfered with more than is absolutely necessary'', to meet conditions set by major subscribers to the building fund. Some haggling over costs produced a revised estimate of about £10,000 excluding architect's fees, seating, fittings and fixtures, without any undertaking by Burke Downing to do other than his best to devise a scheme within that sum; and on this basis his appointment was confirmed in September 1923. By December, Burke Downing gained the Building Committee's approval for amended plans and these – though lacking a specification – were submitted to the Ecclesiastical Commissioners. They provided for the addition of three bays to the existing nave, with a south aisle, and a chancel with an organ chamber, clergy vestry and sacristy, also on the south side. Caröe & Passmore criticised the restricted view of the chancel for the occupants of the south aisle but suggested that this could be partly obviated by carrying the west wall of the organ chamber on arches. An illustration of the proposed exterior was later exhibited by Burke Downing at the Royal Academy, and *The Builder* commented that the design was 'marked by a severe simplicity and economy, features no doubt in some measure dictated by conditions of the

The church from the west.

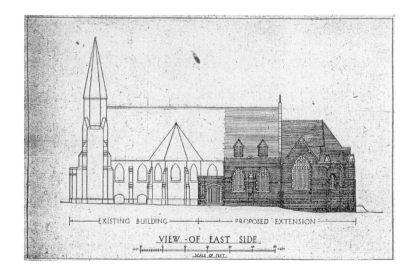

undertaking and the nature of the existing building, but used to aid rather than hinder the achievement of a dignified character'.

Relationships between the architect and his client Building Committee had been uneasy right from the outset and they degenerated into open conflict following a sequence of extraordinary misunderstandings as to the conclusions reached by the Diocesan Advisory Committee on the suitability of Burke Downing's proposals. After a flurry of assertions, rebuttals and explanations

The 1925–6 extension. Above: architect's south elevation. Below: plan, showing the extension; the east end is to the left.

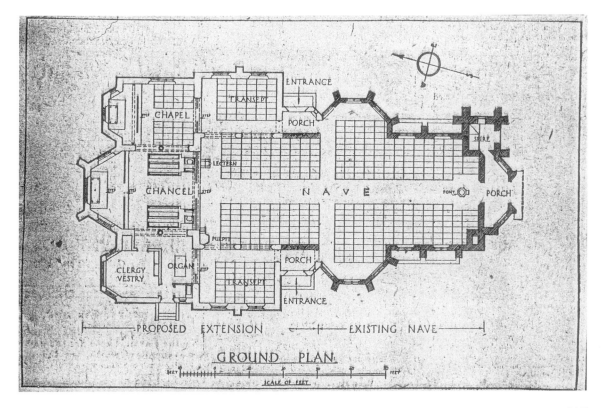

The interior looking east, from an old postcard.

Below: two interior views of the enlarged east end.
Top: looking south-east into the Lady Chapel. Bottom: looking north-east, showing the blocked arches intended to lead to a high-roofed vestry and organ chamber, designed but not built.

involving not only the main protagonists but the Bishops of Southwark and Woolwich and the Archdeacon of Kingston, it emerged that the D.A.C., led by the redoubtable Francis Eeles, were not enthusiastic about the architect's plans; they considered the price 'remarkably high per sitting' and suggested that another architect should be approached for designs 'at a more reasonable price and of greater architectural and artistic interest'. At this, the Building Committee determined to dispense with Burke Downing's services, a decision which provoked his angry reaction and a long wrangle about his fees. He was finally discharged with a payment of 200 guineas.

By now 1924 was well under way, and in July of that year W. A. Forsyth was invited to prepare sketch plans for enlarging the church. He put forward two proposals, preferring one which envisaged an addition to the southern – ritual west – end of the church, but he accepted the choice of a northern extension to meet the wishes of the Taylor family. Alternative tenders were then sought for a comprehensive scheme and one omitting a suggested chapel and eastern transept.

Forsyth's plans appear to have passed the Diocesan Advisory Committee's scrutiny without problem and, for the Ecclesiastical Commissioners, Caröe & Passmore expressed approval although not quite unreservedly. The total outlay was estimated at £10,000 to £11,000, and the completed church was said to allow seating for 504. In June 1925 the building contract was awarded to F. G. Minter Ltd. and, at long last, the project was put under way, the foundation stone for the extensions being laid, in the western wall of the vestry, on 1 October.

The effect of Forsyth's designs and specifications was to double the usable space in the church. The works, subject to a few variations introduced as building progressed, comprised the removal of the former sanctuary and small vestries, the extension of the nave, and the addition of new north and south porches, transepts, and an apsidal chancel flanked to its south by a Lady Chapel and to its north by a clergy vestry and an organ chamber. The walls were constructed of stock brick, plastered within and finished externally with Weldon stone dressings, whilst Bath stone dressings were used internally for arches and doorways. The roof of the nave extension was pierced with two pairs of oak-framed dormer windows and covered with blue Welsh slates to match those on the original nave, whilst the roofs over the chancel and chapel were tiled in red. A Portland stone cross was erected to surmount the nave roof at its ritual east end. Roof timbers were mainly of pitch pine over the nave extension, with deal rafters and joists as on the older parts; but the new chancel, chapel and transept roofs were substantially of English oak, with deal boarding. Lath and plaster ceilings were added. English oak screens were constructed for the Lady Chapel. Despite the use of stock bricks, the essentially Gothic character of the old stone building was preserved, the interior being particularly successful.

Above: the chancel roof. Below: the organ case of 1954.

Repairs were also carried out to the old structure: the original south-west porch was underpinned, pinnacles were re-capped where necessary, part of the interior was re-paved, and the pulpit was given a new base and steps, raising its height.

Some new fittings were introduced at this time. F. G. Minter made the oak pews, A. R. Mowbray & Co. supplied an oak altar, complete with octagonal riddel posts with candle sconces, a Verona tapestry frontal, and Aldershot brocade dorsal and wing curtains; and from John P. White & Sons came a reredos, panelling and altar rails.

The extensions were dedicated on 19 February 1926, by which date only £400 of the anticipated total cost of the enterprise remained to be raised, thanks almost entirely to the efforts of local parishioners and friends. This deficit was quickly cleared, the overall expenditure being finally calculated at £11,920 – an amount, incidentally, which Burke Downing might have recognised as comparable with his own original rough estimate which had so 'staggered' the Churchwardens!

Stained glass windows by Burlison & Grylls were installed in the sanctuary in 1929, and by Kempe & Co. (then under the direction of Walter Ernest Tower) in the Lady Chapel in 1931. In 1933 storm damage necessitated repairs to the tower and spire and to the main porch roof, and the opportunity was taken to fix a Portland stone cross over the ritual west gable, similar to that at the other end of the nave. These works were carried out by T. H. Adamson & Sons under the architect John Rawlinson.

In 1956 came the first reports of cracks opening in the walls of the main porch, and these were followed by the detection of

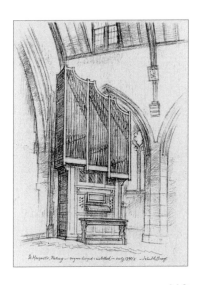

movement in the porch and in the side wall of the church behind the organ; these defects were corrected by structural repairs completed under E. F. Starling in 1961.

The period between the mid-1950s and the mid-1960s also saw many changes to the interior. In 1954 a Faculty was granted for a new organ case designed by Ralph Covell. Then schemes for re-furbishing the east end of the church were devised by the architect T. Manning, and re-decoration was carried out by Campbell, Smith & Co. In the chancel sanctuary the oak work was cleaned, bleached and re-polished, and the enrichments to the reredos and communion rail were picked out in gold leaf and colour; and new altar furnishings were installed. Next, in the Lady Chapel came new fittings including a communion rail and a screen, the latter being dedicated in 1965, in which year the church also received a portable font.

Just off Putney Park Lane, the Church Hall, a brick building with tiled roof and dormer windows, was completed in 1930 to the designs of C. Hamilton Simpson. It was severely damaged by a flying bomb in 1944, and in 1960 was put into the hands of estate agents for letting. A Parish Room, designed by E. F. Starling, was built next to the church in 1962–3.

Granard Lodge was demolished in 1936 and a school was later erected on its site. Housing now covers the area formerly occupied by its park.

RIDDLESDOWN

St James, St James's Road

Completion in 1930 of Church partly built in 1915
Architects: J. E. Newberry & C. W. Fowler
Contractors: Joseph Dorey & Co. Ltd. of Brentford

Proposals for erecting a place of worship and Sunday School at the hamlet of Little Roke in Kenley were put forward by the Rector of Coulsdon in 1899. Four years later, a Mission Church and School were built in Roke Avenue by James Monger of Kenley to the designs of Norman L. Ashburner. Solidly constructed of red brick and white stone, with a ventilating flèche on its red tiled roof, the building was intended to seat up to 180 and was adjudged 'ample for the present needs of the district'.

But by 1909 it had already become necessary to increase the seating capacity, and an extension incorporating a new chancel was provided. The creation of a Diocesan Mission District, from parts of Coulsdon, Kenley and Purley, followed in 1912. Events continued to move rapidly as the local population increased: in 1913 a site was secured for a permanent new church, a Building Fund was opened, and the architects F. H. Greenaway and J. E. Newberry

Riddlesdown, St James from the south, from a drawing used in the church magazine during the 1940s.

submitted designs to the Ecclesiastical Commissioners. The site, a triangular one, was on a steeply sloping hillside overlooking the original community of Little Roke. On it was to be erected a stone-clad cruciform structure with a five-bay aisled nave and a prominent tower rising from the south transept. However, only the western half was to be built at the outset, to provide seating for about 300. The foundation stone was laid on 6 March 1915, and the builders, Joseph Dorey & Co. of Brentford, completed the first portion in time for consecration on 23 October. The building cost was £4,385.

At this stage were constructed the western three bays of the nave with corresponding parts of the north and south aisles, porches on either side, and a baptistry projecting at the west end. The

sanctuary, vestries and east wall were temporary additions in timber and brick.

In 1925 a Consolidated Chapelry was assigned, effectively conferring the status of a separate parish. But the church remained in its truncated state until 1930, when the architects J. E. Newberry and C. W. Fowler – successors to Greenaway and Newberry – exhibited fresh designs at the Royal Academy for the building's completion. With support from private donations as well as from the Twenty-five Churches Fund and the Incorporated Church Building Society, the church was now enlarged to increase the seating capacity to about 500, at an additional cost of approximately a£8,500. The extensions were consecrated on 13 December 1930. What finally emerged from the architects' revised scheme was a four-bay aisled nave adjoined by a baptistry at the west end, and a chancel of the same width as the nave flanked on its north side by a chapel and on its south by clergy and choir vestries and a small sacristy. The originally intended tower was omitted but, to provide a vertical feature, breaking the long horizontal line of the main roof, an octagonal turret was placed at the south-western angle of the projecting choir vestry; the lower part of this contained a circular

The interior looking east.

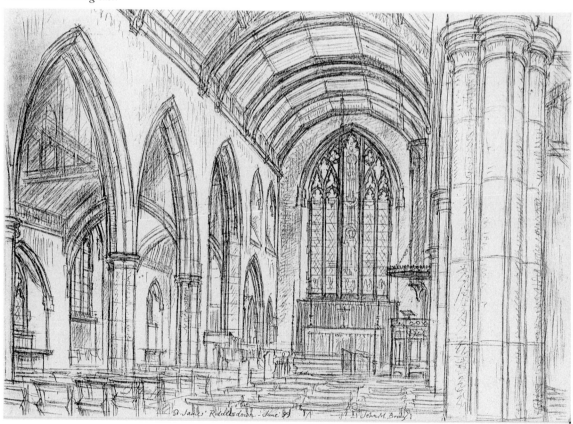

*The north aisle and chapel, from a
mid twentieth-century photograph.*

stone staircase to the organ chamber and the upper part served as a belfry.

Despite the design changes and the fifteen-year interval between the two stages of construction, a satisfying consistency in both style and materials was successfully attained. For this the credit must go to J. E. Newberry who was closely involved throughout. He based the building's architectural style on the fourteenth century Decorated period of English Gothic, adapted to a conception of modern needs and materials. Appropriately traceried windows, including a fine one of seven lights at the west end, were inserted into the walls, which were faced with roughly squared Bargate stone laid in courses. For the earlier portion, Ketton stone was used for the dressed stonework of windows and copings, Monk's Park stone being substituted for the 1930 work. The porches were paved with Portland stone; the roof, continuous across nave and aisles and unbroken from east to west, was covered with Cornish green slates. Internally, Ketton stone was used for the arcade piers, which were each given four clustered shafts with moulded capitals and bases; the arches were treated throughout with wave mouldings, a feature which, like the window tracery, was characteristic of the fourteenth century. The inside walls were plastered. The main roof, of Oregon pine trusses and dark-stained boarding above the nave, was panelled and barrel-vaulted over the chancel where it was originally left in its natural colouring though the design provided for it to be painted; this latter embellishment was carried out some years later. The chancel and chapel floors were paved with red quarry tiles; an intention to replace these later with stone or marble was never realised.

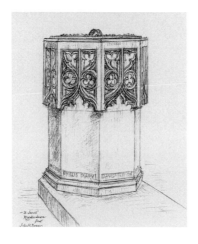

Top: pulpit; centre: aumbry of 1937 by Douglas Purnell; bottom: original font.

The appearance of the well-crafted church interior is enhanced by the quality and beauty of its fittings and artwork. Of particular interest is a collection of five stained glass windows designed by Martin Travers, whose name is recorded in the Book of Remembrance at the east end of the south aisle, with the date of his death, 25 July 1948. The earliest of these windows are a pair, each of three lights, designed in 1915 and placed in the south aisle: one portrays Joan of Arc with St Elizabeth of Hungary and St Patrick, and the other St Francis of Assisi with St Swithun and St Hugh, shown respectively as Bishops of Winchester and Lincoln. In the north aisle is the three-light 'Missionary Window' designed by Travers in 1916 to commemorate Mary Bloxam of the Universities Mission to Central Africa. A later three-light Travers window, depicting a seated Blessed Virgin Mary with the Holy Child, is in the east wall of the Lady Chapel. In 1946 Travers also prepared designs for a four-light window, illustrating the Annunciation, to be placed in the north wall nearby, but this seems not to have been executed. Then, in 1947, he designed a complete scheme for the chancel, including a rood, altar furnishings, reredos, and pictorial glass for the five-light east window. This project was left unrealised at the time of Travers's sudden death a few months later, but his design for the east window was executed by Lawrence Lee, with minor variations, and dedicated in November 1949; a fine work, it has a figure of Our Lord in its centre light and five biblical scenes across the base.

The church also contains small stained glass figures of St Francis de Sales and St Cecilia in the north porch, and a colourful window of 1974 in the south porch displaying a vigorous swirling design.

Some of the original furniture was designed by the architects, including the handsome octagonal stone font which is enriched by Gothic tracery set above cusped ogee arches. Among the later additions, the organ, installed in 1932, was dedicated by Bishop Garbett in his last ceremonial service in Southwark Diocese prior to his enthronement as Bishop of Winchester. On the east wall of the south aisle is a striking tripartite war memorial; between the hinged outer panels which list the names of the fallen is a colourful naturalistic painting of St George and the Dragon, signed by D. Purnell. Douglas Purnell also designed and executed the ornate aumbry in gilded and painted wood, fitted on the north wall of the Lady Chapel and bearing the date 1937; its beautiful detailing incorporates an angel's head said to have been found in the Caledonian Market. Of more recent date are finely carved wooden statuary in the chancel and Lady Chapel; these, with various other fittings including kneeling rails, were made by Roland Barnes.

The one-time mission church at Little Roke has continued in service as a parish hall. In 1966–7 it was extended and remodelled for additional use as a youth centre, as part of a development programme which also resulted in the erection of a prefabricated parish room close by the western end of the church.

For its setting, exterior stonework and internal spacial design and artwork, the present church building must rank as one of the most satisfying and beautiful of all the Southwark Diocese 'Twenty-five'.

ST HELIER
Church Hall, Arras Avenue

New Hall, built 1930–31
Architect: Geddes Hyslop
Contractor: Stanley Dale of Mitcham

During its career as a Church Hall, this building has functioned under various names, including Ravensbury Church Hall, St Peter's Parish Hall, and latterly St Francis's Church Hall. An anomaly is that, although within the parish of St Peter which covers much of St Helier, it lies in an area of privately-built housing just outside the St Helier estate.

It is possible to trace the Hall's roots back to 1864, when the Bidder family moved into the newly-built Ravensbury Park House which was situated near where the present Bishopsford Road is joined by Seddon Road. Attached to the house were grounds which sloped down to the River Wandle. From about 1905 part of this estate was being split up for the erection of villas but, in 1912, Lieut. Col. Harold F. Bidder, an archaeologist, had Ravensbury Manor House built on a new site near the junction of Morden Road and Wandle Road.

About 1921, the Rector of Morden arranged with Lt. Col. Bidder for regular evening services to be held in part of the latter's stable

St Helier, Church Hall, from the east.

Detail, showing brickwork at east end.

and garage block in Wandle Road, for the residents of the Ravensbury Park Estate. This facility became known as the Ravensbury Chapel. Bidder furnished it and is said to have frequently conducted the services himself; later the services were continued with a small body of laymen.

In 1929 Bidder sold his Ravensbury Manor property and moved away. The Rector contacted the purchaser's agent concerning the future provision of facilities for worship but, by then, it was becoming clear that a much larger and more permanent alternative would have to be found. Not only was the Manor House demolished in 1930 to make way for speculative housing but, even more significantly, the London County Council had in 1926 and 1927 acquired a vast area of Morden and Carshalton for the erection of their St Helier estate. Building of this began in 1928 and was to continue through to 1936.

Bishop Garbett involved himself in negotiations aimed at ensuring that his Southwark Diocese had an adequate foothold in the new estate, but these proved to be protracted and difficult. By May 1930, when the first residents arrived in St Helier, he had managed to appoint a priest-in-charge to be responsible for the Ravensbury area to the east of St Helier Avenue, and on 5 June of that year he there dedicated the first of the new churches on the new L.C.C. estate. But this was quite unlike any church he had ever dedicated before, as it took the form of a marquee! The next step was to set up a Mission Hut on a newly acquired site facing Arras Avenue, but on 22 November, before this was ready, the 'marquee church' was wrecked in a gale. Some of its contents were rescued but services had to be suspended until the hut could be opened. The marquee, though short-lived, had earned a unique niche in history as having provided St Peter's with the distinction of being the only known case of an Anglican parish church having originated in a tent.

The Mission Hut was dedicated on 13 December 1930. Built by the Merton Abbey Joinery Works at a cost of £342, it was a wooden structure sheathed in corrugated iron and could seat 100 to 130 people at services. For a short time this modest building formed the centre of church activities in the new Anglican St Peter's parish, which was created on 18 December, but a larger and more permanent building was already under construction.

Its site in Arras Avenue had been purchased with the aid of a £500 grant from the City Parochial Charities Fund, and the foundation stone had been laid by Lt. Col. Bidder on 25 October 1930. Within five months the dual-purpose Church Hall was ready for occupation, becoming the first permanent building to be set up for religious purposes to serve the St Helier estate. The Mission Hut was retained as an annexe. The new building was dedicated on 16 March 1931. Its cost of £4,200 had been borne from the

Twenty-five Churches Fund apart from a residue of expenses amounting to £450 which the local congregation were to raise.

The new Church Hall, designed by Geddes Hyslop and erected by Stanley Dale of Mitcham, was basically a simple structure, of Kent stock bricks and steel roof trusses surmounted by black glazed pantiles. The large steel-framed windows were generally of standard pattern, though at the end fronting on to Arras Avenue there was some ornamental treatment of the adjoining brickwork, including a rough cross quartering a diamond-set window high under the gable; this motif was employed again in Hyslop's second St Helier church, dedicated to Bishop Andrewes (q.v.). The plain, somewhat utilitarian, outward aspect sheltered an interior which, at the time of its dedication, was described as 'a blaze of magnificent colour'. The internal brick wall surfaces were painted white above a blue dado edged with a mauve border. The ceiling was of ash plyboard and the floor of rift sawn Oregon pine, wax polished. Modern-style electric light bowls gave a diffused light, except in the chancel which was brilliantly illuminated by concealed flood lights. The chancel was fitted with a rolling drop shutter to separate it from the main body of the hall when the latter was used for entertainments, for which purpose a stage was provided at the opposite end, together with dressing room accommodation. Adjoining the chancel were the priest's vestry, a kitchen and offices. The building could seat 250 at services and 350 at other meetings.

The name of St Francis which eventually became attached to the Church Hall originated with the foundation there, in 1930, of the St Francis Settlement, comprising a group of three whole-time women church workers whose stipends were supported by a grant, renewable every three years, from the City Parochial Charities Fund.

In 1963 the Church Hall was sold to the Surrey County Council for use as a Youth Centre. As a church, it had long since become redundant; as a hall its use had become infrequent and it was not earning its keep. In its new role, it would be used for youth service training courses and other specialised purposes, not as a youth club. The church authorities, in making the sale, stipulated that the building should not be hired or bought by any other religious denomination.

The building is now known as the Wyvern Youth Centre. The brick cross under its gable facing the road has partly disappeared, as if to illustrate the conversion to a secular role.

St Helier, Bishop Andrewes's church from the south.

ST HELIER

Bishop Andrewes's Church, Wigmore Road

New church, built 1933
Architect: Geddes Hyslop
Contractors: H. M. Nowell Ltd., of Enfield

Concurrently with their decision to buy land for erecting a centrally-placed church for the new St Helier estate (see St Helier, St Peter) St Peter's Building Committee resolved in 1931 to purchase a site from the London County Council for a district church to serve an ultimate population of at least 12,000 in the Lower Greenwrythe Lane area, closer to Carshalton. The site, between Wigmore and Welbeck Roads, cost £350 and, measuring about 190 feet by 130 feet, was large enough to provide for a parsonage house and a parochial hall as well as a moderately sized church. Geddes Hyslop, who had designed the new Church Hall in Arras Avenue for the northern end of the estate, was appointed architect and was asked to prepare plans for a building to hold at least 400 people. Economy was to be very much in mind, though generous financial assistance would be provided from the Twenty-five Churches Fund and this was later supplemented by grants from Marshall's Charity.

Until the district church could be built, there was an urgent need for a temporary building for use as a Mission Church. This was met in 1932 by the erection of a wooden hut in Welbeck Road, which became the Church Hall when the permanent building was completed.

By the summer of 1932 Hyslop produced his proposals for both a church and a parsonage house, and secured the L.C.C.'s approval. The general building contract was then awarded to H. M. Nowell Ltd. of Enfield, their contract price being £6,498 excluding seating and furnishing which would cost an additional £250.

On 14 January 1933 the foundation stone was laid by the Master of the Coopers' Company and a mere five months later, on 15 June, the building was consecrated, as a Chapel of Ease to St Peter's. The consecration ceremony was attended by the Revd Lancelot Andrewes, Major E. Andrewes and the Revd Canon Andrewes, an Honorary Canon of Winchester Cathedral, all of them connected with the family of Bishop Lancelot Andrewes to whom the church was dedicated. This was in fact the first church to be dedicated to the great scholar, bishop and saint who was one of the chief translators of the Authorised Version of the Bible. The idea of the dedication, which seems to have originated with Bishop Garbett, arose from Andrewes's many years of association with the region

Plan, east towards the right. The north transept is a chapel, and the south contains the font. The small enclosed space on the north of the sanctuary is the sacristy cupboard. Notice the cross on the floor of the crossing.

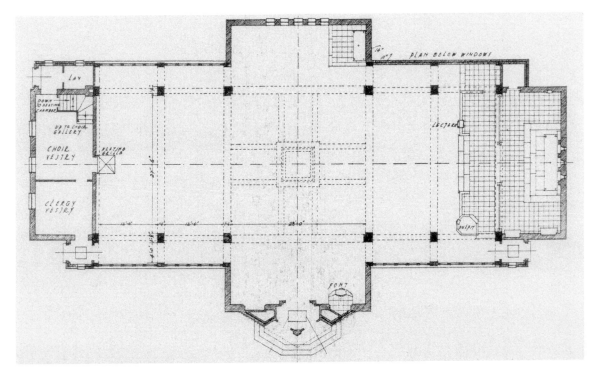

The church from the south, from an old postcard.

The church from the south, from an old postcard.

now included in the Diocese of Southwark. After early education at the Coopers' School at Ratcliff and at the Merchant Taylors' School, he had become Rector of Cheam and, as a subsequent Bishop of Winchester, he resided in Southwark at Winchester Palace. His tomb was placed in what is now Southwark Cathedral, on the south side of the high altar.

While the church's design was fundamentally simple, it was and remains architecturally quite interesting, particularly for its extensive use of reinforced concrete and ornamental exterior brickwork. Caröe & Passmore, the consultants to the Ecclesiastical Commissioners, were less than happy with some aspects of the construction but only minor changes seem to have been made in response to their criticisms. The building's plan was cruciform and almost symmetrical in its outline. The large central crossing space had shallow transepts extending to north and south, and three-bay arms to east and west, each with narrow passage aisles except at the extreme end bays. In the western-most bay were vestries with a gallery over, and the sanctuary occupied the eastern end. The main entrance, facing Wigmore Road, was in the south transept. The seating capacity was claimed to be 400. The total interior length was 109 feet, the width across the aisles 39 feet and across the transepts 55½ feet. The crossing was 28 feet square.

Externally the church's appearance has scarcely changed since it was built. Its dominating feature is the pale grey tower, which closes the vista from Welhouse Road. This is square and low but very broad, with a slightly recessed plain parapet which conceals the church's solitary bell on the south side and a centrally placed square lantern. The tower is of reinforced concrete with horizontal bands of brick, the concrete having been scrubbed down 24 hours after being placed, to expose the Thames ballast aggregate. Of similarly-treated concrete, though containing a finer aggregate, are the triangular hood over the main entrance and the surrounds to the rectangular aisle windows, the mullions and sills of which were pre-cast. The steep roofs, which descend unbroken over the aisles, are covered with red sand-faced pinion pantiles. The walls are faced with brownish-red bricks, darker well-burnt bricks being used for the projecting ornamental work, which includes courses along the aisles and porch, and crosses under the east and west gables as at the Hall in Arras Avenue.

The use of reinforced concrete characterises the internal structure. The crossing tower rises above four large two-centred arches, springing from near floor level. Similar arches, set transversely, divide the chancel and nave into bays to the east and west, and smaller narrow-pointed arches span the aisles at corresponding intervals. The concrete walls and arches were initially lime-plastered and given a rough stippled finish, left undecorated, whilst the side walls of the chancel and aisles were coated with plaster on expanded metal. Skirtings were buff-coloured. The timber roofs were lined with sound-absorbent acoustic board between the painted purlins, a similar material being applied to the front of the west gallery.

Except for a band of Irish green marble round the altar, the chancel floor was paved with squares of reconstructed Purbeck stone in two shades. Elsewhere, the flooring was of teak blocks, 'laid basket fashion'. Set in the floor under the central tower was a

The interior looking east, from a photograph taken in 1933. Notice the north chapel, and how the congregational seating continues into the eastern extension of the church.

Section through the transepts looking east, showing the north chapel, the narrow north and south aisles, and the lantern arrangement in the tower.

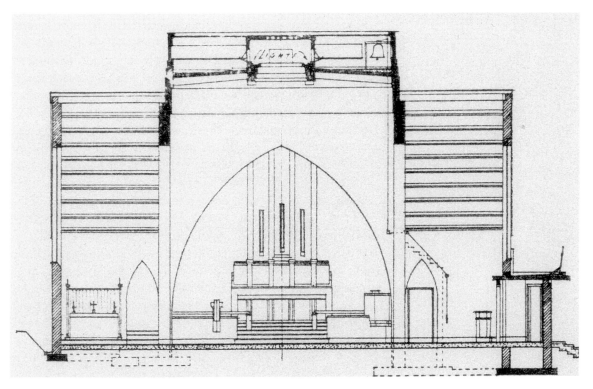

Elevations, showing the brickwork decoration. Left: east end. Right: west end.

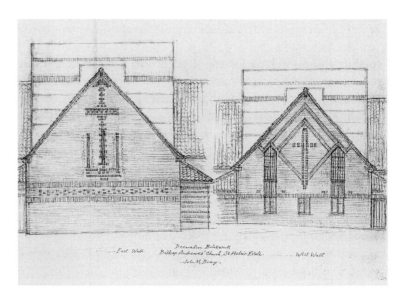

cross formed in oak and ebony, a device repeated with circular glass lenses in the square lantern above.

Fronting the chancel was a low divided balustrade integrated with a lectern and a pulpit, all of concrete. Behind the altar was placed a reredos of beige Lunel Rubane marble, with bands of Irish green and Verde Antico, in which were set four panels with incised and gilded figures representing Bishop Andrewes and his contemporaries Archbishop Laud, Richard Hooker and George Herbert; these were carved by Donald Hastings. Above, the three narrow windows in the east wall were filled with small pieces of stained glass. The altar table, altar rails, reading desks, riddel posts and clergy chairs, all in oak, were designed by the architect and made by A. G. Scott Ltd. of Creed Lane, Ludgate Hill, as were the red and gold light fittings which were of Larana wood. The font, of Purbeck stone, was sited in the south transept, east of the main entrance. In 1939 these fittings were supplemented by sanctuary desks and altar rails, presumably for the chapel in the north transept; these came from the demolished St Matthew's Church at Sydenham. The modest Stations of the Cross were added twelve years later.

By 1954 the population of the area had risen to 17,000, excluding the occupants of the large St Helier Hospital. In the following year, work was begun on erecting a new Church Hall on the site of the earlier one, the builders being the REEMA Construction Company. This was opened in 1956. The building has since been disposed of, and the social functions associated with church life have been concentrated within the church itself by means of a radical reconstruction of the interior, effectively dividing it into three compartments. Normal services now take place in the re-ordered section east of the crossing; there is a small sanctuary with a modern altar table, without communion rails, set forward of the east wall. Seating is all in chairs. The central section, occupying the crossing and transepts, is usable as an alternative or additional worship area as well as for social purposes: it contains a south-facing altar in the north transept and, although the eastern and western sides are now walled in, a wide folding screen has been set into the east wall to permit extension, when required, of the area reserved for normal services. The third compartment, west of the crossing, is equipped for dispensing refreshments and is suitable for meetings and other purposes associated with a parish room. The entire spacial effect has of course been drastically altered by these rearrangements, and most of the original furnishings seem to have been stripped out; but the eastern arm, at least, has an intimate atmosphere which is by no means displeasing.

ST HELIER
St Peter, Bishopsford Road

New Church, built 1932–3
Architect: Sir C. A. Nicholson
Contractors: Wooldridge & Simpson Ltd. of Oxford

The London County Council's huge St Helier estate, constructed between 1928 and 1936, sprawled across the Urban District of Merton & Morden and that of Carshalton, and penetrated a small part of the Borough of Sutton & Cheam. In 1927, before building had commenced, the area was included by the Twenty-five Churches Fund Committee in a list of locations where new churches would be required. Bishop Garbett foresaw a need to build three churches and two church halls to serve the area, and by mid-1929 he had ensured the availability of about £27,000 in the Fund for this purpose and was taking steps towards securing additional grants from the City Parochial Charities Fund.

Garbett's plans for creating a single new parish to cover the whole of St Helier were thwarted by objections from the Rector of Morden and his patrons, so that in 1930 he had to settle for a division of the estate into two New Districts, separated along the line of St Helier Avenue. The western portion became St George's, and the eastern St Peter's. The negotiations occupied much of 1930 and, by the time of their conclusion, other church denominations were already becoming active in the region, necessitating urgent action to ensure an Anglican welcome for the newly arriving residents. Those settling in the northern part of the estate were conveniently served by the arrangements being established there (see St Helier, Church Hall) but, once the new St Peter's District was formally constituted in December 1930, it became imperative to secure a more centrally placed site for a parochial church and a parsonage house. This was achieved in the summer of 1931 by the purchase from the L.C.C. of land at the junction of Bishopsford and Middleton Roads. About the same time, a temporary Church Hut was erected in Love Lane at the southern end of the estate.

Developments now proceeded apace. Sir Charles Nicholson was selected as architect for the new church, and by November 1931 his preliminary designs and specification were submitted to the Ecclesiastical Commissioners and approved almost without qualification. Geddes Hyslop, the architect of the recently erected Church Hall in Arras Avenue, also prepared designs but had to be content with a consolation prize: appointment as architect of a 'daughter' church to be built farther south. (See St Helier, Bishop Andrewes.)

Nicholson's proposals envisaged a lofty and quite stately church, about 129 feet long, comprising a six-bay clerestoried nave with north and south aisles and, additionally, a narrow outer passage aisle on the north side and an outer 'Children's Aisle' on the south, the latter having an altar at its east end. Oddly, no attempt was made to align the clerestory lancets with the spacing of the nave arcades and aisle windows below; this remains a feature of the executed design. The short, almost square, chancel was to be flanked by a small chapel to the north and vestries to the south. There would be a broad projecting west porch, and a smaller porch on the north side leading across the passage aisle into the main north aisle.

St Helier, St Peter, plan, with east to the right.

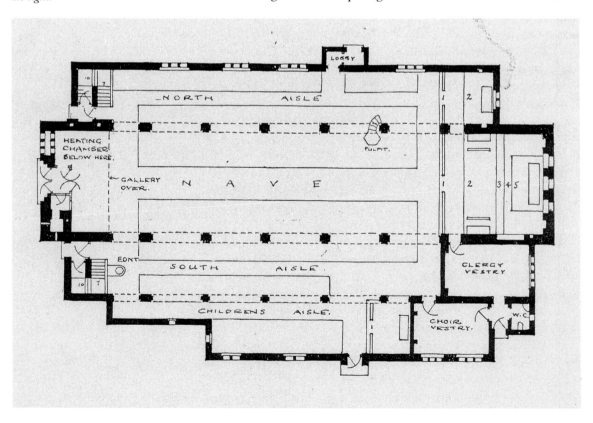

— St. Peter's, Bishopsford Road, St. Helier   *— John M. Bray.*

The church from the south-west. This drawing omits the mural on the west end.

Provision was made for a baptistry at the west end of the inner south aisle, a west gallery to accommodate an organ and choir, and a belfry offset to the south of the nave's west front. The designed maximum seating capacity was 799.

At the outset it was not thought that funds would allow completion of the church in its entirety, and the initial exclusion of both of the north aisles and the outer south aisle was accepted. Furthermore, the Bishop's Advisory Committee asked for the building to be shortened by one bay. Building tenders for the resultant first stage of construction were invited, and the contract was won by Wooldridge & Simpson of Oxford. The total cost was put at £12,750, made up of £1,050 for the site, £11,038 for the builders' contract and £662 for the architect's fees. To meet this, a sum of £12,000 was assured, comprising £11,000 from the Twenty-five Churches Fund and the City Parochial Charities Fund, and £1,500 from Marshall's Charity. The relatively small balance of £250 would have to be found by the parish.

Work on the foundations began early in 1932, and on 14 June the foundation stone was laid by Bishop Garbett. He claimed this as the first foundation stone he had laid in the Southwark Diocese, but it was also to be the last as he had already been effectively translated to

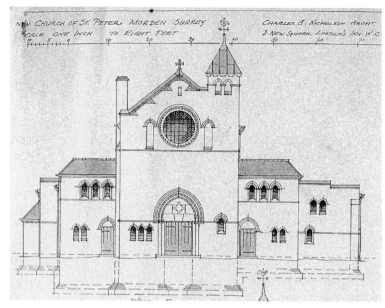

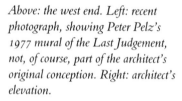

Above: the west end. Left: recent photograph, showing Peter Pelz's 1977 mural of the Last Judgement, not, of course, part of the architect's original conception. Right: architect's elevation.

the See of Winchester: his enthronement there took place just one week later.

At this stage, the proposal was made for an all-out attempt to raise, within three months excluding August, the £2,000 needed for erecting the omitted north and south aisles, as an alternative to abandoning any thought of completing the church for the foreseeable future. This ambitious target was reached on 13 October, with promises from some 500 supporters who were later revealed to include parishioners in Sutton, Roehampton, Epsom and Wimbledon. Nicholson's designs were modified slightly to reduce the

The east end. Below: from a photograph taken soon after completion. Right: architect's elevation.

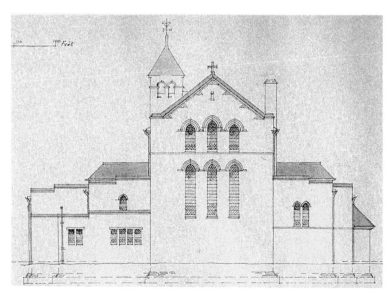

size of the outer south aisle, and to balance it by extending the north one while leaving out the outer passage aisle on that side. The consequent seating capacity, though inevitably curtailed, was still over 700.

On 27 May 1933 when the completed church was consecrated, the building was still completely surrounded by fields, but would not be for much longer. Local labour had been extensively used in its construction, and costs, now estimated at over £15,000 including furnishing – a figure which rose eventually to £17,384 – had been almost completely covered.

T. P. Stevens in the *Southwark Diocesan Gazette* called the church 'a very impressive building', and added 'it bears marks of originality'. He found 'something Italian about the outside' but felt that the 'general appearance of the inside is Gothic'. The round-headed windows coupled internally with the sturdy square-sectioned and only slightly pointed arches, might be said rather to owe their inspiration to a Romanesque/Early English transitional style.

The church was built almost entirely of brick and timber, the use of stone being restricted to steps, pavings and the tympanum of the west doorway. The continuous roof over nave and chancel was clad in copper. Exterior decoration was minimal: the brick arch over the west portal was given inconspicuous billet moulding, and a simple cross was set into the tympanum, whilst the bell turret was finished with a copper-covered pyramidal roof. Within, the brick surfaces were plastered and whitewashed, and the windows glazed almost exclusively in clear glass, giving a rather stark background which was perhaps intended to enhance the effect of the decorative features. Prominent among these was a fine oak roof over the nave and chancel, painted in green, red and white. A similar colour scheme was applied to the panelled front of the west gallery, which was reached by two concrete staircases. Some of the furniture was designed by the architect, and executed in English oak; the elegant

The south chapel of St Francis, partitioned off and unfurnished except for a statue to the saint.

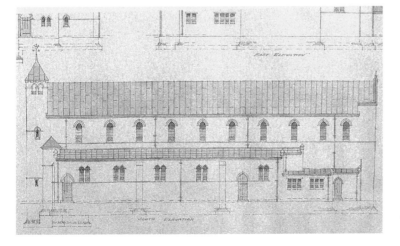

Architect's south elevation of the church.

Right: relief carving on pulpit. Below: the interior looking east.

— St Peter's Church, St Helier. Shallow relief carving on pulpit. – Sept '99 —John M. Bray

pulpit has panelled sides surmounted by a carved frieze. In the Lady Chapel, on the north side of the chancel, were placed a pair of stained glass windows by A. K. Nicholson. Between 1939 and 1941 Martin Travers produced designs, apparently unexecuted, for furnishing the outer south aisle as a Chapel of St Francis; they included stained glass for two small windows in the east wall, as well as altar furnishings and communion rails.

It is clear from the architect's drawings that he intended the west gallery to house an organ designed with two end towers and perhaps a much shorter one in the middle, so as not to obscure the penetration of light from the circular window mounted high in the west wall to the rear. As at Bellingham, his intentions do not seem to have been realised; at any rate, the gallery now has two organs, one behind the other, neither of which corresponds to Nicholson's ideas although they are both of some interest. A report of 1983 by

— St Peter, St Helier – Sept '99   —John M. Bray A.R.C.A.

Matthew Copley shows that the instrument at the rear was originally presented by King George III to the Huguenot Chapel in Spitalfields. When, in 1897, the chapel was converted into a synagogue the organ was moved to the Wesleyan Methodist Church in Hackney Road, London. In 1933 it was rebuilt by Henry Speechly & Sons, and in 1956 it was removed and re-erected in St Peter's by N. P. Mander who fitted a new two-manual console. Its painted wooden case, apparently of late eighteenth-century date, was retained in its upper parts, including two half-round end towers and a taller central one, but the lower portion did not survive in its original state. In November 1992 this organ was displaced by a smaller instrument from St John's Church, Clapham, built by Hill's and re-erected here by Matthew Copley.

The west-end gallery and two organs, one behind the other.

St Peter's has succeeded in attracting national interest – some might say notoriety – in its time. In 1973 the enterprising incumbent commissioned from Peter Pelz, a self-taught artist residing in the vicarage, a series of fifteen remarkable mural paintings in a spectacularly expressionist style. Most of them were executed on hardboard roundels mounted on the spandrels of the nave arcades; representing the Stations of the Cross, they depicted biblical scenes against a modern inner-city background complete with buses, advertisements and hippies. Another, on the front of the organ case, featured a sunburst surrounded by the faces of the choir and topped by a figure playing the organ. These paintings were officially 'opened' by Jennie Lee – later Baroness Lee of Asheridge – in her capacity as the first Minister of the Arts, a post created by Harold Wilson. Then in 1977 another work by Pelz was added, with the approval of the Diocesan Advisory Committee: a gigantic mural painted directly on to the exterior of the church's west wall. This depicted The Last Judgement.

The subsequent departure of the commissioning vicar to St James's, Piccadilly, led to a surge of opposition to the pictures. The Parochial Church Council voted three times to have them removed but were thwarted by the objections of a small number of parishioners. Eventually the fate of the paintings was placed in the hands of a Consistory Court which, in 1991, reached a verdict, in the interests of pastoral unity, that would have done credit to King Solomon: the Stations of the Cross were to be removed, but the external Last Judgement should remain 'because it was already a landmark in the area'. The painting on the organ front has also survived but is now partly concealed by the Hill organ set up in 1992.

Other introductions have included a striking banner by Thetis Blacker, illustrating 'The Resurrection of the Phoenix' (1980).

SANDERSTEAD

St Mary the Virgin, Purley Oaks Road

New Church, built 1925–6
Architects: F. H. Greenaway & J. E. Newberry
Contractors: George Everitt & Sons Ltd., of Croydon

A mission church of iron and wood, to serve Lower Sanderstead at the northern end of All Saints' parish, was dedicated on 24 February 1908. Erected in Purley Oaks Road on land donated from the Arkwright Estate, it could seat well over 200 worshippers but was apparently never intended as more than a temporary expedient, since discussions on building a more substantial church were under way a mere two years later. These led to the production in 1914 of designs for a big stone structure based on fourteenth century precepts including traceried windows, a tower and spire. A funding campaign was launched but the first World War caused the proposals to be postponed, the only advance being the addition in 1915 of an extension to the temporary building.

By the end of the war, building costs had doubled, increasing the funding difficulties and creating a need to work to a lower budget. It was therefore decided to make do with a smaller church and to

Sanderstead, St Mary the Virgin. Below: from the south-east. Opposite: from the north-east.

St.Mary's, Sanderstead - Sept '99
- John M Bray.

economise in the choice of design and materials. To this end, a limited architectural competition was held in 1920, with H. P. Burke Downing as the assessor; the winning design was that prepared by F. H. Greenaway and J. E. Newberry. Further progress had to await the provision of adequate funding, and it was not until March 1925, when a sum of over £7,000 was said to be 'in hand', that the architects submitted their drawings and specifications to the Ecclesiastical Commissioners. By this time a grant of £800 had been allocated, presumably at Bishop Garbett's behest. Approval of the architects' proposals was followed in July 1925 by the appointment of George Everitt & Sons as the contractors and, later in the year, by the constitution of a separate District, formed from All Saints', Sanderstead, and St Augustine's at Croydon, with patronage vested in the Bishop of Southwark. Meanwhile, the temporary mission building was said to be 'beginning to decay rapidly'. According to a contemporary report it was actually shortened at this stage, but the reason was not given.

The foundation stone of the new church was laid on an adjoining site on 31 October 1925. During the ensuing construction more economies were made: in particular, an intended fourth bay at the west end of the nave, together with the main entrance porch on the

— St Mary's Sanderstead — May '99.

The interior looking east. Right: from an old postcard. Below: a modern drawing.

north side, were left for completion at a later date. The truncated west end was filled in with temporary framing covered with weatherboarding, the thrust of the western arches of the nave arcades being counteracted by tie rods and timber shores. A makeshift porch was constructed with timber framing standing on a brick base.

As built, the three-bay nave was about 52 feet long by 21 feet wide, with north and south aisles providing additional width; the unaisled chancel, about 37 feet long, was flanked by a chapel on its north side, dedicated to St John, and by vestries and a small sacristy on the south. An organ chamber was provided above the choir vestry. As with some of J. E. Newberry's other churches, in order to gain the greatest effect of height and space for the least expenditure the nave, chancel and aisles were made relatively narrow, the walls and arcades being kept as lofty as was consistent with stability. Apart from the temporary west end, the walls were entirely of brick, those on the exterior being purplish red and of rough texture whilst greyish white sand bricks were used within to face arches and responds as well as the walls. The nave piers were of Portland stone, without capitals; and a plain cross set into the east gable was the only external feature of this material. The main roof, continuous from end to end and covered with red hand-made tiles, was carried down over the aisles, dispensing with a clerestory. No provision was made for a tower or flèche, but an inconspicuous bellcote was added over the north side of the chancel. All windows were simple lancets.

Inside, the boarded main roof, reinforced with tie-beams, was constructed of unstained Oregon pine and open to the ridge. Seating capacity was assessed at about 417. The chairs, choir stalls and temporary pulpit were all initially stained green as part of a plan to add colour to the interior. The communicants' benches were inlaid with black and white wood; the riddel posts by the high altar were painted black and white and capped with pewter sconces. The plain stone font, with an octagonal bowl tapering to an octagonal stem, was placed at the west end.

Thus equipped, the church was consecrated on 4 October 1926. The total building cost, including the provision of heating, lighting and unusually deep foundations, reached £9,112, some £2,500 short of the outlay which would have been needed to cover completion of the west end at that time. For the next few years, however, priority was given to improving the interior fittings, though not all proposals were put into effect. A design for a rood screen, for example, was exhibited by J. E. Newberry and C. W. Fowler at the Royal Academy in 1930 but does not seem to have been executed. A decade later, Newberry submitted a design for a Gothic-traceried altar to replace the temporary one in the north chapel. In 1935 new choir stalls were fitted, and a new organ was built into the chamber adjoining the chancel, with a detached console on the north side, at a cost of £1,400. Its pipework is concealed behind a traceried timber screen; the console bears the name of Rushworth & Dreaper of Liverpool. The carved timber pulpit is a replacement for the original green-painted one. Other

The west end, completed 1970 by Stephen Dykes Bower. Above: from the south. Below: two interior views.

The pulpit, a replacement of the original.

additions include stained glass in the north chapel and in the chancel east windows.

In 1956, following the appointment of Stephen Dykes Bower as architect, fund-raising was begun with a target of £12,000 and plans for completing the church, erecting a modern hall and replacing the vicarage. Dykes Bower is said to have 'expressed great admiration for the style of the church', adding that it had an 'atmosphere of devotion' which few churches could claim. Inflationary pressures on costs must have increased the difficulty of financing the improvements but by 1968 the timber shores supporting the church's temporary west wall were rotting, and the structure was showing signs of movement. Dykes Bower was commissioned to design a new permanent west end, with an entrance porch, baptistry and upper room, and these additions were largely completed in 1970 and dedicated on 25 February 1971.

Externally, the new work is restrained and unobtrusive, care having been taken to match the brickwork with that already existing. The nave's west gable is faced with tiles; below it, under a lean-to roof, projects a full-width extension containing, in its centre portion, the baptistry. The main entrance porch is on the north side. Within, the baptistry occupies an open recess beneath a lofty upper storey. The latter is fronted by a lateral arcade of three big pointed arches with square-topped windows of clear glass under blind tympana, so that the room behind is visible from the nave and vice versa. The whole composition, capped by bold timbering high in the west gable, has an almost dramatic quality which belies its modest exterior.

Apart from its west end, the church may be regarded as the archetypal ecclesiastical design from the practice of Greenaway & Newberry, and it served as the model upon which All Saints' Church at East Sheen (q.v.) was based. Newberry's churches at Furzedown and Wallington (q.v.) have similar characteristics.

In 1976 the parish hall, which began life in 1908 as the temporary mission hall, was said to be 'now approaching the end of its distinguished life of service', and rebuilding was considered. It is still serving its purpose today, though some alterations have been made.

SOUTH BEDDINGTON

St Michael and All Angels, Milton Road

Completion in 1929 of church partly built 1906–7
Architect: W. D. Caröe
Contractors: Burnand & Pickett, of Wallington

About 1870 a wooden mission church with slate roofing was erected in Sandy Lane to serve the Bandon Hill area at the southern end of

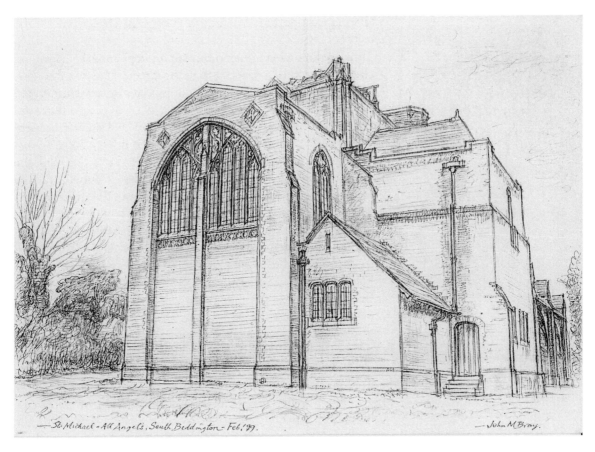

St Michael & All Angels, South Beddington - Feb.'99. — *John M Bray.*

Beddington parish; it provided seating for 250 to 300 persons. This was followed in 1896 by the acquisition of a site at Bandon Hill for a permanent church to be dedicated to St Michael and All Angels, but building had not begun by the time a separate parish was sanctioned in 1904 from parts of Beddington and Wallington. In the following year, this site was exchanged for a new one nearby in Milton Road, which was large enough to accommodate a parish room and a vicarage as well as a church. W. D. Caröe was commissioned as architect, and his specification and plans for the church were approved in 1906, the foundation stone being laid on 16 June in that year.

At that time the local population was estimated at about 5,000, but the expected advent of trams was thought likely to attract more people to the area. The cost of building a complete new church was put at around £7,300 and, towards this, some £5,300 had already been subscribed or promised, including £1,500 from the Diocese. Because of the shortfall, it was decided to build the chancel, morning chapel and part of the nave first, leaving a projected tower and two further bays of the nave to be added 'when funds allow'. The building contract was awarded to E. J. Burnand.

South Beddington, St Michael and All Angels. The east end, with the incomplete tower just visible

145

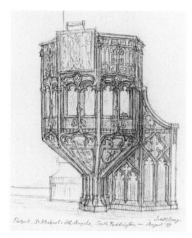

The pulpit.

The partly completed building was consecrated on 17 July 1907; three days earlier, a deconsecration service had been performed at the old mission church in Sandy Lane. Caröe's overall design had provided for a church to seat 800, with a nave of five bays, chancel, morning chapel, vestries and central tower, so the conception was quite an ambitious one. Even shorn of its western two bays, the building could still accommodate 540. A Consolidated Chapelry was assigned in November 1907.

The question of enlarging and completing the church, while not set aside completely, was not actively pursued for another twenty years, during which period a parish hall was built in 1908, a smaller hall in 1920, and a vicarage in 1924. The apparent lack of motivation may have stemmed from delays in the expected influx of new residents: the 1921 census showed the parish population to be 5,593, not much higher than estimated in 1906, whereas it climbed to 9,584 by 1931.

In 1927 the Southwark Diocesan Directory included St Michael's in its list of churches to be completed or enlarged with help from the Twenty-five Churches Fund. £2,000 was allocated from the Fund for this purpose, and in 1928 a local appeal for donations was launched to find the balance of the £4,000 expected

The interior looking east.

to be required. The options for completing the west end were placed before the annual parochial meeting in April, and the decision was then taken to accept Caröe's proposals to modify his original designs by omitting one of the two extra nave bays, simplifying the west end, and erecting the tower 'in a more economical form'. Burnand and Pickett of Wallington, who quoted a contract price of £3,656 plus architect's fees and other expenses, were engaged as builders.

By April 1929 work was in progress, and on 23 September the finished west end was dedicated. The completion of the tower, however, was put into abeyance, and even today it appears as no more than a vestigial stump, with exposed brickwork contrasting in colour with that of the rest of the exterior.

Except at the west end, which faces the road, the church is now rather hemmed in so that it is not easy to view the structure as a whole, though the general impression is of a building of majestic proportions. The west front is impressive, its breadth being accentuated by a low narthex and its height by a tall five-light window with Perpendicular tracery. The walls are faced with red brick, laid in English bond, with white stone dressings confined mostly to parapets and windows. The main windows to the nave and aisles are recessed under bold arches, and buttresses also are given prominence. Roofs are red-tiled.

Within, strongly defined arches are again a feature of the design, and they are an effective contribution to what has been described as 'possibly Caröe's most accomplished suburban church interior'.

Sir John Betjeman described the church as 'full of cleverness and built on whims'.

South aisle windows, recessed under an arch.

Above and below: Southend, St John the Baptist, two early sketches by the architect.

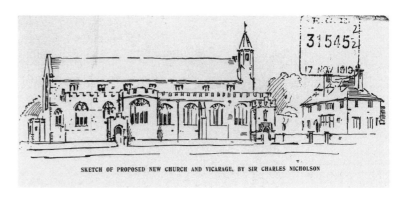

SKETCH OF PROPOSED NEW CHURCH AND VICARAGE, BY SIR CHARLES NICHOLSON

SOUTHEND (Catford)
St John the Baptist, Bromley Road

New Church, built 1926–8
Architect: Sir C. A. Nicholson
Contractor: E. Bowman & Sons, Stamford, Lincs

The first place of worship recorded in this part of Catford was a proprietary chapel, erected in 1824 by the Forster family who occupied Southend Hall and owned Southend hamlet. In 1916 this chapel, a small building with a cupola and a Tuscan west porch, was given as a place of public worship under the patronage of the Bishop of Southwark. A separate ecclesiastical district was then created, in anticipation of a huge population influx arising from ambitious building plans which had been approved by the London County Council as early as 1912. With the chapel, which could seat only 150, the Forsters offered an adjoining site for the erection of a larger permanent church and a parsonage, and the Lewisham Deanery Church Extension Fund promised a substantial grant towards the building cost.

In 1919 the offered site was handed over, and Sir Charles Nicholson prepared the first designs for a new church and vicarage. An appeal for funds was launched in the following year. The

CHURCH OF ST JOHN SOUTHEND VILLAGE

The later design by the architect, seen from the north-west, including a tower.

provision of a vicarage was seen as 'an immediate necessity', with a major church to follow; £50,000 would be needed to finance the complete project, which the Bishop of Southwark – the newly installed Cyril Garbett – considered 'may well prove one of the largest [problems] which will confront the Diocese in the next few years'. The L.C.C. building schemes were by now under way, and the population of the district – which totalled 1,275 according to the 1921 census, including Bellingham and the site of the Downham Estate – appeared likely to rise to 60,000 within ten years.

The vicarage, built to Nicholson's designs by Thomas Crossley & Son of Bromley, was completed in 1921. Two years later, the Revd Ellis Foster Edge Partington was appointed to the living; during his 20-year incumbency he piloted the local Anglicans with immense skill through an extraordinary period of growth, fortified by experience gained through an earlier curacy at Portsea, the training ground which had proved so invaluable to Garbett himself.

Nicholson's earliest designs for the new church, as reproduced in the appeal leaflet of 1919, envisaged quite an impressive Gothic structure with a long continuous roof line over the clerestoried nave and chancel, aisles of almost full length with battlemented parapets, and a stumpy bell turret; within there were to be arcades of pointed arches resting on octagonal piers, and an open timber roof with tie-beams and king-posts. However, the grant by Lord Forster of additional land and finance enabled an even more ambitious scheme to be considered, and completely new designs were approved in 1925. These provided for a tall cruciform Gothic church, with an impressive tower attached to the north transept. The five-bay nave was to have north and south aisles and a clerestory of large three-light windows; the west front would be

A visualisation of the interior of the completed church as originally designed, used to encourage potential donors . This design differs from the church as built in having an east window of five lights, not seven; and piers of octagonal, not circular, section.

St. John, Southend (Catford) - Sept. 97 — John M. Bray.

Above: the church as built, from the north-east. Opposite: from the south.

dominated by a huge six-light richly-traceried window. East of the crossing, the pointed arcades would continue, forming a three-bay chancel with flanking chapels. The seating capacity would be nearly one thousand.

Completed as planned, the church was intended to be 'one of the noblest and most beautiful in the Diocese'; certainly it would have been the biggest and stateliest of all the 'Twenty-five' churches. But this was not to be. Whilst the enlarged site now available would undoubtedly have permitted the construction of a church on a grand scale, realism demanded a step-by-step approach, and it was decided that the scheme should be executed only in part to begin with, omitting the western three bays of the nave, the tower, and the vestries. With new inhabitants of the Downham estate arriving by now at the rate of 1,000 a week, the foundation stone of the truncated church was laid on 17 July 1926 by the Rt. Hon. Lord Forster, P.C., G.C.M.G., and blessed by Bishop Garbett. In his address, the Bishop explained 'I have always hoped that in this parish there might be tried the experiment, which has proved so successful elsewhere, of a great central parish church, standing up beautiful and splendid, surrounded by smaller churches, and with the whole of the large parish being worked from a common centre, with a common life and common spirit pervading it. If that is to be done successfully in this or any other parish it is essential that the parish church shall have both size and dignity. We are thankful that the plans prepared for this church are plans worthy of a great church.' Garbett clearly had Portsea in mind as his role model.

The Bishop returned on 28 January 1928 to consecrate the partly-completed church. It had cost some £26,000, including architect's fees, to build and furnish. £5,000 had been contributed directly from the Twenty-five Churches Fund, and there had been substantial grants also from other ecclesiastical sources, as well as generous gifts from private donors. In addition to providing the site and adjoining grounds, Lord and Lady Forster had financed the construction and equipment of the north chapel.

As erected, the church consisted of two of the intended five bays of the nave, with a temporary brick wall blocking the west end; wide north and south aisles; north and south transepts; and a chancel with flanking chapels. An elevated organ chamber was provided in the south transept. The walls were substantially of brick, but finely tooled Weldon stone was used for window surrounds and tracery, doorways, buttress weatherings and the internal arcading. The shallow-pitched main roof, continuous from east to west, and those of the transepts, were covered in small slates.

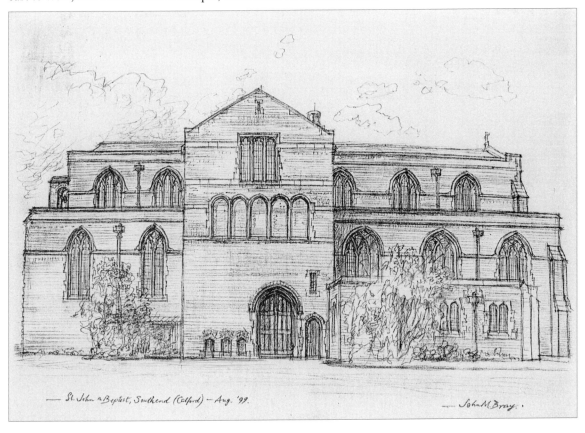

— St. John n Baptist, Southend (Catford) — Aug. '99.　　　　　　— John M Bray.

Above: the west end, still incomplete.
Below: two views of the east end.

Pevsner later called the church 'not original, but sensitive in the details', whilst Basil Clarke described it as 'traditional, sound and pleasing'. The nave and chancel were each 58 feet wide across the aisles and chapels, and the overall length was about two-thirds of the 170 feet which had been planned. Total seating capacity was assessed at 546, well below the intended target on completion.

The temporary west front – still in position today – is the plainest feature of the exterior, with prominent brick buttresses to counter the thrust of the nave arcade. The church's outward appearance also suffers from the omission of its intended tower and from its unbalanced proportions. The east wall, which has the foundation stone built into it, is of interest for the finely traceried seven-light sanctuary window and, set on high, the carved arms of the sees of Canterbury, Rochester and Southwark. The five-light north transept window also has good tracery. There are windows of three lights in the clerestory and of two lights in the aisles.

The internal design was undoubtedly impressive, though very conservative for its date. The effect is lofty and spacious. There is stone paving to the chancel and passages, and the walls are plastered. The arcades to nave and chancel are of uniform design, with cylindrical piers carrying pointed Gothic arches which, like the capitals, are heavily moulded. In contrast, the responds to the much loftier arches across the shallow transepts lack capitals and are square-sectioned and set diagonally with chamfered edges. There are no crossing arches to nave and chancel. The splendid oak roofs are finished with boarded and panelled ceilings featuring elaborately carved and gilded bosses, some 150 in all, and no two alike; tracery with quatrefoils fills the spandrels above the tie-beams.

Early views of the interior. Right: the north chapel [courtesy of Lewisham Local History Centre]. Opposite: looking north-east into the sanctuary [reproduced by permission of English Heritage. NMR].

Most of the original furniture was made by the church contractors, E. Bowman & Sons; the choir stalls and much other woodwork were in oak. The Forster Memorial Chapel, on the north side of the chancel, was furnished at the expense of Lord and Lady Forster. On its north wall were affixed memorial tablets, transferred from the old chapel, to members of the Forster family, including John (d.1834) and Elizabeth (d.1837), both by R. W. Sievier; and Harriet (d.1839), by M. W. Johnson. The centrepiece, however, is a superb memorial made by Cecil Thomas in 1923; it takes the form of a bronze recumbent effigy on a free-standing stone table, representing Lieut. Alfred Henry Forster of the Royal Scots Greys, one of two sons of Lord Forster who fell in the first World War. Cecil Thomas is said to have occupied a bed next to the younger son in a military hospital where both lay seriously wounded. This memorial established Thomas's name as a sculptor; it was exhibited in the Royal Academy, and a replica was given by Lord Forster to All-Hallows-by-the-Tower in London, as a representation of Youth. Two further casts were made: for Exbury (Hampshire) and Australia.

On the south side of the church, the east end was equipped temporarily as a guild chapel and a vestry. New vestries to Nicholson's designs were added in 1932 by E. Bowman & Sons, enabling the space south of the chancel to be used wholly as a chapel; Pevsner drew attention to glass of 1933 by Karl Parsons and E. Liddall Armitage in what became the chapel's east window.

Whilst the nave has never been completed beyond the two bays originally constructed, and the church's external appearance has scarcely changed since Garbett consecrated it, the interior of the

St John's, Southend
(Catford)
John M.Brew.

John Hayward's octagonal corona, over the central altar.

building underwent a radical transformation in 1977, when a major reordering took place under a scheme drawn up by Gordon Cook. His initial proposals envisaged the provision of a 'central' altar mounted on a platform at the crossing, with a symbolic artistic feature suspended above; this would be encompassed by seating on all four sides. The arcades were to be walled in to enclose the congregation. An upper floor would be installed at the west end, but the old sanctuary and chancel floor levels would be lowered; the chapels at the east end would be modified, though the architect suggested that the Blessed Sacrament Chapel 'must be preserved as a private and peaceful place' and the Forster Memorial Chapel 'should probably be preserved on historical grounds alone'.

This scheme was not implemented in full, but the executed portions are nonetheless striking. The square central altar sits on its platform at the crossing, with seating for the congregation around it as proposed. An immense jagged octagonal corona, designed by John Hayward, hangs overhead. The former sanctuary at the east end, now redundant, has been blocked off by a wooden screen and its fittings removed, though three sedilia and a shelved piscina have been left in position. A panelled wooden screen, which appears to have been placed originally at the west end of the Lady Chapel, has been remodelled and re-positioned inside the north-west entrance door.

The present organ was installed about 1981.

STREATHAM
Holy Redeemer, Churchmore Road

New Hall, built 1927–8
Architect: Sir C. A. Nicholson
Contractors: Walden & Son, Henley-on-Thames

New Church, built 1931–2
Architects: Martin Travers & T. F. W. Grant
Contractor: none – built by direct labour, with builder Joseph Hastings acting as general foreman

The Hall

Although designed by Sir Charles Nicholson and not by any means an insubstantial building, this hall was destined to be quickly eclipsed by a church with a significance extending far beyond the new parochial boundary, so that very little information about the hall has ever been published.

Construction began in 1927, in reaction to a developer's proposal, reported in the previous year, to build 4,000 houses during the next four years across the parish of St Andrew, Streatham. At a ceremony conducted on 24 September 1927 an inscribed stone was unveiled by the Mayor of Wandsworth and is now to be seen forming the tympanum above the building's main entrance doorway, facing Churchmore Road.

The hall was formally dedicated on 17 March 1928, by which time all but about £200 had been raised towards the cost of the site, building and furnishings, totalling some £4,500. Support had been provided from the Twenty-five Churches Fund. A Diocesan missioner was appointed to hold services there, and by the middle of 1929 most of the Sunday services in the projected new District – at that stage known unofficially as St Luke's, Streatham Vale – were taking place in the new hall rather than in the older St John's District Church and the Mission Church of the Good Shepherd.

The building is of brick, and lacks pretensions of conformity to any historical 'style'. Featured in its main front is a battery of nine simple straight-headed windows, each under a semi-circular plain white tympanum: three are on each side of the centrally placed entrance doorway and another three, admitting light to an upper storey, are in the gable above. The wide roof, covered in red tiles, is unbroken from end to end and sweeps down boldly to low side walls. Piercing the roof are dormer windows and what appears to have been designed as a combined chimney stack and belfry, though the bell-opening is now empty.

Within was set up a shallow sanctuary, as commonly found in dual-purpose halls; and an early commentary referred to 'white-coated pillars and walls', and 'dark oaken beams'. A pulpit, installed about the beginning of 1930, had spent its previous two years in the mission hall which preceded the construction of St Olave's Church at Mitcham (q.v.); prior to this it served at East Horsley. The hall

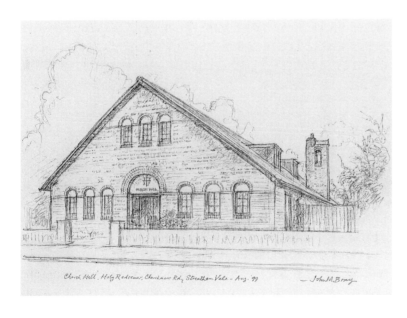

Streatham, Holy Redeemer church hall, from the west.

was repaired after bomb damage in 1940. Since then it appears to have led a quiet life in the shadow of its neighbouring church.

The Church

Set into the wall of Holy Trinity Church at Clapham is a tablet, designed by H. P. Burke Downing, commemorating the so-called Clapham Sect. This term, first applied derisively by Sydney Smith but later acquiring a significance of honour and respect, was attached to a group of men who, in the late eighteenth and early nineteenth centuries, resided in or were connected with the Clapham area. Best-remembered among them was William Wilberforce, but they also included Charles Grant, Chairman of the East India Company; Zachary Macaulay, ex-Governor of Sierra Leone; Henry Thornton, banker; Baron Teignmouth who, as Sir John Shore, was lately the Governor-General of India; Granville Sharp; and James Stephen. Their fame rests on their determined efforts to secure the abolition of the slave trade and on their influence in founding three notable evangelical undertakings: the Church Missionary Society, the Religious Tract Society and the British and Foreign Bible Society.

About 1909 Canon Erskine Clark opened a fund for erecting a memorial church to members of the Sect on a site he acquired for the purpose on the Thornton Estate in South Battersea. Realisation of this scheme was prevented by the first World War and Canon Clark's own death, and in 1929 arrangements were made to sell the site, which by then was judged to be 'totally unsuitable', and to apply the proceeds towards building a church elsewhere. Streatham Vale was chosen as an appropriate location, being one of the largest of the proposed new Districts in the Southwark Diocese and also the nearest geographically to the Clapham area. Acceptance of this arrangement involved placing the patronage of the future District in the hands of the Trustees of the evangelical Church Pastoral Aid Society, but Bishop Garbett, aware that this would unlock funds totalling more than £3,000 already collected by Canon Clark and from the sale of the Battersea site, was content to waive his usual proviso that assistance from the Twenty-five Churches Fund would be conditional on the Bishop of Southwark being nominated as patron; he also knew that the parishes from which the District was to be formed were evangelical in their tradition and he hoped to attract gifts from other evangelicals who might not otherwise have felt able to support the Twenty-five Churches Fund. In the event the Fund contributed generously towards the enterprise.

One other stipulation arose from deeds left by Erskine Clark: that the memorial church should be dedicated to the Holy Redeemer, in recognition of the redemptive work done by the Clapham Sect. Thus was this dedication, instead of the previously intended one to St Luke, applied to the new District when it was formed in May 1930 from parts of Lower Streatham, Streatham Common and Mitcham.

A renewed fund-raising appeal, aimed nation-wide, enabled firm progress to be made in the latter half of 1930, by which time Martin Travers had been asked to submit designs for a church which 'must possess dignity, simplicity and beauty'. His preliminary plan was for a building, 156 feet long, to seat 600 worshippers but by the end of the year a revised design was approved for a shorter, broader church, about 113 feet long internally and 56 feet across the aisles, which could accommodate over 500. The ceremony of cutting the first turf, on the site secured at the junction of Streatham Vale and Churchmore Road, was carried out on 10 January 1931, and digging for the foundations commenced two days later. The foundation stone was placed in position on 28 March; and the complete church was ready for consecration on 5 March 1932. Travers had designed much of the furniture and fittings as well as the detailing of the building itself, whilst his associate T. F. W. Grant, as usual when these two worked together, provided the structural expertise. Construction was carried out by direct labour, under the supervision of builder Joseph Hastings – an arrangement adopted earlier at the Church of the Good Shepherd, Carshalton

Streatham, Church of the Holy Redeemer, plan (east to the left).

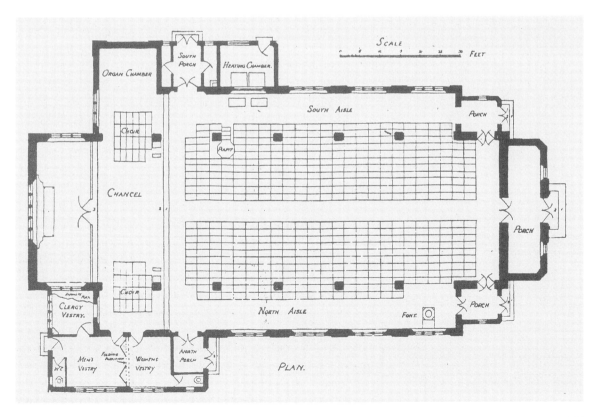

Holy Redeemer, Streatham Vale – Feb. '95.

The church from the west.

Beeches (q.v.). The total cost, including lighting, heating and architects' fees, was £11,775, with an additional £981 for fittings.

The church was erected on a straightforward ground plan: a broad nave with five-bay aisles on each side, and a sixth aisleless bay at the west end flanked by subsidiary porches; the wide main porch projected from the west front. The chancel comprised a single-bay choir without structural division from the nave, and a small aisleless sanctuary. An organ chamber was provided on the south side of the choir, and three vestries on the north, the latter extending eastwards to adjoin the sanctuary also. The walls were constructed of brick, externally Sussex multi-coloured stocks; artificial stone was used for the window tracery and mullions. The impressively large east and west windows, each of five main lights, were Perpendicular Gothic in style; other windows were much

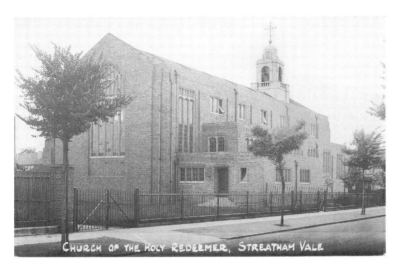

Left: the church from the north-east, from an old postcard. Below: the church from the south-east.

CHURCH OF THE HOLY REDEEMER, STREATHAM VALE

more restrained, with no more than elemental trefoil tracery under square heads. The main roof, covered with copper, was surmounted near its west end by a white wooden bell-turret which deserves description. Of Renaissance inspiration, it is of three stages, the lowest of which is square in plan, with a flat-faced balustrade on each side; above, the recessed bell-stage has round-headed louvred bell openings; and uppermost and further recessed is a small cupola, square-sided but with chamfered corners, crowned by a domed cap with a ball finial and a gilded ornamental cross. Within the turret is a single bell, of 4½ cwt. and 27 inches in diameter, inscribed CANTATE DOMINO CANTICUM NOVUM; it was cast by Mears & Stainbank in 1931 for an exhibition of lettering.

Internally, the church's architectural features are plain and simple: the pointed arches of the arcades rest on square-sectioned piers without capitals; the roof is carried on steel trusses concealed

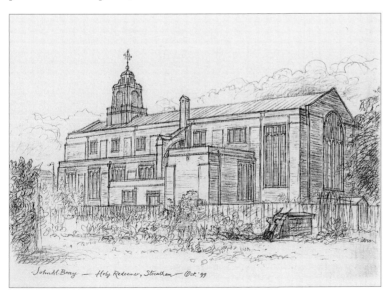

John M. Bray — Holy Redeemer, Streatham — Oct. '99

The interior, looking east, a view published not long after completion.

above barrel vaulting which, like other surfaces, is covered with cream-coated plaster. But Travers provided numerous ornamental touches to enliven what might otherwise have been a rather monotonous and undistinguished scene. The prominent corbels supporting the roof tie-beams and cornices were each finished with a scroll decoration picked out in scarlet. The pendant electric light fittings in the main body of the church were shaped like brass helmets and inclined towards the east end, so concealing the bulbs from view by worshippers, whilst the wall-mounted aisle lights were designed with ornamental back-plates and tripartite framed glass shields. Most of Travers's decorative features, however, were concentrated in the chancel, backed by the great east window which Travers envisaged as containing pictorial glass. An illustration of the general scheme was exhibited at the Royal Academy in 1933. On either side of the window were placed thickly-framed text boards, with gold lettering on a red ground. Travers produced several designs for the red and gold reredos, backed by dark wooden wall panelling (one is shown on the front cover). The one selected featured linenfold carving, with a simple cross in the centre; the carving was reported to have been the work of a parishioner, S. Kisby. The altar frontal also was ablaze with red and gold. The full-width timber altar rails were balustraded. Choir and clergy stalls were likewise designed by Travers, but the carved wooden eagle lectern came from St John's Church at Streatham. In

Holy Redeemer, Streatham — June '99.   *John M Bray.*

the nave was installed a plain octagonal stone font; instead of chairs, oak pews were supplied for the congregation at an extra cost of £200. The organ was specially designed for the church but only partly built to begin with, lacking one of its three manuals.

The building's connection with the Clapham Sect is marked by a board in the church grounds recording its building 'to commemorate the work of William Wilberforce 1759–1833 and his Friends'.

In 1964 the architect David Bush directed the re-decoration of the church by Campbell, Smith & Company.

Travers and Grant produced proposals for a vicarage to be constructed between the church and the hall, but these were abandoned in favour of a house erected in 1938–9 to the designs of David E. Nye.

A recent view of the interior, looking east. The original light fittings have now gone, but much of the chancel furniture is still in place.

TOLWORTH

St George, Hamilton Avenue

New Hall, built 1934
Architect: T. F. Ford
Contractors: Limpus & Son, of Kingston-upon-Thames

The opening of the Kingston by-pass in 1927 inevitably attracted much residential development to this part of Surbiton. By about 1930, some 1,300 houses and 57 shops had been constructed there, bringing over 6,000 new residents – and the numbers continued to swell. The local Anglicans had been served by St Matthew's Church, an impressively large building completed in 1875 to the designs of C. L. Luck, and by the nearer though diminutive Mission Hall which had been erected in Pyne Road in 1883.

The need for additional facilities for worship was first suggested in 1929, and early in the following year it was accepted that the Pyne Road hall was now too small and that the time had come to provide another building and to enlarge the parish hall which was situated in Douglas Road. An appeal was made for £3,000 to finance the scheme, and plans were prepared for securing a site for a new hall on the other side of the by-pass. In 1931 the site was re-considered; land was acquired in Hamilton Avenue, close to the by-pass but on its north-western side, and the appeal for funds was renewed. By 1933 £1,000 had been granted from the Twenty-five Churches Fund on condition that a permanent structure would be erected; a bank loan of £1,000 had been obtained; and an anonymous donation of £500 received. Plans for a new hall could now be implemented. Thomas F. Ford was appointed architect, and the building contract was awarded to Limpus & Son of Kingston. Construction was under way by February 1934, and on 13 June the building was dedicated as St George's Mission Hall. The site was capacious enough to allow for a large area to be set aside for the 'erection of a church when the time comes'.

The main body of the hall was designed as a straightforward unaisled parallelogram, with outer walls of dark red Claygate brick and a pitched roof covered in tiles. Inside, the walls were finished in cream above a dado of lime-treated Oregon pine. Space was available to seat up to 320 people. The dual-purpose nature of the building was given effect by the provision, at one end, of a stage platform together with a kitchen and a small vestry, whilst projecting from the other end was a shallow chancel under a separate concave-hipped roof covered in copper. This feature, coupled with some modest ornamentation to the brickwork below, relieved an otherwise plain and utilitarian exterior. Within, a roller-shutter was positioned to segregate the sanctuary from the main hall.

Exterior view of Tolworth, St George's Church Centre, from the west. On the left of the picture is the original hall, now the church; on the right the current hall, built in the 1980s.

Overall, a total of £5,354 was expended, on purchasing the site, erecting the hall and meeting associated costs such as fees and equipment. Of this, £850 remained outstanding as mortgage on the land, but this debt was paid off in 1943. After the second World War the original aim of adding a purpose-built church on the site was revived; the old hall in Pyne Road was sold in 1947 and most of the proceeds were invested with this end in view. However, a quotation of £50,000, obtained in 1950, effectively put these aspirations out of court, in favour of more modest proposals. At the end of 1955 the Church Development Fund stood at just £2,657, to which could be added a donation of £600 to 'beautify the church' when built. With the Diocese plainly in no position to offer adequate financial assistance for ambitious projects, it was finally agreed to settle for constructing a simple new hall and converting the existing building so as to function solely as a church. For these works, Kenneth B. Wood was appointed as architect, with Bailey's of New Malden as contractors.

The new hall, to seat 250, was designed to be placed at right-angles to the older one, and to share an entrance foyer with it. A committee room was to be included, for use also by the Sunday School. Construction was to be of load-bearing brick end walls and laminated timber portals supporting a flat roof of prefabricated timber trough units covered with spar-finished built-up felt. The remaining open space in front of the hall was to be developed as gardens. The hall's foundation stone was laid on 29 September 1956 and the completed building was dedicated on 23 February 1957. The cost, which reached £10,241 including fees, landscaping, furnishing and other expenses, was met with the aid of a £5,000 loan from the Diocese.

The east end of the hall, now church.

The next step was to convert the original building into a full-time church. Kenneth Wood's proposals for this were approved in November 1958. They involved interior remodelling including removal of the dado panelling and part of the stage, sealing some of the windows and doors and re-designing the chancel area so as to give it higher definition and a more dignified setting for the sanctuary. The estimated cost was about £2,500. This scheme, executed in 1959, culminated in the transformation of the former stage end into a baptistry, using the £600 donation received a few years earlier. Kenneth Wood designed a new font, which was dedicated on Easter Day 1960. A Compton organ was introduced in 1962.

Unfortunately it was not long before problems began to arise. In 1973 the sanctuary panelling had to be removed following the discovery of woodworm; the walls were plastered and painted instead. Three years earlier, the new hall had been found 'in need of much repair and redecoration'; the flat roof was leaking badly in heavy rain. Local funds were being placed under strain, leading to a proposal to sell part of the church land for house building. This was initially rejected but maintenance problems persisted and in 1979 the decision was taken to sell a piece of land, including the site of the hall, for residential development. The hall was pulled down early in 1980, and almost immediately construction work began, by Barratt Developments on a small estate of houses and maisonettes, and by Lywood Contractors Ltd. of Tadworth on a replacement hall. This latter building, of multi-coloured brick with a tile-covered pitched roof, was erected alongside Thomas Ford's original hall and parallel with it, but on the opposite side from Kenneth Wood's demolished structure.

The replacement hall was dedicated on 17 May 1981 and the whole complex became known as St George's Church Centre. Seen from Hamilton Avenue, the profile is now of two simple and compatible buildings side by side, with an entrance porch in the middle. Inside, a vestibule and passage-way give access to the hall on the right and the church on the left. Within the church, a major reordering has resulted in the Holy Table being positioned midway along what was the ritual south wall. The baptistry remains at the former stage end.

TOOTING
St Augustine, Broadwater Road

New Church, built 1929–31
Architect: H. P. Burke Downing
Contractors: Dorey & Co. Ltd., of Brentford

The erection in 1884 of an 'Iron Room' at Tooting, known as St Andrew's, was followed six years later by the opening of a small iron-clad mission church on a neighbouring site in Selkirk Road; this was dedicated to St Augustine, the former name being abandoned apparently because of its adoption for a new church at Earlsfield. In 1896 St Augustine's became the centre of a Diocesan Mission District.

In 1900 the recently constituted London County Council acquired Totterdown Fields as its first site for mass housing, under the provisions of the 1890 Working Classes Act. Intended ultimately to contain over 1,200 dwellings, the site attracted a work force of building tradesmen to St Augustine's Mission District, and construction of the estate proceeded rapidly.

A hall in Broadwater Road was bought in 1914 for use as a temporary church for St Augustine's Mission. An adjoining site for a permanent church was acquired at the same time, giving a total road frontage of 190 feet. Initially this hall was named the Emmanuel Mission Church but in 1918 the dedication reverted once more to St Augustine's.

The first development on the new site was the erection of a parsonage, built in 1923 by G. P. & H. Barnes of Streatham to the designs of H. P. Burke Downing. In the following year Bishop Garbett warned that the District, then populated by about 4,000 souls, was growing rapidly and would need parochial status within a few years. This sparked off a swift application to the Ecclesiastical Commissioners for a Conventional District to be established, backed by the promise of a £1,000 grant from the City Parochial Charities Fund, but it was not until 1926 that the appropriate Order in Council was made. The new District's population was then already estimated to be in excess of 6,000 and to rise shortly to about 10,000 with the inclusion of the Bell Estate. The Bishop of Southwark was awarded patronage of the living by virtue of his having contributed £2,000, with the promise of £2,000 more, from the Twenty-five Churches Fund towards the cost of erecting a permanent church. Grants were also secured from other ecclesiastical sources.

Burke Downing was appointed architect for the permanent church, and in both 1928 and 1929 his initial proposals were illustrated in *The Builder*. They were to provide seating for 585 persons in a five-bay aisled nave with a chancel and south chapel.

Tooting, St Augustine. Right: from the south-west. Opposite: from the south-east.

The south aisle was to be considerably broader than the north; a baptistry would project one bay to the west; a richly traceried five-light east window was to illuminate the chancel; and rising above the vestries on the chancel's north flank was to be a gabled bell-turret. The total external length would be 123½ feet, with a width across the aisles of 52½ feet. Burke Downing's designs were exhibited at the Royal Academy in 1929 but, by the time building commenced, they had been scaled down a little and it was in the

Plan, with east to the right.

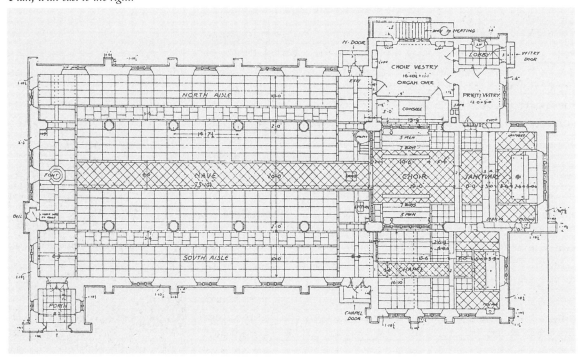

modified form that approval was obtained from the Ecclesiastical Commissioners. At the west end, the baptistry would no longer project; the aisles would be of equal width; the south chapel would be simplified, with an almost flat lean-to roof; the chancel east window would lose its exuberant tracery – though its smaller counterpart in the south chapel would gain some – and the bell-turret would be re-sited at the west end of the church. Dimensions would be cut back to about 112 feet in length and 44 feet across the aisles. Seating capacity would be reduced to 516. The total cost was estimated at £12,215.

On St Andrew's Day, 30 November 1929, the foundation stone was laid by H. M. the Queen Mother, who was then Duchess of York; the completed church was consecrated on 10 March 1931. As usual, Burke Downing had done a sound, if conservative, job in fourteenth century style and the Ecclesiastical Commissioners' consulting architects had no qualms about approving the building as suitable for use as a parish church. Bishop Garbett described it as 'simple, beautiful and dignified', and T. P. Stevens as 'lofty and spacious'. Basil Clarke, however, rated it as less successful than Burke Downing's earlier churches.

The exterior, faced with brown Crowborough bricks with quite liberal dressings of stone, also featured a red-tiled main roof embracing the aisles and continuing unbroken over nave and chancel. The main entrance porch, south-facing at the western end of the south aisle, had a pointed archway and an ornamental stone finial to the gable. A large five-light window with subdued tracery heads was set into the chancel's east wall, whilst the west front of the nave contained three stepped two-light windows, again traceried in rather elemental fashion. The crowning piece of

The east end.

Above: the communion rail. Opposite: the pulpit. Below: the interior, looking east and across into the south aisle.

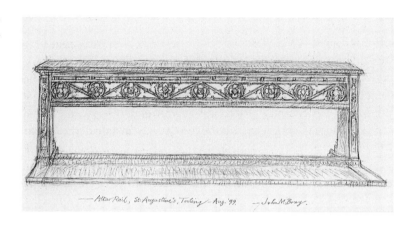

fenestration was reserved for the south chapel, which was given a broad five-light east window with lavishly flamboyant tracery. The brick bell-turret, at the west end but offset to the south, was capped with a gable supported on stone buttresses; the bell within was later recorded by G. P. Elphick as of 4½ cwt and possibly 'a Croydon casting'.

Inside the church, the walls were mainly plastered; piers and arches were built of stone. The open timber roof was boarded and

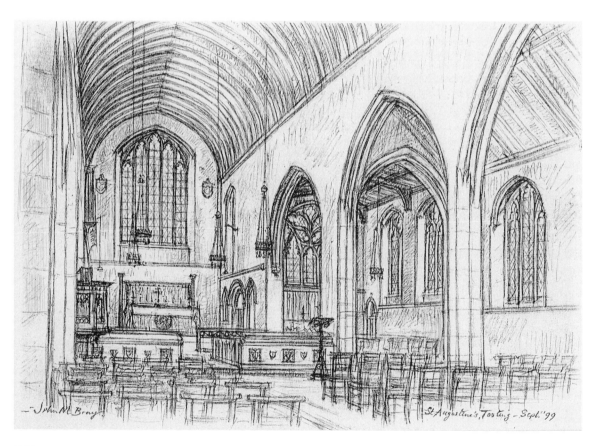

left 'without colour or gilding'. The floors of the choir, sanctuary and passages were paved with white Mansfield and Ancaster rag stone. Most of the furniture was designed by the architect: altars, doors, benches and stalls were all in oak in natural colour. The electric light fittings and pendants were also specially designed. The stone font was centrally placed at the west end of the nave. In the organ chamber, above the choir vestry, was installed the organ which had been erected some forty years earlier in the iron mission church; prior to that, it had apparently served in almshouses and a school. In 1927 it had been cleaned and renovated by G. H. C. Foskett & Co., who also enlarged and re-voiced it, and further additions were made on its removal to the new St Augustine's.

The final cost of building the church and installing its furniture and fittings proved to be remarkably close to the estimate: £12,265, including £695 for fees and £846 for extra foundations to an additional depth of 12 feet. The church was re-dedicated in 1954 after the completion of extensive war-damage repairs. About 1967 the choir vestry was set on fire by arsonists, damaging the organ, housed above, so severely that it had to be replaced. A two-manual instrument was built by Fr. Watson, a monk and organ-builder from Prinknash Abbey, re-using much material from the old organ, but by 1987 this in turn was reaching the end of its useful life. An attempt to purchase the organ from Christ Church, Brondesbury, was abandoned as too costly; no doubt the erection of a new hall, followed about 1983 by a complete re-roofing of the church, had drained the coffers of available funds. Eventually an instrument was obtained free of charge from St Peter's Church, East Dulwich, where it had been lying unused. Built for that church by T. C. Lewis in 1875, the organ was restored and re-constructed in St Augustine's by Saxon Aldred in 1995.

WALLINGTON

St Patrick, Park Hill Road

New Church, built 1932
Architects: J. E. Newberry & C. W. Fowler
Contractors: James Burges & Sons Ltd. of Wimbledon

A plot of land for building a place of worship at the Woodcote end of the parish was purchased by local parishioners in 1909, but this was exchanged in the following year for a nearby site in Park Hill Road which, at 210 feet by 150 feet, was intended to be large enough to accommodate a church, a hall and a parsonage. On St Patrick's Day in 1910 a parish meeting was held to consider erecting a church on the site and, as a result, a contract was placed with Harrison & Sons of Camberwell for putting up a temporary building to seat 294 people; this, an 80-feet structure of timber clad with corrugated

Wallington, the temporary church, from an old postcard.

iron, was dedicated on 1 April 1911. A hall, also built by Harrison's, followed in 1920, by which time over £1,200 had been accumulated in a Building Fund for a permanent church.

In 1924 a Mission and Sunday School were opened at Little Woodcote and, with the launch of the Twenty-five Churches Fund, a new source of financial support soon became available for building the intended permanent church. In 1930 J. E. Newberry & C. W. Fowler exhibited designs of three ecclesiastical works at the Royal Academy, one of which depicted their proposal for a new church of St Patrick at Wallington. This was selected in preference to those of other architects who were consulted; a typical example of their style, it was in fact an adaptation of their design for All Saints' Church at East Sheen (q.v.). James Burges & Sons Ltd. were then awarded the building contract, the estimated cost being £9,700 including removal of the organ from the temporary church to the new one. In June 1931 the architects' drawings and specification passed the scrutiny of Caröe & Passmore, the Ecclesiastical

Wallington, St Patrick, the east end, from an old postcard.

Commissioners' consultants, and preparations for the church's construction were thereupon set in train.

The foundation stone was laid on 23 January 1932. Surrounding it in the east wall were set some stones said to have come from the remains of a medieval chapel of ease on Butter Hill nearby, the site of which had been excavated in 1921.

Progress towards completion of the building seems to have proceeded at quite a brisk pace. The consecration date was fixed for 12 November but, with barely a fortnight to go, the new Bishop of Southwark, Dr Parsons, declared that, instead of consecrating the church, he would only dedicate it and license it for Divine Worship. Consecration would have to wait until the matter of patronage had been settled; the normal practice established by his predecessor Bishop Garbett was for patronage to be surrendered to the Bishop as a condition under which financial assistance was awarded from the Twenty-five Churches Fund. In the case of Wallington parish, patronage of the living was at the time vested in the National Church League Trust. To this day, St Patrick's remains unconsecrated, the patrons now being the Church Society Trust and its incumbent a minister-in-charge responsible to the Vicar of Wallington.

Above: an early drawing of the east end. Below: from the north-east.

St Patrick's, Wallington – April '94. – John M. Bray.

The interior looking east. Opposite: from an old postcard. Below: a modern view.

The church is reported to have cost £9,467 to erect. It was provided with a four-bay nave with narrow north and south aisles. The chancel had a Lady Chapel on its south side and a small aisle or return way to its north; adjoining this were vestries for choir and clergy. The organ chamber surmounted the choir vestry and to its rear was a separate ladies' vestry. North and south entrance porches were added at the west end. The nave measured about 65 feet long and 25½ feet wide, the aisles together adding 19½ feet to the width. The chancel was 34 feet in length and 21 feet wide, excluding the return way. Total seating capacity was 425.

Brick was used almost entirely in the church's construction: externally the walls were faced with multi-coloured purplish bricks, whilst the internal walls, piers and arches were of creamy sand-lime bricks, with dados of blue-grey. Stone was used only in the jambs, mullions and tracery of windows. Outside, a single roof of thick hand-made red-brown tiles spans the nave and aisles and continues unbroken to cover the chancel; the Lady Chapel and vestry block are separately roofed. A slender flèche, of timber covered with copper, rises from the main ridge. A tall five-light Gothic-traceried window is set into the chancel's east wall, and there are clerestory windows on the flanking sides. The nave has a

St. Patrick's, Wallington: Interior   John M Bray

large seven-light traceried window in its west wall, and five-light traceried windows in the aisles.

Within, the effect has been described as 'lofty, spacious, well lighted and, above all, reverential'. The open roof of the nave and chancel has arched principals and is of British Columbian pine. The chancel and chapel floors and the nave passages are paved with tiles. A novel feature is that the floor of the nave and aisles was made to slope slightly upward from east to west. The east windows of both chancel and chapel were filled with deep yellow glass, 'to obviate glare'.

Some of the fittings came from the temporary church: these included the communion table, pine chancel seats and pews, lectern and organ. The organ seems to have been built about 1890 and was bought from the Royal Academy of Music in 1911 for installation in the newly-constructed temporary church. It was overhauled by N. P. Mander in the 1960s, and its console was then re-positioned. The church bell is said to date from 1815 and to have come from Woodcote Hall. The stone font, communion kneeling benches, and the communion table in the chapel were all designed for the church by the architects.

When the new permanent church was opened, the old temporary building of 1911 was put into use as a hall, whilst the former hall of 1920 was moved to Little Woodcote for service as a mission hall. The 1911 building lasted until 1964, when it was burned down; by that time it was in any case nearing the end of its useful life as its timbers were affected by woodworm. A new hall, designed by Roger Symes and built by Robert Marshall (Builders) Ltd., at a cost of £29,000, was opened in 1965. It is situated on the north side of the church.

The church underwent liturgical reordering in the 1970s, during the course of which a bookstall displaced the font at the west end of the nave, and the font migrated eastwards. In the chancel, the

Communion table, from the original temporary church.

communion table was brought forward to a more central position, the organ console was moved slightly back, and the choir stalls were re-located at the far east end, to face the congregation.

WELLING

St Mary the Virgin, Shoulder of Mutton Green

Site for new church, hall and parsonage house, acquired 1933
Hall and church later built outside the aegis of the Twenty-five Churches Fund

The replacement, in 1933, of East Wickham's diminutive medieval church of St Michael by a much larger structure did not in itself fully solve the problem of providing for the perceived spiritual needs of the parish's burgeoning population. The establishment of two subsidiary centres of worship was soon envisaged, and arrangements for the first of these were put in train before the year was out.

The site chosen was a mile or so to the west of the new parish church, alongside Shoulder of Mutton Green at the Welling end of the winding Wickham Street. Its acquisition for the erection of a church, hall and parsonage house was sufficiently far advanced to warrant inclusion as the final entry in the list of churches, halls and sites which was produced at the Service of Thanksgiving, held in Southwark Cathedral on 25 January 1934, for the work of 'those who raised the Twenty-five Churches Fund'. This was almost certainly the last commitment from the Fund before its closure and the transfer of its functions to the Bishop of Southwark's Council for New Districts.

Designs for a hall on the site, to be known as St Mary's Mission Hall, were drawn up by the architect Thomas F. Ford. For an estimated cost of about £4,000 they offered seating for 350 in a brick building with a tiled roof, measuring 87 feet by 30 feet. John Garrett & Son Ltd. were appointed contractors, and the structure was erected in 1934.

Financial support for the Mission building, in the form of cash grants, was given in the 1930s by the South London Church Fund and the Council for New Districts; and the promise of an additional £2,000 from Diocesan sources was announced at the annual parochial meeting in April 1938, as a contribution towards the cost of building a church on the site. This latter project, planned to commence about two years later, was again placed in the hands of T. F. Ford who prepared designs.

These proposals were suspended on the outbreak of war in 1939 but were revived in 1945 with the launch of an appeal for £2,000. Ambitions were reinforced by the formation of a New District for St Mary's in 1947, but it was not until 9 October 1954 that the foundation stone for a re-designed permanent church was laid,

Thomas Ford once more being the chosen architect. The church was opened in 1955. A simple building faced with red brick, it has a broad frontal aspect, emphasised by a low-pitched nave roof extending unbroken across the aisles. The main entrance, below a sweeping round-headed arch, overlooks the west side of the Green and reveals the church's reverse orientation. The tympanum recessed beneath the entrance arch is decorated in colour with an interesting example of sgraffito work, in the form of stylised plaster engravings representing scenes from the life of the patron saint. A slender Lombardic-style tower rises on the north (ritual south) side of the church.

Within, there is a five-bay nave with narrow passage aisles to north and south, and a west gallery for the organ and choir. The nave roof is panelled and ceiled in a gentle curve; the aisle bays are separated by transverse arches. The aisle windows, which form the principal fenestration, are simple and round-headed. There is stained glass in the smaller side windows of the shallow sanctuary, but the dominating feature at this end of the church is a large mural, by Hans Feibusch, depicting the Ascension of Christ. Biblical scenes, painted by Clare Dawson, are displayed on the arches over the aisles. The pulpit, matching lectern ambo and communion rail are all in white. On the ritual south side of the sanctuary is a small chapel dedicated to St Thomas of Canterbury, reflecting the proximity of the nearby route from London once taken by Canterbury pilgrims. The chapel contains a carved wooden reredos.

The church is now listed in the Southwark Diocesan Directory under the district name of Welling.

NOTES AND INDEX

ABBREVIATIONS

BAL   British Architectural Library
CCC   Council for the Care of Churches
CERC Church of England Record Centre
ICBS   Incorporated Church Building Society
LB   London Borough
LCC   London County Council
LMA   London Metropolitan Archives (formerly Greater London Record Office)
LPL   Lambeth Palace Library
LS   Local Studies Centre/Library
PCC   Parochial Church Council
RIBA   Royal Institute of British Architects
SDD   *Southwark Diocesan Directory*
SDG   *Southwark Diocesan Gazette*
SRO   Surrey Record Office

1. Not all of this movement was within the Southwark Diocese itself: some of it represented an influx from elsewhere. Between 1921 and 1931 the Diocese experienced a population increase of 7.3% to reach over 2.5 million, according to census returns.
2. Reference to Thomas Jefferson, in J. B. MacMaster, *History of the People of the United States*, (1883–1913), Vol II, p. 586.
3. For a more detailed exposition and analysis of the problem see 'Some account of the Southwark Diocese' by William Woodcock Hough, Bishop of Woolwich (South London Church Fund, 1928).
4. Charles Smyth, *Cyril Forster Garbett, Archbishop of York* (London, Hodder & Stoughton, 1959).
5. To some extent, Garbett himself stirred the cauldron by actively helping to promote the growing campaign for slum clearance and the provision of new low-rent housing. See e.g. Margaret, Prioress of Whitby, *Archbishop Garbett – A Memoir* (London, Mowbray, 1957) & Garbett's own book, *In the Heart of South London* (London, Longman's, Green & Co., 1931).
6. Garbett, op. cit., p. 132 *et seq.*
7. Smyth, op. cit., p. 155.
8. J. A. B. Robertson, *Notes on the Ancient Parish of Saint Mary, Lewisham* (Lewisham, *c.*1957).
9. See *London Housing* (pub. LCC, 1937).
10. For an excellent illustrated survey of church building on Portsea, see Rodney Hubbuck's *Portsea Island Churches* (No. 8 of the Portsmouth Papers, pub. by Portsmouth City Council, 1969).
11. See under Morden St George & the three St Helier entries in the gazetteer section.
12. Smyth, op. cit., pp. 152–3.
13. Ibid., p. 154.
14. Ibid., p. 156. See also *SDD*, 1927.
15. Smyth, op. cit., p. 154.
16. W. W. Hough, Bishop of Woolwich, *The History of the Diocese, part VI – The Beginning of a New Era, 1911–28* (Insert to *SDG*, March 1928).
17. *SDG*, December 1925.
18. *Wandsworth Borough News*, 26 February 1926, for example. The event received good publicity in the national as well as the local press.
19. *SDG*, January 1928. Also e.g. *Eltham and District Times*, 9 December 1927.
20. *SDG*, June 1928.
21. *SDG*, August 1928. Also Smyth, op. cit., p. 158.
22. Sums raised locally and applied directly to approved local schemes brought the overall total collected to one quarter of a million pounds, according to *SDG*, January 1934.
23. *SDD*, 1934. Also *SDG*, January 1934.
24. *SDG*, March 1934.
25. *SDD*, 1927.
26. Form of Service at Southwark Cathedral, 25 January 1934. This includes a list which is complete except for the omission, no doubt unintentionally, of the Hall at St Barnabas's, Downham.
27. *SDG*, January 1935.
28. Suspicion for example, at Malden & Mitcham; hostility at Morden.
29. The Church of the Holy Redeemer, Streatham Vale, was designed on evangelical lines.
30. CERC file 90364: report dated 26 August 1926.
31. 'Bad taste in churches', RIBA Journal, 24 May 1930.
32. H. P. Burke Downing, 'Churches for the new centres of population', *ICBS Annual Report*, 1929.
33. N. F. Cachemaille-Day, 'Ecclesiastical architecture in the present age', *RIBA Journal*, 14 October 1933. Based on a lecture to the St Paul's Ecclesiological Society.
34. Report on meeting of Architecture Club on 6 March, in *Builder*, 9 March 1934, p. 411.
35. Report on dedication of St Dunstan's, Bellingham, in *Lewisham Borough News*, 25 November 1925.
36. Review by Sir C. A. Nicholson of the book *New Churches Illustrated* (ICBS, 1936), in *RIBA Journal*, 6 February 1937.
37. Commentary by Maurice E. Webb on Auctioneers' & Estate Agents' Institute, Lincoln's Inn Fields, designed by Greenaway & Newberry, in *Architectural Review*, 1925, vol. 57, p. 95.

38. S. E. Dykes Bower, 'The improvement of churches', in supplement on 'Churches new & old – their fabric & furniture', *Manchester Guardian*, 29 March 1935.

39. He could not have known it at the time, but Dykes Bower was destined to become directly involved in the eventual completion of one of the Twenty-five churches: St Mary's at Sanderstead. See gazetteer section.

40. Smyth, op. cit., p. 11.

41. Margaret, Prioress of Whitby, op. cit., p. 61.

42. Ibid., pp. 107 & 109.

NOTES TO THE GAZETTEER

Sources for the history of each building are presented in alphabetical order. Sources / locations of illustrations used in this book are marked with an asterisk.

BELLINGHAM St Dunstan, Bellingham Green

Bellingham & Downham Tenants' Handbook (LCC, 1934) • Church Survey File: Bellingham, St Dunstan (CCC) • Colley, J., *A History of St Dunstan's Church, Bellingham, and the Bellingham Estate* (1985) • Ecclesiastical Commissioners' archives: files 50975 & 90150 (CERC) • *ICBS Annual Report, 1924 • Kentish Mercury*, 28 Jul 1922, 17 Oct 1924 • *Lewisham Borough News*, 26 Jul 1922, 6 Dec 1922, 15 Oct 1924, 25 Nov 1925 • *London Housing* (LCC, 1937) • *Nicholson, Sir C. A.: Deposited Drawings (LMA): Bellingham, St Dunstan's Church, LCC/VA/DO/R306 • *SDG*, Nov 1924.

CARSHALTON BEECHES The Good Shepherd, Queen Mary's Avenue

Betjeman, Sir J., *Guide to English Parish Churches* (1958; revised N. Kerr & repub. Harper Collins, 1993) • Church Survey File: Carshalton Beeches, Good Shepherd (CCC) • Ecclesiastical Commissioners' archives: file 83897 (CERC) • *London Borough of Sutton Local Studies Department, photograph: SBC 726 • London Gazette*, 2 Nov 1965 • Maufe, E., 'The furnishing of churches' (*Architectural Review*, Oct 1934) • Molesworth-Roberts, H. V., article in *Wallington & Carshalton Times*, 5 Jun 1930 • Moore, Jean, *Theoretical & stylistic sources of Martin Travers's design for the Church of the Good Shepherd, Carshalton Beeches – a case study* (1975) (Sutton LS, 590820) • *Moore, Parsons & Tuffield, The Church of the Good Shepherd – A Short History & Guide* (1980) • *New Churches Illustrated* (ICBS, 1936) • Southwark Diocesan Archives (LMA): Office pps., DSOP/1966/31 • *SDG*, Oct 1929, Jun 1930 • Souvenir booklet on laying foundation stone of church, 26 Jun 1929 • *Sutton & Cheam Advertiser*, 27 Jun 1929 • Travers, Martin: Deposited Designs (RIBA Drawings Collection): Carshalton, Church of Good Shepherd – windows & furnishings; also, with T. F. W. Grant, church structure. Ref. W16/4, 1–4 • *Wallington Advertiser*, 7 Jun 1984, 2 May 1985 • *Wallington & Carshalton Times*, 4 Jul 1929, 15 May 1930, 30 Mar 1972, 22 May 1980, 26 Sep 1985.

CASTELNAU (BARNES) Estate Church Hall, Stillingfleet Road

Barnes & Mortlake Herald, 16 Jun 1928 • *Daily Telegraph*, 11 Dec 1993 • *Ecclesiastical Commissioners' archives: files 26478 & 91421 (CERC) • London Housing* (LCC, May 1937) • Parish magazines, Castelnau Holy Trinity: 1926–9; 1939–41, 1946–8 • Parish Record Index, Castelnau Holy Trinity (SRO) • Parish Records, Castelnau Holy Trinity (SRO): Corresp. & other pps., 1940–42, 1946–52, 1959 & 1963–7 (refs. 3676/4/14–16 & 3788/3/9); Quinquennial Survey Report on Castelnau Estate Hall, by Thos. F. Ford & Ptnrs., Aug 1963 (ref. 3676/4/17) • Paton L. R., *et al.*, *The History of Castelnau* (pub. Holy Trinity Church, 1968) • *Richmond & Twickenham Times*, 3 May 1968 • *Richmond Herald*, 4 May & 28 Sep 1929; 5 Jan 1968.

CHEAM St Alban the Martyr, Elmbrook Road

Burgess, F., *Cheam, Belmont & Worcester Park – A Pictorial History* (Phillimore, Chichester, 1993) • Cherry, B., & Pevsner, N., *Buildings of England, London 2, South* (Penguin, 1983) • Church Survey File: Cheam St Alban (CCC) • Ecclesiastical Commissioners' archives: file 24413 (CERC) • *Illustrated Sutton & Epsom Mail*, 21 Mar 1930 • *London Borough of Sutton Local Studies Department, photograph: SBFC 726 • Marshall, C. J., *A History of Cheam & Sutton* (revised edn. SR Publishers, 1971) • *SDG*, Jul 1934 • *Surrey Comet*, 6 Apr 1929 • *Sutton & Cheam Advertiser*, 11 Apr 1929, 20 Mar 1930, 1 Jan 1931, 22 Jun 1933 • *Sutton Times & Cheam Mail*, 23 Jun 1933 • *Wallington & Carshalton Advertiser*, 14 Feb 1929 • Wild, Laurence, 'Surrey's barn buildings' (*Surrey Life*, Sep 1974).

CHEAM St Oswald, Brock's Drive

The Builder, 20 Nov 1936 • *Building*, 23 Dec 1966 • Church Survey File: Cheam St Oswald (CCC) • Ecclesiastical Commissioners' archives: file 24413 (CERC) • Marshall, C. J., *The Story of the Churches of Cheam* (British Publishing Co., n.d.) • Rochester & Southwark Diocesan Church Trust: Report for 1934 • *Surrey Comet*, 17 Oct 1936, 10 Mar 1937, 26 Apr 1952, 14 Feb 1953 • *Sutton & Cheam Advertiser*, 11 Mar 1937 • *Sutton Times & Cheam Mail*, 16 Jun 1933, 16 Oct 1936.

COULSDON St Francis of Assisi, Rickman Hill

Bourne Society Bulletin, No. 94, Nov 1978 • Church Survey Files (CCC): Coulsdon St Francis, and Coulsdon St John the Evangelist • *Coulsdon & Purley Advertiser*, 23 Aug 1957, 11 & 18 Dec 1987, 15 Jul 1988, 7 Apr 1989, 8 Nov 1991 • *Coulsdon & Purley Weekly Record*, 20 Jul & 19 Oct 1928 • *Croydon Advertiser*, 21 Jul 1928 • Ecclesiastical Commissioners' archives: file 90878 (CERC) • Elliot-Binns, Michael, *The North Downs Church* (1983) • Finch, Joyce, article on St Andrew's, Coulsdon, in *The Surrey Enterprise*, No. 2 • Local History File of cuttings & corresp., Coulsdon St Francis (Purley Reference Library).

DOWNHAM St Barnabas, Downham Way

Cherry, B., & Pevsner, N., *Buildings of England, London 2, South* (Penguin, 1983) • Church Survey File: Catford (Downham) St Barnabas (CCC) • Dalton, L., *St John's Birthday Book: The Story of the Church of St John the Baptist, Southend Village, Lewisham (c.*1950) • Ecclesiastical Commissioners' archives: file 90469 (CERC) • Fincham, E.: Deposited Drawings (LMA): Downham, St. Barnabas's Hall, GLC/AR/BR/19/4218 • Greenfield, J., *St Barnabas – The Early Years* (St Barnabas's Church, *c.*1989) • ICBS Annual Report, 1930 (CCC) • *Kentish Mercury*, 25 Jun 1926, 24 Dec 1926, 12 Oct 1928, 19 Jul 1929 • *Lewisham Borough News*, 23 Jun 1926, 29 Dec 1926, 10 Oct 1928, 17 Jul 1929 • Lewisham Local History Society: *Newsletter* No. 88, Apr 1992 • London County Council: *Housing, With Particular Reference to Post-War Housing Schemes* (LCC, 1928) • Nicholson, Sir C. A.: Deposited Drawings (LMA): Downham, St Barnabas's Church & Hall, LCC/VA/DD/R266 • St Barnabas's Church Newsletter: Nov 1992 • *SDG*, Feb 1927, Mar 1928 • *The Times*, 6 Mar 1929 • Wood, A. W., *Christopher Boone's Charity, Lee* (Merchant Taylors' Co., *c.*1983).

DOWNHAM St Luke, Northover

Baker, L. A. J., *Churches in the Hundred of Blackheath* (Greenwich & Lewisham Antiquarian Society, 1961) • Dalton, L., *St John's Birthday Book – The Story of the Church of St John the Baptist, Southend Village, Lewisham (c.*1950) • Ecclesiastical Commissioners' archives: files 90469 & 94014 (CERC) • Harbrow, William, Ltd.: Deposited Drawings (LMA): Downham, Proposed Parish Hall for St Luke's, LCC/VA/DD/R322 • *Kentish Mercury*, 19 Sep 1930 • *Lewisham Borough News*, 1 Feb 1928, 21 May 1930, 17 Sep 1930 & 23 Mar 1937 • *Lewisham, Lee & Catford Journal*, 4 Apr, 23 May, 5 Sep & 19 Sep 1930 • Nicholson, Sir C. A., & T. J. Rushton: Deposited Drawings (LMA): Downham, St Luke's Church, Jun 1935, LCC/VA/DD/R360 • ★St Luke's Church: architect's drawing • South London Church Fund: Annual Report, 1934 • Southwark Diocesan Archives (LMA): Consecration pps., DSCP/1938/2.

EAST SHEEN All Saints, East Sheen Avenue

All Saints' Church, East Sheen: Church archives 1950–66 (courtesy of incumbent); Commemorative Handbook of the Consecration, All Saints' Day, 1929; Inscription on Wall of Clergy Vestry • ★*Architects' Journal*, 19 Mar 1930 • *Barnes & Mortlake Herald*, 17 Mar, 16 Jun, 20 Oct & 27 Oct 1928; 12 Oct & 2 Nov 1929 • Braithwaite, David, *Building in the Blood: Dove Brothers of Islington* (Godfrey Cave & Dove Bros., 1981) • *The Bridge* (Southwark Diocesan Newspaper), No. 2, Oct 1996 • Ecclesiastical Commissioners' archives: file 90364 (CERC) • ★Ford, John A., *A Short History of All Saints' Church, East Sheen, with contributions on organs & choir by Ronald S. Peck* (1973, revised 1979) • Kennington, Revd J. Paul, information supplied orally • Monroe, Revd Horace, 'Church extension at Mortlake' in *Church Builder*, Jan 1914 • Parish Magazines, Mortlake with East Sheen: 1928–30, 1950, Nov 1957, Feb 1960, Jul & Dec 1964, 1966, 1967 • Parish Records: East Sheen, All Saints (SRO): 2414/2/81, letter describing church, 1940; 2414/2/301, leaflet (n.d.) appealing for funds to build church in Clifford Ave.; 2414/2/306, pps. *c.*1909–29 re conveying of site & building of church; 2414/2/307A, Order of Service for Laying of Foundation Stone by HRH the Duchess of York, 24 Oct 1928; 2414/2/310–315, citations, 1949–66 • Peck, Ronald S., see Ford, John A. • *Richmond & Twickenham Times*, 27 Oct 1928, 2 Nov 1929, 30 Jul 1966, 6 May 1967 • *Richmond Herald*, 26 Nov 1965, 29 Jul 1966, 5 May 1967 • Southwark Diocesan Archives (LMA): Consecration pps., DS/CP/1929/5; Office pps., DS/OP/1926/7 • *SDG*, Dec 1929 • ★Yeandle, Revd W. H., & Watts, W. W., *The History of the Churches in Mortlake & East Sheen* (pub. R. W. Simpson, 1925).

EAST WICKHAM St Michael, Upper Wickham Lane

Anon., *St Michael's Church, East Wickham* (leaflet, *c*.1933) • *Bexleyheath Observer & Kentish Times*, 15 Jul 1932, 24 Feb 1933 • Caley, Frank: *The Churches of the Parish of St Michael, East Wickham, Welling, Kent* (Church Publishers, Ramsgate, *c*.1968) • Carr, M. C., 'The development & character of a metropolitan suburb: Bexley, Kent' in F. M. L. Thompson (ed.), *The Rise in Suburbia* (Leicester University Press, 1982) • Church Survey File: East Wickham St Michael (CCC) • Clouston, R. W. M.: corresp. with Revd M. Sweet re church bell, 1971 • Ecclesiastical Commissioners' archives: files 63934; 84228; 92082; 92241 (CERC) • Kennett, John: *The Eltham Hutments* (Eltham Books, 1985) • *London Gazette*, 21 Mar 1933 • *Manchester Guardian*, 24 Feb 1933 • Parish Records, East Wickham St Michael (Bexley LS): Deed of Conveyance dated 5 Jul 1926; PCC minutes, 1920–72; Service Register, 1933–5 • *The Record*, Aug 1932, Mar 1933 • Southwark Diocesan Archives (LMA): Consecration pps., DSCP/1933/3; Office pps., DSOP/1973/62 • *SDD*, 1928–29; 1934 • *SDG*, Jan 1926 • Spurgeon, Darrell, *Discover Woolwich & Its Environs* (Greenwich Guide-Books, 1990) • Tester, P. J., *East Wickham & Welling: A Short History* (London Borough of Bexley, 1979).

ELTHAM St Barnabas, Rochester Way

Anon., 'Our church in retrospect' in *Review – St Barnabas Church, Re-Dedicated Jun 1957* • *Anon., print of the Royal Dockyard Chapel of 1858 • *The Bridge* (Southwark Diocesan Newspaper), No. 4, Christmas 1996/New Year 1997 • *Church Survey File: Eltham St Barnabas (CCC) • Clarke, B. F. L., *Parish Churches of London* (Batsford, 1966) • *Clerical Journal*, 1867 (issue date not established) • Cole, David, *The Work of Sir Gilbert Scott* (Architectural Press, 1980) • Ecclesiastical Commissioners' archives: file 90630 (CERC) • *Eltham & Kentish Times*, 3 Aug & 7 Sep 1928, 13 Oct 1933, 23 Apr 1937, 28 Jun 1957 • Ford, Thomas F., 'The rebirth of St Barnabas' in *Review – St Barnabas Church, Re-Dedicated Jun 1957* • Franklin, J. V., & Percival, Joyce D. (compilers), *Buildings of Local Architectural or Historic Interest* (London Borough of Greenwich, 1977) • Glencross, Alan, *The Buildings of Greenwich* (London Borough of Greenwich, 1974) • Kennett, John (1) 'Eltham in 1935 – some aspects of a Silver Jubilee Year' in *Some Eltham Local History Records* (Eltham Society, 1977); (2) *The Eltham Hutments* (Eltham Books, 1985) • *Kentish Independent*: 2 Sep 1932, 13 Oct 1933, 23 Apr & 31 Dec 1937, 28 Jun 1957, 21 Sep 1972 • Murdock, Ian, 'Well Hall & the Progress Area' in *Looking Into Eltham* (Eltham Society, 1980) • Nairn, Ian, *Nairn's London* (Penguin, 1966) • Order of Service for Golden Jubilee Thanksgiving & Dedication, 7 Oct 1983 • South London Church Fund & Southwark Diocesan Board of Finance: Annual Report, 1936 • Southwark Diocesan Archives (LMA): Consecration pps., DSCP/1957/2/B • *SDD*: 1934 • *SDG*, Jun 1936 • *Surrey Comet*, 23 Sep 1933 • Watling, R. A.: Deposited Drawings (LMA): Well Hall (Eltham), St Barnabas Hall, 19 Aug 1933 (GLC/AR/BR/19/909) • Young, Barbara: *Pilgrim Church – A History of St Barnabas's, Eltham* (1983).

ELTHAM St Saviour's Mission Hall, Mayerne Road

Cook, Deaconess Gwen: letter dated 8 Nov 1997 to author • District Surveyor's Returns, Woolwich South (LMA): 1929 (LCC/AR/BA/4/498/42 & /43) • *Ecclesiastical Commissioners' archives: file 92241 (CERC) • *Eltham & Kentish Times*, 10 Aug & 14 Sep 1928, 8 Mar & 17 May 1929, 30 Oct 1931, 30 Sep 1932, 7 Jul 1933, 15 Mar 1957 • Kennett, John, 'The Page Estate & Eltham Green' in *Looking Into Eltham* (pub. Eltham Society, 1980) • *Kentish Independent*, 17 May 1929 • *London Housing* (LCC, 1937) • *SDD*: 1929–30 • *Woodbridge, Mrs. Joyce: letter dated 1 Dec 1997 to author, with photograph.

ELTHAM St Saviour, Middle Park Avenue

*Anon., 'All Saints' Church, New Eltham, S.E.9: an appeal for church building' (CCC) • *Architect & Building News* 30 Jun 1933 • Caple, Revd Stephen: information supplied orally • Church Survey File: Eltham St Saviour (CCC) • Clarke, B. F. L., *Parish Churches of London* (Batsford, 1966) • Ecclesiastical Commissioners' archives: file 92241 (CERC) • *Eltham & Kentish Times*, 22 Feb 1931, 25 Nov 1932, 7 Jul 1933 • Franklin, J . V., & Percival, Joyce D., *Buildings of Local Architectural & Historic Interest* (London Borough of Greenwich, 1977) • *Kentish Independent*, 7 Jul 1933, 9 Jul 1937 • King, Laurence, obit. of N. F. Cachemaille-Day, *RIBA Journal*, Nov 1976 • Lookback Group, *Middle Park Past & Present* (1984) • Maufe, Sir Edward, 'The furnishing of churches' (*Architectural Review*, Oct 1934) • *New Churches Illustrated* (ICBS, 1936) • Saunders, Ann, *The Art & Architecture of London* (Phaidon Press, 1984) • *SDG*, Aug 1933 • Taylor, Margaret, 'Middle Park' in *Looking Into Eltham* (pub. Eltham Society, 1980) • Woodbridge, Mrs. Joyce: letter of 1 Dec 1997 to author.

ELTHAM PARK St Luke, Westmount Road

Baker, L. A. J., *Churches in the Hundred of Blackheath* (Greenwich & Lewisham Antiquarian Society, 1980) • Buckley, L. G., 'Stained glass in London's churches' (unpub. list, n.d.) • *Building News*, 15 Jun 1906 • *Church Survey File: Eltham St Luke (CCC) • Clarke, B. F. L., *Parish Churches of London* (Batsford, 1966) • Corbett Estate, Eltham: information folder (Greenwich LS) • Ecclesiastical Commissioners' archives: file 80714 (CERC) • *Eltham & District Times*, 12 Jul 1907 •

• *Eltham & Kentish Times*, 23 Feb 1934; 19 Nov 1948 • Goodhart-Rendel, H. S., 'The Work of Temple Moore' in *RIBA Journal*, Vol. 35, No. 14, 26 May 1928 • Kennett, John, *The Eltham Hutments* (Eltham Books, 1985) • *Kentish Independent*, 23 Feb 1934 •*London Gazette*, 29 Mar 1963 • Parish Magazines, Eltham St Luke (LMA): 1905–18 (P97/LUK/3, 262 & 263); 1923–6 (P97/LUK/19–22); 1932–4 (P97/LUK/28–30); 1940–47 (P97/LUK/32) • Taylor, Margaret, & Gus White, 'Eltham Park & the Corbett area' in *Looking Into Eltham* (pub. Eltham Society, 1980) • Thewlis, Revd Dr John C. (1) *Growth in a Parish – Saint Luke, Eltham Park, 1904–1940* (pub. 1992) (2) information supplied orally • ★Tolhurst, J. B. L.: elevation for new south aisle (RIBA Library Drawings Collection; copy held by church) • Tomkinson, Revd H. F., & James Hall, *The Life Story of Our Parish – St Luke's, Eltham* (Kentish District Times Co., 1927).

FURZEDOWN (STREATHAM) St Paul, Welham Road

Balham News, 24 Apr 1931 • Buckley, L. G, 'Stained glass in London's churches' (unpub. list, n.d.) • Church Survey File: Furzedown St Paul (CCC) • Clarke, B. F. L., *Parish Churches of London* (Batsford, 1966) • Ecclesiastical Commissioners' archives: file 82860 (CERC) • Greenaway, F. H ., & J. E. Newberry: Deposited Drawings (LMA): Furzedown – St Paul's Church, 1924–6 (B/FN/183–285); Parochial Hall, 1910–11 (B/FN/286–98); Vicarage, 1926 (B/FN/299–321) • ICBS Annual Reports, 1924 & 1926 • ★St Paul's Church, Furzedown:photograph of interior • Southwark Diocesan Archives (LMA): Consecration pps., DSCP/1926/2; Office pps., DSOP/1926/4 • *Streatham News*, 17 Sep 1926, 2 Sep 1927 • Symondson, Cyril: see Thomas, Audrey J. • Thomas, Audrey J*., Diamond Jubilee 1986 – A Brief History of St Paul, Furzedown* (incorporating notes by Cyril Symondson on stained glass windows) (St Paul's PCC, 1986) • Travers, Martin: Deposited Designs (RIBA Drawings Collection): glass in 3–light window, ref. TRAV(164).

HACKBRIDGE AND NORTH BEDDINGTON All Saints, London Road

All Saints' Church Magazine: 21st anniversary edition, 1952 (Sutton LS, SBAW726) • ★*The Builder*, 26 May 1922, 26 Aug 1927 • *Building News*, 5 Jan 1923 • Ecclesiastical Commissioners' archives: file 68377 (CERC) • ★ICBS Annual Report, 1928 (CCC) • *London Gazette*, 27 Mar 1934 • Parish Record Index (SRO) • Parish Records, Hackbridge All Saints (SRO): Deed of Conveyance, 1 Apr 1887 (2813/2/8); Easter Vestry Minute Book, 1916–28 (3848/2/1); PCC Minute Book, 1922–6 (3848/2/2) • *Royal Academy Exhibitors 1905–70*, Vol. IV, (EP Publishing, 1981) • Souvenir Programme of Consecration, 19 May 1931 (Sutton LS) • *Wallington & Carshalton Advertiser*, 12 Jul 1928, 21 May 1931 • *Wallington & Carshalton Times*, 13 Feb 1930, 21 May 1931.

MALDEN St James, Bodley Road

Anon., *St James's Golden Jubilee, 1933–1983* (pub. St James's Church, Malden, 1983) • Church Survey File: Malden St John the Baptist (CCC) • Ecclesiastical Commissioners' archives: file 91764 (CERC) • Parish Magazines, Malden St James: 1934–9; 1943–48; 1952–59; 1964–6; 1970; 1973–4 • Parish Records (SRO): Malden Christ Church – 3965/5/44, docs. re building of St James's Mission Church, 1902–11); Malden St James – 3965/2/15–19, docs. of 1929 re creation of new District & vesting patronage; Malden St John the Baptist – 2473/4/1, PCC minute book, 1919–31 • Photographic Archives (Kingston Local History Room): Malden St James, Mission Church, K2–393/394 • Southwark Diocesan Archives (LMA): Consecration pps., DSCP/1929/7 & DSCP/1933/5; Office pps., DSOP/1929/7 • *SDG*, Oct 1933 • *Surrey Comet*, 8 & 15 Oct 1932, 23 Sep 1933, 18 Oct 1947, 25 Sep 1954, 4 Oct 1958, 19 Oct 1966.

MERTON St James the Apostle, Beaford Grove

Ecclesiastical commissioners' archives: file 92860 (CERC) • *Kelly's Surrey Directory*, 1938 • Parish Magazines, Merton St James: Aug 1938, Dec 1951, Jan, May & Jun 1956, Jun, Jul & Aug 1957, May, Jun, Sep & Oct 1958, Sep 1959, Nov 1962, Feb 1963, Apr & May 1965 • Parish Records, Merton St James (SRO): 2061/4/1–4, designs, 1907, by J. Alick Thomas for proposed new church; 2061/4/14, corresp. etc., 1938–50, re hall & proposed church; 2061/4/15, corresp. etc., 1952–9, re building church • St James's Church Hall, District Notes: Jan 1940 • Southwark Diocesan Archives (LMA): Consecration pps., DSCP/1957/5; Office pps., DSOP/1938/7 • Southwark Diocesan Directories: 1927, 1928 • Southwark Diocesan Pastoral Committee: Letter DPC/Gen/PDA/S of 11 Apr 1990 • *Surrey Comet*, 10 Feb 1934 • *Wimbledon Borough News*, 13 Apr 1934.

MITCHAM St Olave, Church Walk

Balham, Tooting & Mitcham News & Mercury, 3 Feb & 9 Mar 1928, 9 May 1930, 23 Jan & 20 Mar 1931 • *The Builder*, 24 Aug 1928 • Church Survey File: Mitcham St Olave (CCC) • Ecclesiastical Commissioners' archives: file 91151 (CERC) • ★ICBS Annual Report, 1930 • *Kelly's Surrey Directory*, 1927: Mitcham • *Mitcham Advertiser*, 8 May 1930, 22 Jan 1931 • *Norwood News*, 9 Jan 1931 • Parish magazines, Mitcham St Olave: various issues, 1928–81 • Parish Record Index, Mitcham St Olave (SRO) • Parish Records, Mitcham St Olave (SRO): 2051/4/2, corresp. 1951 re installation of Stations of the Cross; 2051/4/3, photographs, *c.*1928, of hall interior; 2051/5/1 & /2, PCC minutes etc., 1928–36 & 1936–50; 2051/5/3, brochure, 1960, on life of church & parish; 2051/5/4, photographs for brochure pub. 1960; ★2051/8/1–23, photographs of church, *c.*1950–60; 2252/2 & /3, PCC minutes etc., 1967–72 & 1972–4; 2252/5, PCC corresp., 1970–73; 2252/15 & /16, dedication of new porch & vestibule, service pps.; 2635/1/1–24, Golden Jubilee, 1981 – various docs. • *RIBA Journal*, 14 Oct 1933 • Riley, W. E., *Report on architectural history of St Olave's, Southwark* (LCC, 1918) (Southwark LS) • St Olave's, Tooley Street: file PC 283 St O. (Southwark LS) • ★St Olave's, Mitcham: plan and elevations • Southwark Diocesan Archives (LMA): Consecration pps., DSCP/1931/7; Office pps., DSOP/1973/61 & DSOP/1974/3 • *SDD*: 1934 • *SDG*, Mar 1928, Oct 1929, Mar 1931, May 1933, Apr 1951 • *Sutton & Cheam Advertiser*, 17 Jul 1929, 1 Jan & 22 Jan 1931 • *Wallington & Carshalton Advertiser*, 11 Apr 1929 • Watkinson, Amy E., *The Parish of St Olave, Mitcham* (1981).

MORDEN St George, Central Road

Anon., *Fifty Years On: The Story of St George's, Morden, 1932 to 1982* (St George's Church, Morden, 1982) • *Crockford's Clerical Directory*, 1930 • Ecclesiastical Commissioners' archives: files 92082 & 92150 (CERC) • Livermore, Revd Canon T. L., revised W. J. Rudd, *The Story of Morden and its Churches* (St Lawrence's Parish Church, Morden, 1968, revised 1983) • *Merton & Morden News*, 7 Jan 1938 • *Morden Chronicle*, 20 Mar 1931 • Parish Records, Morden St Lawrence (SRO): PCC minutes, 1927–34 (2269/9/1), 1934–7 (2269/9/2); Pps. 1944–50 re St George's Church (2269/10/29) • Thanksgiving & Re-dedication, 22 Jun 1976, on completion of St George's Church & Family Centre: Service Sheet • Ward's Croydon Directory: 1930 • *Wimbledon Borough News*, 11 Jan 1929, 5 Jun & 27 Nov 1931, 4 Mar 1932, 7 Jan 1938.

MOTSPUR PARK Holy Cross, Douglas Avenue

Bendell, Bruce S., 'Illustrations & memories of West Barnes Lane & Motspur Park from about 1920' (unpub. Ms., 1990) • Biography File: R. G. C. Covell (BAL, RIBA) • Church Survey Files: Raynes Park Holy Cross & Raynes Park St Saviour (CCC) • *Crossing* (Holy Cross Church Magazine), Jan 1990 • Ecclesiastical Commissioners' archives: file 82581 (CERC) • Jowett, Evelyn M., *Raynes Park, with West Barnes & Cannon Hill – A Social History* (Merton Historical Society, 1987) • *Merton & Morden News*, 28 Jan 1949, 2 May 1958 • Parish Record Index, Raynes Park St Saviour (SRO) • *SDD*, 1927–1932 & 1934 • *SDG*, Mar 1949 • Southwark Diocesan Pastoral Committee: Letter DPC/Gen/PDA/S dated 21 Feb 1992 • *Surrey Comet*, 19 Oct 1966 • Thanksgiving at Southwark Cathedral, 25 Jan 1934: Form of Service • *Wimbledon Borough News*, 7 Nov 1908, 18 Apr & 27 Jun 1914, 25 Nov 1921, 23 Apr 1926.

NEW ELTHAM All Saints, Bercta Road

The Builder, 23 Aug 1929 • Bunce, Thomas G., *New Eltham Methodist Church – Fiftieth Anniversary* (1980) • ★Church Survey File, New Eltham All Saints (CCC) • Ecclesiastical Commissioners' archives: files 71818 & 91151 (CERC) • *Eltham & Kentish Times*, 22 May 1931, 25 Jun, 6 Aug & 17 Dec 1937 • Everness, Mrs Pat, information supplied orally • Kennett, John, *Eltham – A Pictorial History* (Phillimore, 1995) • *Kentish Independent*, 22 May 1931, 17 Dec 1937 • Kingston, Revd M., *The Church & Parish of All Saints, New Eltham – Golden Jubilee, 1979* (All Saints' Church, 1979) • Rochester Diocesan Archives (LMA): Consecration pps., DRCP/100 • Shepherd, F., 'New Eltham' in *Looking Into Eltham* (pub. Eltham Society, 1980) • Silvester, Walter P.: Deposited Drawings (LMA): New Eltham All Saints – Proposed Hall (GLC/AR/BR/19/3295) • Southwark Diocesan Archives (LMA): Consecration pps., DSCP/1931/3; Office pps., DSOP/1963/8; Orders in Council, DSOC/1929/6, DSOC/1931/7, DSOC/1954/3.

NORTH SHEEN (KEW) St Philip the Apostle and All Saints, Marksbury Avenue.

Anon., *The Barn Church of St Philip & All Saints, North Sheen* (leaflet, n.d.) • Anon., *The Barn Church 1929–99 – Planning for the Millennium* (*c.*1994) • Church Survey File: North Sheen, St Philip & All Saints (CCC) • Consecration of the Barn Church, North Sheen, 4 Feb 1929: Brochure & Order of Service • Darby, Revd Nicholas, information supplied orally • Ecclesiastical Commissioners' archives: files 71818 & 83965 (CERC) • Foundation stone inscription • ★Lambert, Uvedale junr, *The Barn Church of St Philip the Apostle & All Saints, North Sheen – A Brief Account of the Building & its Conversion into a Parish Church* (1936) • Lambert, Uvedale junr, 'The story of the barn church' (pub. in 6 parts in *Barn Church Magazine*, Jan–Jun 1950) • Lambert, Uvedale junr., 'The Lamberts of Blechingley' (*Bourne Society Local History Records*, 1980) • Lyons, Peter, & Gregorowski, Paul, *Harvests to the Barn: The Jubilee Story of St Philip & All Saints, North Sheen* (St Philip & All Saints PCC, *c.*1979) • Mee, Arthur: *Surrey*, King's England series, Hodder & Stoughton, 1938 &c • ★*New Churches Illustrated* (ICBS, 1936) • Parish Magazine, St Luke, Richmond: Apr 1926 • Parish Magazines, St Philip & All Saints, North Sheen: Jun & Jul 1928, May 1950 • Parish Records, North Sheen St Philip & All Saints (SRO): 2068/1/14 – 2068/3/46, PCC minute books & various other docs., 1910–68 • *Richmond & Twickenham Times*, 18 Jun 1927, 5 May 1928, 2 & 9 Feb 1929, 4 Nov 1933, 4 Jul 1936, 9 Dec 1967 • *Richmond Herald*, 5 May 1928, 9 Feb 1929 • Southwark Diocesan Archives

(LMA): Consecration pps., DSCP/1929/7; Office pps., DSOP/1968/23 •*SDD*, 1994 • *Thames Valley Times*, 6 Feb 1929 •Woodward, H. J., *A Short History of the Barn Church of St Philip the Apostle & All Saints* (Graham Cumming, 1962).

OLD MALDEN proposed new church

Parish Records, St John's, Malden (SRO): PCC Minute Book, 1919–31, ref. 2473/4/1 • Sampson, June, *All Change – Kingston, Surbiton & New Malden in the 19th Century* (pub. St Luke's Church, Kingston-upon-Thames, 1985) • *Southwark Diocesan Directories*, 1927, 1928, 1929–30, 1931–32.

PURLEY St Swithun, Grovelands Road.

Barker, Celia, *It's Up the Ladder to Heaven* (St Mark's, Woodcote, PCC, 1985) • Bourne Society, *Bulletin*, No. 106 (Nov 1981) • *Coulsdon & Purley Advertiser*, 1 May 1953, 16 May 1958 • *Coulsdon & Purley Weekly Record*, 28 Jan 1927 • *Croydon Advertiser*, 27 Apr 1929, 21 Jul 1939 • *Croydon Times*, 1 May 1929 •Ecclesiastical Commissioners' archives: file 94457 (CERC) • Elliot-Binns, Michael, *The North Downs Church* (1983) • *Kelly's Directory of Kent & Surrey*, 1930 • Local History Index (Croydon LS): Purley, St Mark • Parish Magazines: Purley (Woodcote) St Mark, 1927–32; Purley St Swithun, 1972–8 • Parish Record Index (SRO): Purley (Woodcote), St Mark • *Purley Review*, Apr & May 1929 • *Sixty Post-War Churches* (ICBS, 1956) • Southwark Diocesan Archives (LMA): Consecration pps., DSCP/1961/2 • Southwark Diocesan Board of Finance: Annual Report, 1937.

PUTNEY St Margaret, Putney Park Lane

★*The Builder*, 5 Sep 1924 • Campbell, Kenneth L. J., *Campbell, Smith & Co. 1873–1973 – A Century of Decorative Craftsmanship* (Campbell, Smith, 1973) • Church Survey File: Putney St Margaret (CCC) • Clarke, B. F. L., *Parish Churches of London* (Batsford, 1966) • Court copy of Will, Alexander Angus Croll, died 7 Jun 1887 (Somerset House) • Crotch, Arthur, 'The story of Putney Churches' *(Wandsworth Borough News*, 12 Apr 1935) •Ecclesiastical Commissioners' archives: file 85013 (CERC) • *Kelly's Directory of Wimbledon, Merton, Mitcham & Morden*, 1911/12 • Loobey, Patrick, *Putney & Roehampton – Positive Pastimes from Picture Postcards* (pub. author, 1988) • Loose, Jacqueline, *Roehampton – The Last Village in London* (London Borough of Wandsworth, 1979) • MacRobert, Scott, *Putney – A Brief History* (Putney Soc., 1977) • Parish Magazines, Putney St Margaret (LMA): 1957–9 (P95/MGT/80/1); 1960–66 (P95/MGT/80/32–107) • Parish Records, Putney St Margaret (LMA): Citations & Faculties 1918 & 1954–61 (P95/MGT/39/1–5); Corresp.: 1922–4 re formation of parish etc. (P95/MGT/26), 1923–8 re church enlargement etc. (P95/MGT/28 /30 & /32), 1925–8 re church furnishings etc. (P95/MGT/45 & /46) & other pps. re stained glass windows (P95/MGT/47); Documents re repairs after storm damage, 1933 (P95/MGT/48); Inventory of removable church property, begun 1924 (P95/MGT/40); Licence for solemnisation of marriages, 3 Mar 1920 (P95/MGT/25); Licences for temporary building at rear of church (P95/MGT/27); Misc. pps. 1910–36 (P95/MGT/34); Misc. pps. 1932–63 (P95/MGT/68); Specification for Church Hall, 1929 (P/95/MGT/54); Specification of works for church additions, 1925 (P95/MGT/33) • *Post Office Directories*: City Of London, 1875; London, 1911–20 • *Putney Newsletter*, 15 & 29 Jun 1912 • Simpson, C. H., Deposited Drawings (LMA): Putney (Roehampton Estate), Proposed Church Hall, 1929 (ref. LCC/VA/DD/R301); Putney, St Margaret's Parish Hall, 1929–30 (ref. GLC/AR/BR/19/4177) • Southwark Diocesan Archives (LMA): Office pps., DSOP/1911/6/12 • *SDG*, Apr 1926 • *The Times*, 16 Jun 1887, obit. to Alexander Angus Croll • Underwood, A. C., *A History of the English Baptists* (Baptist Union Publication Dept. 1947) • Wallis, Revd Philip C. B., *Saint Margaret's, Putney Park Lane – A Short History of the Church and Parish* (1959, repr. 1974) • *Wandsworth Borough News*, 12 Feb & 11 Oct 1912, ★2 Oct 1925, 26 Feb 1926 . • Whitley, W. T., *The Baptists of London, 1612–1928* (Kingsgate, London, 1928).

RIDDLESDOWN St James, St James's Road

Bates, Paul, *Saint James's Church, Riddlesdown* (pub. *c.*1993) • Broadberry, Revd Canon R. StL., information supplied orally • Church Survey File: Riddlesdown St James (CCC) • *Coulsdon & Purley Advertiser*, 25 Oct 1958, 19 Feb 1965, 7 Nov 1966, 6 Jun 1967 • *Croydon Advertiser*, 12 Dec 1903, 2 Oct 1909, 13 Mar & 30 Oct 1915, 20 Dec 1930, 11 Jun 1932 • *Croydon Chronicle*, 12 Dec 1903 • *Croydon Guardian*, 12 Dec 1903, 13 Mar 1915 • Ecclesiastical Commissioners' archives: file 85963 (CERC) • Elliot-Binns, Michael, *The North Downs Church* (1983) • ICBS Annual Report, 1930 • Parish Record Index, Riddlesdown St James (SRO) • *Purley, Caterham & Oxted Gazette*, 12 Dec 1903 • ★Purley Library Local History Collection: F4/58• *Royal Academy Exhibitors, 1905–70*, Vol. V, LAWR–SHER (EP Publishing, 1981) • ★St James', Riddlesdown: Parish Magazine, February 1941 (CCC) and original architect's drawing • Southwark Diocesan Archives (LMA): Consecration pps., DSCP/1930/3; Orders in Council, DSOC/1925/1 • *SDD*, 1928–9, 1929–30 • *SDG*, Jul 1940 • Sykes, Christopher, et al, *The Jubilee Story of St James's Church, Riddlesdown 1915–1965* (1965) • Travers, Martin: Deposited Designs (RIBA Drawings Collection): Windows & furnishings, refs. TRAV[127] 1 –3, TRAV[128] 1–4, & W16/10(2).

ST HELIER Church Hall, Arras Avenue

Anon., *Ravensbury Manor House & Park* (Merton Historical Society, 1981) • Denbigh, Kathleen, *History & Heroes of Old Merton* (C. Skilton, London, 1975) • Ecclesiastical Commissioners' archives: file 92082 (CERC) • Jowett, Evelyn M., *History of Merton & Morden* (Merton & Morden Festival of Britain Local Committee, 1951) • *Kelly's Surrey Directory*, 1927 & 1930: Mitcham • *London Housing* (LCC, 1937) • *Merton & Morden News*, 23 Aug 1963 • Mitcham St Olave Parish Magazine, Jul 1930 • *Morden Chronicle*, 29 Nov & 20 Dec 1930, 10 Jan 1931 • Parish Records, Morden St Lawrence (SRO): PCC minutes, 1927–34 • *St Helier Estate: Design Guide* (London Borough of Merton, *c*.1992) • *SDG*, Apr 1931 • *Sutton & Cheam Advertiser*, 19 Mar 1931, 1 Jun 1933, 22 Aug 1963 • *Sutton Times & Cheam Mail*, 2 Jun 1933 • *Wallington & Carshalton Advertiser*, 19 Mar 1931 • *Wimbledon Borough News*, 5 Apr 1929, 31 Oct & 19 Dec 1930, 24 Apr & 29 May 1931.

ST HELIER Bishop Andrewes's Church, Wigmore Road

★*Architect & Building News*, 17 Nov 1933 • *The Builder*, 10 Aug 1934 • Chronicle of the Parish Church of St Peter & the Church of Bishop Andrewes: Oct 1955 • Church Survey File: Mitcham St Olave (CCC) • Ecclesiastical Commissioners' archives: files 92082 & 92964 (CERC) • Hyslop, Geddes: Deposited Drawings (LMA): St Helier, Bishop Andrewes's Church, 1932, LCC/VA/DD/R208 • *Lewisham Borough News*, 9 May 1939 • Parish Records, Mitcham St Olave (SRO): Corresp. re Stations of the Cross (2051/4/2) • Southwark Diocesan Archives (LMA): Consecration pps., DSCP/1933/8 • *SDG*, Aug 1933, Apr 1951 • *Sutton & Cheam Advertiser*, 5 & 19 Jan 1933, 22 Jun 1933 • *Sutton Times & Cheam Mail*, 4 Mar 1932, 23 Jun 1933 • *Wimbledon Borough News*, 5 Jun 1931.

ST HELIER St Peter, Bishopsford Road

Architects' Journal, 6 Jun 1935 • Chronicle of the Parish Church of St Peter and the Church of Bishop Andrewes: Aug 1954, Dec 1955 • Church Survey File: Morden (St Helier) St Peter (CCC) • *Daily Telegraph*, 20 Mar & 14 Sep 1991 • *Dictionary of National Biography*, 1951–60 • Ecclesiastical Commissioners' archives: file 92082 (CERC) • ICBS: Annual Report, 1932 & ★1935 • *Independent*, 5 Sep 1991 • *London Housing* (LCC, 1937) • *Morden Chronicle*, 10 Jan 1931 • ★*New Churches Illustrated* (ICBS, 1936) • ★Nicholson, Sir C. A.: Deposited Drawings (LMA): Morden (St Helier), Church of St Peter, 1931, LCC/VA/DD/R394 • Our Parish News (St Peter & Bishop Andrewes): Feb 1933 • Southwark Diocesan Archives (LMA): Consecration pps., DSCP/1933/9 • *SDD*, 1927 • *SDG*, Mar, Oct & Dec 1932, Jul 1933 • *Sutton & Cheam Advertiser*, 2 Jun, 16 Jun, 20 Oct & 3 Nov 1932, 1 Jun 1933 • *Sutton Times & Cheam Mail*, 4 Mar 1932, 2 Jun 1933 • Travers, Martin: Deposited Designs (RIBA Drawings Collection): Furnishing & decorating chapel in St Peter's Church, St Helier, refs. [166] 1–3 • *Wimbledon Borough News*, 8 May, 5 Jun, 4 Dec & 11 Dec 1931.

SANDERSTEAD St Mary the Virgin, Purley Oaks Road

Anon., *Church of St Mary the Virgin, Sanderstead – Golden Jubilee 1926–1976* (pub. *c*.1976) • Anon., 'The parish church of St Mary, Sanderstead' (*Sanderstead News*, No. 30, Summer 1973) • Church Survey File: Sanderstead St Mary (CCC) • *Coulsdon & Purley Advertiser*, 25 Apr 1958, 5 Mar 1971 • *Croydon Advertiser*, 29 Feb 1908, 7 Nov 1925, 2 & 9 Oct 1926, 21 Sep 1935 • *Croydon Chronicle*, 29 Feb 1908 • *Croydon Times*, 9 Oct 1926 • Ecclesiastical Commissioners' archives: file 86640 (CERC) • Elliott-Binns, Michael, *The North Downs Church* (1983) • Mortlake with East Sheen Parish Magazine: Sep 1928 • *Purley, Caterham & Oxted Gazette*, 29 Feb 1908 • *Royal Academy Exhibitors 1905–70*, Vol. V, LAWR–SHER (EP Publishing, 1981) • Southwark Diocesan Archives (LMA): Orders in Council, DSOC/1925/8 • *SDG*, Dec 1925.

SOUTH BEDDINGTON St Michael and All Angels, Milton Road

Betjeman, Sir J., *Guide to English Parish Churches* (Collins, 1958, rev. N. Kerr & re-pub. Harper Collins 1993) • Church Survey File: S. Beddington St Michael & All Angels (CCC) • *Croydon Times*, 21 Jul 1928 • Ecclesiastical Commissioners' archives: files 68377 & 74498 (CERC) • ICBS Annual Reports, 1925, 1929 • ICBS Grants List 1818–1927 (LPL) • *London Gazette*, 8 Nov 1907 • Southwark Diocesan Archives (LMA): Office pps., DSOP/1908/4 • *SDD*, 1927 • *Sutton & Cheam Advertiser*, 26 Sep 1929 • *Sutton & Epsom Advertiser*, 22 Jun 1906 • *Wallington & Carshalton Times*, 19 Apr 1928, 19 & 26 Jul 1928, 11 Apr 1929, 19 & 26 Sep 1929 • *Wallington & Carshalton Weekly Record*, 18 Jul 1907.

SOUTHEND (CATFORD) St John the Baptist, Bromley Road

Cherry, B. & Pevsner, N., *Buildings of England, London 2, South* (Penguin, 1983) • Church Survey File: Catford St John the Baptist (CCC) • Clarke, B. F. L., *Parish Churches of London* (Batsford, 1966) • Dalton, L., *St John's Birthday Book: The Story of the Church of St John the Baptist, Southend Village, Lewisham* (*c*.1950) • ★Ecclesiastical Commissioners' archives: file 50975 (CERC) • ICBS Annual Report, 1926 • *Kentish Mercury*, 23 Jul 1926, 3 Feb 1928 • *Lewisham Borough News*, 23 Jun & 21 Jul 1926, 1 Feb 1928, 25 Sep 1929 • ★*London Borough of Lewisham Local Studies Centre, photograph PH70/3341* • ★National Monuments Record: filed under Lewisham, St John the *Evangelist* • ★St John the Baptist, Southend: architect's drawings, exterior and interior • Southwark Diocesan Archives (LMA): Office pps., DS/OP/1916/3 & DS/OP/1919/5 •

Southwark Diocesan Committee for the Care of Churches: Reordered & Remodelled Churches, 1960–1978 (Southwark Diocesan Office, 1978) (CCC) • *SDD*, 1928–9 • *SDG*, Sep 1926, Mar 1928 • Southwark Diocesan Leaflet No. 70, Oct 1957.

STREATHAM Holy Redeemer, Churchmore Road

Balham, Tooting & Mitcham News & Mercury, 16 Jan, 20 Mar & 3 Apr 1931; 11 Mar 1932 • Beare, Cyril, 'The church of the Holy Redeemer, Streatham Vale' (*Common News*, Oct 1983) • *The Builder*, 14 Jul 1933 • Campbell, Kenneth L. G., *Campbell, Smith & Co., 1873–1973 – A Century of Decorative Craftsmanship* (Campbell, Smith 1973) • Church Survey File: Streatham Vale, Holy Redeemer (CCC) • Clarke, B. F. L., *Parish Churches of London* (Batsford, 1966) • District Surveyor's Returns, Wandsworth East: 1927 & 1928 (LMA) • Ecclesiastical Commissioners' archives: file 91834 (CERC) • Humphrey, S . C., *Churches & Chapels of Southern England* ('Blue Guide', A. & C. Black, 1991) • Isaac, I. C. A*., Vale Vistas – The Story of Streatham Vale & Its Parish Church, 1900–1982* (Victoria Publications, London, *c*.1982) • Lambeth Churches, A – J (Minet Library, Lambeth) • *Mitcham Advertiser*, 15 Jan 1931 • *Mitcham & Tooting Advertiser*, 2 Apr 1931, 10 Mar 1932 • ★*New Churches Illustrated* (ICBS, 1936) • *Norwood News*, 9 & 16 Jan 1931, 3 Apr 1931, 4 & 11 Mar 1932 • Parish Lists (LMA): Vol. 88 – P95 Wandsworth • Parish Magazines, Mitcham St Olave: Feb 1928, Feb 1930 • *Royal Academy Exhibitors 1905–70*, Vol. VI, SHERR–ZUL (EP Publishing, 1982) • *Sign, The*, May 1932 • Smith, E. E. F., *Clapham Saints & Sinners* (1987) • Southwark Diocesan Archives (LMA): Consecration pps., DSCP/1932/3; Orders in Council, DSOC/1930/1 • *SDD*, 1934 • *SDG*, Jan 1926, Apr 1932 • *Southwark News*, Dec 1979 • *Streatham News*, 2, 23 & 30 Sep 1927, 2 Dec 1927, 23 Mar 1928, 3 Apr 1931, 4 & 11 Mar 1932 • *Sutton & Cheam Advertiser*, 13 Jun, 17 Jul & 14 Nov 1929; 15 Jan 1931 • *The Times*, 9 Mar 1929, 7 Feb 1930 • ★(front cover): Travers, Martin: Deposited Designs (RIBA Drawings Collection) – Streatham Vale, Holy Redeemer Church, furniture & fittings, and with T. F. W. Grant, plans, sections & elevations (refs. RAN24/M/5(8) & W16/5(1–10) (renumbered PB95/5(1–10) • Ward Album of Photographs (Minet Library, Lambeth).

TOLWORTH St George, Hamilton Avenue

Architects' Journal, 7 & 14 Mar 1957 • *Architectural Review*, Jan 1956 • *Kelly's Directory of Surrey*, 1930 • Owen, Betty*, St George's Church, Tolworth – The First Fifty Years, 1934–1984* (pub. *c*.1984) • *Surrey Comet*, 16 Jun 1934, 15 Nov 1958 • Ward, Patricia J., *From Talworth Hamlet to Tolworth Tower – St Matthew's Parish, Surbiton, 1875–1975* (pub. author, 1975)

TOOTING St Augustine, Broadwater Road

Balham News, 6 Mar 1931, quoting W. E. Morden's *The History of Tooting Graveney* (pub. 1897) • *Balham, Tooting & Mitcham News & Mercury*, 27 Jan & 9 Mar 1928, 20 Mar 1931, 23 Jul 1954 • Black, Alistair, *The Building of the L.C.C. Downham Estate, S.E. London* (1981) • Booth, Charles*, Life & Labour of the People in London – Religious Influences* (Macmillan, London, 1902–03) • *The Builder*, 21 Sep 1923, 22 Jun 1928, 3 May 1929 • Butler, John, *Holy Trinity, Upper Tooting – A History of the Church & Parish* (1955) • Church Survey File: Tooting St Augustine (CCC) • Clarke, B. F. L., *Parish Churches of London* (Batsford, 1966) • Ecclesiastical Commissioners' archives: file 75885 (CERC) • ICBS Annual Report, 1929 • ★*New Churches Illustrated* (ICBS, 1936) • *Royal Academy Exhibitors, 1905–70*, Vol. II, CAS–D (EP Publishing, 1977) • Southwark Diocesan Archives (LMA): Consecration pps., DSCP/1931/1 • *SDG*, Jan 1930, Apr 1931 • *Tooting & Balham Gazette*, 7 Dec 1929 • *Wandsworth Borough Guardian*, 17 Aug 1995.

WALLINGTON St Patrick, Park Hill Road

Anon., *St Patrick's, Wallington: Facts About the Organ* (Leaflet, 1964) • ★Church Survey File: Wallington Holy Trinity (CCC) • Ecclesiastical Commissioners' archives: file 92433 (CERC) • Fisher, A., *St Patrick's Church, Wallington, 1932–57* (1957) • Fisher, A., *The Unfinished History of St Patrick's Church, Wallington* (*c*.1982) • Fisher, H. B., *Wallington Church and Parish* (British Publishing Co., 1960) • *Kelly's Directory of Wimbledon*, 1936 • *Royal Academy Exhibitors 1905–70*, Vol. V, LAWR–SHER (EP Publishing, 1981) • Southwark Diocesan Archives (LMA): Consecration pps., DSCP/1932/7 • *SDD*, 1995 • *Sutton & Cheam Advertiser*, 10 Oct 1963 • Sutton Library Photographs Collection, ref. SBAW 726 • *Wallington & Carshalton Times*, 28 Jan & 17 Nov 1932 • *Wallington & Carshalton Weekly Record*, 6 Apr 1911.

WELLING St Mary the Virgin, Shoulder of Mutton Green

Bexleyheath Observer & Kentish Times, 15 Oct 1954 • Parish Records, East Wickham St Michael (Bexley LS): PCC minute books, 1933–55 • South London Church Fund & Southwark Diocesan Board of Finance Annual Reports, 1934, 1937, 1939 • *SDD*, 1994 • Spurgeon, Darrell, *Discover Woolwich & its Environs* (Greenwich Guide–Books, 1990) • Tester, P. J., *East Wickham & Welling – A Short History* (London Borough of Bexley, 1979) • Thanksgiving at Southwark Cathedral, 25 Jan 1934: Form of Service.

Where a PLACE NAME consists of two elements, it will be found under the first of the two: for example, 'North Sheen' is under 'North' rather than 'Sheen'. CHURCHES are listed under their dedication, cross-referenced by place name. Thus St John the Baptist, Southend is under 'St John the Baptist', rather than 'Southend', but a cross reference will be found under 'Southend'.

INDIVIDUAL ARCHITECTS, CONTRACTORS, ARTISTS AND CRAFTSMEN will be found grouped under the following headings: architects, artists, bell founders, contractors, furniture & fittings, icons, mural painters, organ builders, sculptors, stained glass artists, stonemasons.

The Ecclesiological Society

The Ecclesiological Society is the society for all those who love churches. It was founded in 1879, acting as a successor to the Cambridge Camden Society of 1839. The Society has a lively programme, including lectures, an annual conference, and visits to a range of locations in Great Britain. Members receive the Society's periodical, Ecclesiology Today, *three times a year. From time to time the Society publishes monographs, of which this volume is an example.*

Membership is open to all. For further details, see our website at www.ecclsoc.org, or write to us at the address on the reverse of the title page.